Kids, Computers, & Homework

JAMES

G.

LENGEL

AND

DIANE

S.

KENDALL

RANDOM HOUSE, INC.

New York

Kids, Computers, & Homework

Composed by Daryl Marie Erbach

Manufactured in the United States of America

First Edition

0 9 8 7 6 5 4 3 2 1

ISBN 0-679-76007-5

New York   Toronto   London   Sydney   Auckland

This book is dedicated to Molly and C.J. and all the other kids who use their computers to do their homework.

contents

introduction

From Browser to Builder

- If you are a passenger, this book will help you become a pilot.
- If you are a player, this book will help you become a creator.
- If you are an admirer, this book will help you become an architect.
- If you are a reader, this book will help you become an author.
- If you are a browser, this book will help you become a builder.

The personal computer is the invention of our time. Just as in previous generations when television, movies, radio, the telephone, and the light bulb transformed our society, the computer is changing the way we work and the way we live, and the way our children do their homework. Computers will soon be in about one out of every two American homes. Each new computer household moves into the midst of a revolution in the way we deal with information.

But like other revolutions, this one has the potential to go off in different directions. Do we want our home computers used to watch cartoons and sitcoms? Or to interact with excerpts from the latest adventure movie? Today, three of the four best-selling software titles for home computers are of the shoot-'em-up variety.

A home computer is now capable of much more than playing games. It can read CD-ROMs, connect to the Internet, compose digital photographs, and produce live-motion video. Many of them come equipped right from the factory with the software tools for students to create their own desktop publishing and multimedia homework projects. This book teaches parents and their kids how to create simple essays and multimedia slide shows, all designed to produce more interesting and better-quality school assignments. Each chapter presents several cogent ideas for turning a homework assignment into a creative computer project, as well as step-by-step instructions on building each part.

We wrote this book to help families move toward using their computers as ideally envisioned—as a source of information and a tool to enlighten and alleviate some of the burden of everyday tasks and homework. We want to inspire you to use the computer for both practical and creative purposes.

Why This Book?

. . . .

A few years ago, my daughter's English teacher refused to accept her homework essay on Roman aqueducts. Nothing was wrong with the grammar, syntax, length, or spelling. The problem was the teacher. She required that "All first drafts must be written by hand." My daughter had to copy her essay from the nicely printed pages into longhand on yellow lined paper!

Miss Ring, a good teacher, taught my daughter how to write. But because Miss Ring did not grow up with a word processor she didn't know how it fit into the process of good writing.

We wrote this book to help parents, teachers, and schools learn about the positive aspects of the new technologies. We also want to show how the computer can be a valuable addition to the student's set of homework tools.

More recently, another daughter completed an assignment showing the major population centers of Australia by using an electronic atlas on CD-ROM. When she went to hand in her paper, her classmates turned on her and told her that she couldn't submit it because it "looked too good." Yet most of her classmates do in fact own fully equipped home computers, many of them with the same atlas and printer. The problem was that they and their parents did not know how to apply the computer to complement day-to-day schoolwork.

We wrote this book to help parents understand how computers can help with homework; to help children take full advantage of their home computer for schoolwork; and to help teachers learn how to alter their assignments for students who have computers at home.

One Sunday afternoon I watched four children, aged six through eleven, play Sega Genesis in the living room. I mistakenly thought that the device, built around a computer chip and digital technology, was called "Nintendo," but I was sharply corrected. The hardware setup and TV, which cost almost as much as a home computer, dominated the room and the minds of the children. As they watched, a little birdlike character appeared to move across a landscape of roads and bridges. The mesmerized children controlled it so as to avoid fatal pitfalls and violent enemies.

We wrote this book to help those kids realize that there are more significant ways to apply computer technology to their lives.

But the chief motivation for this book was to help kids move from browsing through the information to building their own ideas. We have watched many kids, in many homes and schools, find in the computer a powerful tool for discovering new ideas and expressing their own thoughts. We have watched them increase their self-esteem as they present their computer-generated works to others; we have listened to them engage in informed discourse with online pen pals; we have witnessed in them a new spirit of openness to learning and exploring new ideas.

We wrote this book so that their experiences could be shared by as many kids as possible. And we wrote this book to support the parents who love them and just need a few clues to help them more fully experience this age of digital wonders.

A Progressive Approach

This book starts simply, with assignments that just about any student can accomplish with the most basic home computer setup (plus a printer). From there we lead you step by step through more substantial tasks that take fuller advantage of the computer's capabilities. We also expand the range of subject matter, from a one-page composition, to a science lab report, social studies research project, and artistic presentation.

As we progress through the chapters, we introduce and teach you how to use many of the peripherals that expand the computer's power. Printer, CD-ROM, scanner, microphone, modem, video digitizer: we show how all these devices—many of them now standard or accessible equipment—can be employed in the completion of homework assignments.

We also explain how to use the software programs that come preloaded on most home computers, especially integrated software programs such as ClarisWorks or Microsoft Works. At the same time we add instruction on using specialized software (such as Kid Pix) and the electronic encyclopedias to help with homework. In later chapters we show how online services, music software, and even the Internet can be put to good use for school assignments.

The homework examples in the first three chapters can be produced on any home computer with a printer. Assignments outlined in chapters 4–6 require access to a CD-ROM drive as well as a modem. Later chapters discuss more sophisticated projects that incorporate the use of a scanner, microphone, digital camera, photo CD, and video digitizer—some of which you may have or have access to or might consider purchasing.

The two most popular types of home computer are those running either the Macintosh or the Windows operating system. These account for over 90% of computers being purchased today. Wherever possible, we show homework examples using cross-platform software—that is, software published in both Macintosh and Windows versions. Where necessary, we explain how the programs work differently on the two platforms. You will be able to re-create just about all the projects in this book with an up-to-date Macintosh or Windows computer.

An up-to-date Windows or Macintosh computer should have, at a minimum:

- 8 megabytes of random access memory (RAM)
- a hard disk drive of at least 230 megabytes
- a mouse
- 8-bit video (256 colors)
- 13-inch color monitor
- Windows: Windows 3.1 or higher operating system, 386 or better processor
- Macintosh: Macintosh System 7 or higher, 68030 or better processor
- a printer

By following this book chapter by chapter and working with your child on various projects, you will gradually increase your child's ability to think creatively about schoolwork and make use of more powerful and complex computer software and peripherals. If the examples in the later chapters seem beyond your capabilities, don't worry—just follow the book and we'll take you every step of the way.

part

. . . .

Author, Author!

chapter 1

It All Starts with an Idea

Writing is hard work. All of us remember how frustrating it was to sit down with a blank piece of paper, hoping the words would flow by themselves. Students in school today have the same problem. They are expected to write every day in several different subjects as well as come home to do book reports, essays, research reports, and more. It's not easy, but the computer can help them get the thinking process off the ground.

Thinking can also be a struggle, but it's the most important step in learning to write well. Once we start to think, the words begin to flow— and one sure way to jump-start the thinking process is through *brainstorming*. With a little instruction from you on how to get started, your child can learn to apply this thought-provoking method of creating and organizing ideas when tackling a variety of school assignments.

This chapter looks at how you can help your kids use the computer as a tool to stimulate and organize the brainstorming process as the first step toward creating a well-written document. We begin with a familiar school writing assignment that C.J., our fictitious sixth-grader in middle school, must complete and demonstrate how she uses her computer step by step to do so. Along the way, we review a variety of software and techniques that can help any student in any

brainstorming—let your brain think of as many ideas as possible, get them down, and share them with others.

grade carry out the thinking, brainstorming, and organization process essential to successful writing.

How Did She Do That?

At first I could not believe Ms. Flores asked us to write an autobiography! After all, I've only been around for eleven years—what is there to tell about me—C.J.? But when I sat down at the computer and began to make a quick list of the ten most important things that ever happened to me, I found that there were lots of things I've done, places I've gone, and people I've met. My storyboard quickly got longer and longer. I've already got at least twenty things to write about in my autobiography!

Every year, it seems as though one of our kids is given an autobiography report to do as a school assignment. If you think about your last parent-teacher meeting at school, you will probably remember seeing some kind of bulletin board displaying student autobiographies, complete with pictures. It's a common assignment, and there are a couple of good reasons for it. First, an autobiography assigned at the beginning of the school year is a good way for the teacher and classmates to get to know each other. An autobiography is also used to help develop kids' self-esteem as they approach adolescence. This is not an easy assignment for students of this age. They do not often think of their lives as a story, and they seldom reflect rationally on the personal events that got them to where they are. Many students find themselves incapable of organizing their thoughts to the task—some never even get past the first sentence! This is where the computer, as a tool, can be used in some interesting ways to overcome these blocks to writing and to turn this sometimes fearsome task into an opportunity for thinking and communicating.

C.J., our student pictured at the beginning of this chapter, just completed the first phase of her autobiography. She ordered the major events of her life and the most important aspects of her personality onto a *storyboard*. Each frame of this storyboard contained an important event or interesting juncture in her personal history, represented by graphics and text. Each frame denoted one paragraph or chapter in her autobiography. Later in this project C.J. turned this storyboard into a written document and then into a multimedia presentation.

storyboard—a set of
panels or frames that
depicts a plot, facts,
or characters in
sequential scenes—like
a comic strip.

C.J. constructed this storyboard using Kid Pix, a drawing program from Brøderbund, available on her computer. First she drew pictures of some of the events in her life that she could remember, using the mouse as a paintbrush or employing the "rubber stamps" that Kid Pix provides. Her first pictures were simple line drawings, but they were more than adequate to represent the various events she was thinking about. As she browsed through the collection of stamps, she culled some of the familiar items she found there—a baby's face to represent her birth, a horse for the summer she spent on her grandparents' farm, and an airplane and birthday cake for her trip to Disney World. Using the stamps was inspiring and easy. She quickly added the stamp to the screen, then wrote some simple words describing the event. As she created each frame, she saved it with simple descriptive words such as "birth" or "first pet" to identify the frame for future reference. After a break from her work, she came back to the Kid Pix program, opened each frame, and wrote a longer description for each picture. On one frame she recorded her own spoken description of the event, using the computer's microphone and Kid Pix's recording feature.

Brainstorming is an essential first step in the act of writing, and the computer can be invaluable here. As C.J. created the scenes of her life, she was using the computer as a brainstorming tool, an aid to remembering ideas and recording them quickly. Note that her ideas were represented by both words and images. For writers of all

KidPix

Kid Pix from Brøderbund is a basic drawing program for kids. All kinds of easy-to-use tools let the child draw lines, boxes, and circles; fill in colors, patterns, and mixtures; paint in various styles; and add text and erase. There's also a Hidden Pictures feature and a Pages feature from a coloring book. Rubber stamps let kids add icons to their pictures. Kids can also record an oral description of what they've drawn on each screen. (This recording works with all Apple Macintosh computers but requires the addition of a sound digitizer to an MS-DOS or Windows computer.) Kid Pix also includes a Slide Show feature that lets kids put their work into a presentation for display on the computer screen, complete with either previously recorded sounds or sounds of their own creation, short animated movies of miscellaneous things such as spooky ghosts or jumping dogs, and even a chance to add transitions between slides. Pictures created in Kid Pix can be printed or exported into word-processing documents. Newer versions of the program also include the ability to import photos from photo CDs and videotape, work with animated stamps, play with digital puppets, and create animated pictures with tools that have a life of their own. Whether you have an old or new version, this program has aged well, has a good future, and is flexible enough to be used in a variety of ways.

ages, images are an important source of ideas. Too often we expect students to be able to sit with a blank sheet of paper and instantly create a string of words. Better writing often comes by starting with ideas and images. When Albert Einstein was asked how he began his thinking, how he came up with the ideas for his writings, he explained that he constructed *pictures in his mind*, images that moved around one another. It was by thinking about these images that he crystallized his ideas. Only later did he write them down.

All of us learn through images. When we hear words, we paint pictures in our minds of what the words mean. When we think of events or feelings, we think first of an image, and later we describe it with words. Child development research has found that without well-developed images to represent ideas, the child cannot later develop the more abstract concepts necessary for full adult understanding.

Onward and Upward

. . . .

Like Einstein, C.J. next committed her ideas to paper. She printed out her storyboard pages and showed them to her older brother and to her parents. They suggested some parts of her life that she had not included—a writing contest she'd won and her soccer team's championship season—so she returned to Kid Pix and made a few new pages. Then she took all these printed pages and sorted them on the dining room table. She put them as best she could in chronological

Born in New York City, June 4, 1984

Got my dog Split when I was 3

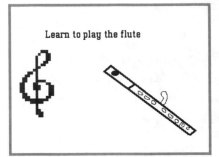

Learn to play the flute

Went to Disney World for my birthday

8

C.J. created storyboard pages in Kid Pix of important events in her life.

order. Then she went back into the Kid Pix program and used the Slide Show feature to put them in order, moving them around on the screen and using the drawing board of Kid Pix to improve many of them along the way. Eventually each page contained a graphic, a sentence about the event, and a number representing its order. On some pages her voice was also recorded.

In this example, the computer helped C.J. think. It provided a convenient forum for her to record her ideas. It provoked new ideas with its store of images and words. It allowed her to reorder her events and communicate them with others. The computer did no thinking of its own; in fact, the computer knows nothing about C.J.'s life. The computer did not do the homework. It did not substitute its brainpower for C.J.'s; instead it acted as an amplifier and recorder of her own thinking. Throughout this book we will stress these important aspects of computing.

Note also the parents' and siblings' role in this example. They did not do the homework; they served as sources of facts, reviewed her work, suggested fresh ideas and new avenues for thinking. But like the computer, her family expected C.J. to think for herself.

How to Do It: Brainstorming

1. Start from ground zero—create a storyboard or a list.
2. Type or draw your thoughts into the computer with an art program or a word processor. Record your own voice. Use single words or short phrases that can be embellished later.
3. Show your ideas to other people and get their advice. What should you add or take away?
4. Put items into the right order either chronologically or in order of importance, make them steps in a process, or group them by common elements.
5. Revise your list, improving it and making it consistent.
6. When you feel you have enough to have a beginning, middle, and end to your writing project, take a break and then get started. Don't be afraid to change your list around a bit as your project unfolds.

More Tools for Brainstorming with the Computer

Although an autobiography is only one example of a school assignment, the process we have described will work in many areas. Composing and writing are necessary in just about every subject. The brainstorming process, and the ways the computer can help it along, can be used to create a book report in reading or a research report in social studies. The steps in writing the autobiography in this chapter's example could be used to write a biography of a historical figure or famous scientist. Brainstorming ideas and recording them quickly on the computer screen can help your child problem solve in math, or sequence a story in literature, or complete a creative writing assignment in English.

Kid Pix is just one software tool available to help in thinking and brainstorming. C.J. could have used just about any drawing program—Kid Works from Davidson, ClarisWorks from Claris, Fine Artist from Microsoft, The Amazing Writing Machine by Brøderbund, or even a storybook creation program like Storybook Weaver from MECC or Imagination Express from Edmark—to create the pictures or frames of her storyboard to accomplish this first phase of her project. But if the student at your house is currently putting together a different type of assignment, another kind of software might be a better tool.

Rules of Brainstorming

1. Anything goes—every idea is equal in the brainstorming process.
2. The order of the ideas, questions, comments, and facts brought forth is irrelevant. The computer is an excellent tool for reorganizing these items later in the process.
3. The ideas can be in any form—questions, statements, images, facts, hypotheses, and so on.
4. Write it down as soon as it comes to mind. Don't wait.
5. Think out loud. Talk to the computer if you have to.
6. Work with other people if possible. Talk out your ideas with them or write down your thoughts and let other people comment on them.
7. When the imagination well runs dry, either take a break or stop.

Using a Word Processor

For some projects, a better brainstorming tool might be the simple *word processor*. As ideas come to mind, type them down line by line on a page in the word processor. New idea, new line. Keep going until you run out of ideas, then go back and cut and paste to combine ideas, put them into a different order, or group them. Many word-processing programs such as ClarisWorks come equipped with an outlining function that makes ordering and grouping even easier. The important thing to remember is that you are brainstorming, not composing sentences for the assignment itself. Follow the rules of brainstorming, and you will be processing words in a whole new way.

Thinking with a Thesaurus

Some word processors offer a *thesaurus*, which can be very useful in the brainstorming process. Select a word that represents one of your key ideas. Call up the thesaurus, usually located under the Tools or Edit menu. See what other words it refers you to. Look at those words. Do they foster any new ideas? Any new ways of pursuing the subject at hand? If so, copy them out of the thesaurus and paste them on a separate line of the word processor as the germ of a new idea.

The Value of an Idea Web

Many teachers use an *idea web* to help students with the first stages of the writing process. An idea web links brainstormed ideas graphically, like this:

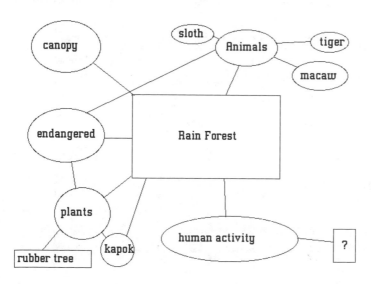

Idea webs help kids see the connections between facts, ideas, thoughts, and questions.

A computer drawing program can help a student generate, compose, and revise such a web, moving elements from place to place, making new links, and so forth. Students simply type in the words they brainstorm, draw a box or oval around them, then draw a line to link the box to other items. By grouping the box and the word (using the Group menu item on most drawing programs or the Moving Van feature of Kid Pix), they are dragged together around the screen. Students can print the web, share it with fellow students, and use it for reference later as they research or write.

The Payoff of a Spreadsheet

. . . .

Even a *spreadsheet* can help in the writing process—at this stage, for example, it can help in the recording and ordering of ideas. As you did with the word processor, type each of your ideas into a new row of the spreadsheet. For now, put them into column B. When it's time to sort the ideas, you can use column A to help you—put a number next to each item, representing its place in order of time or importance. If you prefer, you can use a few common words to label each item and type them into column A. When every idea has been labeled or numbered, use the spreadsheet's Sort function (usually located under the Data or Calculate menu) to sort the list based on column A.

	File	**Edit**	**Format**	**Calculate**	**Options**	**View**

Untitled 1 (SS)

| C19 | ×✓ |

	A	**B**	**C**
1			
2	In Order #1	In Order #2	Parts of the Story
3			
4	3	4	Make a plan to get into the castle.
5	1	5	Encounter the beast.
6	4	7	Put plan into action.
7	6	2	Meet the good witch.
8	5	3	Discover the ruby ring.
9	7	9	Melt the wizard.
10	8	8	Get the treasure.
11	9	6	Lose my way.
12	10	10	Escape.
13	2	1	Find a hidden castle.
14			
15			
16			

Try experimenting with the order of the elements of a fantasy story by using a multi-column spreadsheet.

Taking Advantage of a Timeline Program

. . . .

For an assignment like a biography, a history, or anything that takes place over time, a timeline program such as Timeliner from Tom Snyder Productions may help in the thinking process. These programs allow the student to enter items onto a timeline, then organize them on the screen, cross-reference them, annotate them, and print them out. Timelines can be as short as a day or go from the past to the future. They can also be compared to sample timelines of American or world history that come with the programs.

The Life of Rebecca Jane Gilleand Fisher

1820	1840	1860	1880	1900	1920	1940

▶ Rebecca Jane Gilleland is born in Philadelphia
 ▶ Family moves to Texas
  ▶ Parents killed by Comanche, children kidnapped
  ▶ Rescued by Albert Sidney Johnston
   ▶ Enters Rutersville College
    ▶ Marries Orceneth Fisher, has 6 children
     ▶ Travels to California
      ▶ Helps found Corvallis College in Oregan
       ▶ Helps found Daughters of the
        Republic of Texas
          ▶ Dies in Austin,
          Texas

C.J. created a timeline to help her remember the order of the key events in her great great grandmother's life.

Sequencing a Slide Show

. . . .

To make a quick storyboard, older students can use the Slide Show function of programs like ClarisWorks, Claris Impact, Microsoft PowerPoint, or Aldus Persuasion. Let each page or each slide represent one event or one idea that you've brainstormed. Use words or images to represent each idea. Images can come from your drawing or from a collection of clip art that often accompanies slide show programs. It's easy to reorder and revise your slides and then to present them to others to get advice on your ideas.

Talking It Out

Students who have trouble writing down their ideas, even in the simple ways we have described above, can often brainstorm effectively by *talking*. Let them record their spoken brainstorms onto the computer with a program like Kid Pix (one recording on each picture) or HyperCard (one recording on each card). When they are done brainstorming they can listen to their oral reports while writing (on the same screen or the same card) the essence of the idea. When they're done, they can reorder and revise their list as described above.

Younger students or those who speak English as a second language may benefit from a talking word processor like Kid Works from Davidson, with its ability to go back and forth between the spoken and the written word. The computer can speak the words the student writes and record their voices. Kid Works can also represent

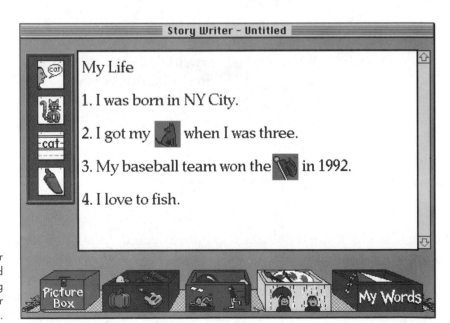

The talking word processor and rebus features of Kid Works can help young students collect their thoughts.

words with pictures, switching back and forth easily between the image and the word. For younger students, this kind of program is a useful aid to thinking and recording ideas.

Stimulating Stories

Storybook creation programs such as Storybook Weaver from MECC and Imagination Express from Edmark can also help get the creative juices flowing when your child is called upon to do some more creative writing. All the elements of a classic fairy tale, legend, fable, or science fiction story are available in each of these programs, including great scenery, classic and not-so-classic characters, and all kinds of props. The best way to start a story project is to choose some characters and jot down a few thoughts about how they might interact on each page of the storybook. Enough characters, backdrops, and props are available in these programs to help stimulate a thousand and one tales.

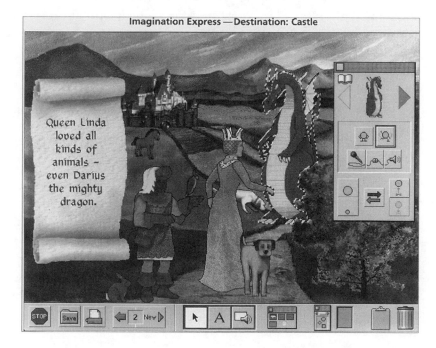

The Castle module of Imagination Express is a great way to stimulate kids to write fairy tales or reports on the Middle Ages.

Courtesy of Edmark

Asking Questions

Asking yourself *questions* is another good way to brainstorm. On your word processor or drawing program, make a "Who, What, When, Where, and Why" form. Ask yourself questions such as *Who* is the person or place? *What* happened first to them? *How* did it affect their lives, the people in their family, their friends, or their community? *Why* was this important? *What* other events did it cause? *What* came before? *What* are some interesting details I can add? Asking questions can help you describe the details from beginning to end, from top to bottom, and from the outside in.

What to Look for in Software Tools

The basic tools for this stage of thinking and brainstorming are the word processor and the drawing program, with their associated extra functions. Just about any brand or version can be useful at this stage, but certain features may make one more valuable than another. Look for software that

- allows you to enter text, images, or sounds (the student's voice or other sounds) into a single frame of your story-board.
- contains images—clip art, rubber stamps, and so on—that can be used to stimulate the student's thinking.
- permits you easily to move information around within the document or storyboard, using cut, copy, and paste tools.
- provides the opportunity to import and export text, graphic, and sound items to other programs for the next stages of the project.
- allows you quickly and easily to print out your work at any stage along the way.

- features a slide show that allows you to see and reorder a "thumbnail view" of all the items in your collection of brainstorms.

Next Steps

Now that we have our ideas all in order, we'll go to the next chapter and learn how to turn them into prose. We'll see how a word processor can streamline the process of writing and produce a final document that is attractive and easy to read.

chapter 2

Conjuring Up the Right Words

"Why can't I just tell the teacher the answer? Why do I have to write it?" our kids complain. It is much easier to talk than to write. Speaking comes naturally. The words just come out of our mouths—for better or for worse. But getting these same words written on paper is a totally different story. Producing a written page is not an easy task.

Writing is a skill that all students have struggled with at one time or another. These days, with the added emphasis on written communication in schools, most kids face the challenge of producing written works every day. This chapter shows you and, in turn, your children how to use the personal computer as a writer's assistant and how to find within it a set of tools that can help compose words into sentences.

In chapter 1 we suggest how the computer can help in the process of brainstorming and recording ideas on the computer. Armed with those ideas, the students at your house can use the material in this chapter to turn their ideas into sentences and their sentences into paragraphs, stories, essays, and reports. With your help they will learn not only how to use the computer's word-processing software, but also how to plan and organize their writing. Along the way, you can explore techniques for completing the types of writing assignments typically asked of students, from science lab reports to history themes to creative essays.

How Did She Do That?

To complete her autobiography assignment, C.J. (our student from chapter 1) used a word-processing program to turn her ideas into prose. She began by opening up a blank document with the word processor. Then, for each idea recorded in her brainstorm list (again from chapter 1), she composed one sentence stating the essence of the idea. C.J. spoke the sentence aloud, then typed it into her word processor.

This "speaking first, writing second" strategy is a good way to approach the word processor, one that most people can comfortably adopt to turn ideas into sentences. At first C.J. just typed one sentence for each idea. Later she went back to rearrange and edit these

I can't believe it's done. I never thought I'd be able to finish on time. And the computer makes it look so good!

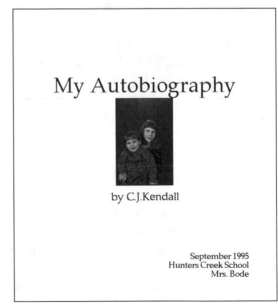

My Autobiography

by C.J.Kendall

September 1995
Hunters Creek School
Mrs. Bode

sentences. She went right through all of her brainstormed ideas until she had a document full of sentences. Since she had already organized her brainstorm list into a logical order, these sentences made some degree of sense when read in a string. But much more work had to be done before the project was complete.

The Keyboarding Question

Before we start in on the project though, we need to say a few words about kids and learning how to type. It's one thing for a kid to type a few sentences, but doing a whole report can seem overwhelming sometimes, especially if the child has not had very much experience with the keyboard. If you are reading this book in advance of any serious project your child has to undertake, now is a good time to prepare him or her to use the keyboard. Children in the third or fourth grade can be introduced to a typing game or program that will help them begin to type with some speed and accuracy. A list of typing programs is included in the appendix for your use.

Courtesy of Sierra, Inc.

Kids Typing from Sierra, with host Spooky the ghost, is a light-hearted way to approach the arduous task of learning to type.

Another area your children need help with when confronted with the prospect of a long project is scheduling. No one should sit at the keyboard for hours to complete a project; it isn't good for anyone either physically or mentally. Help your children break the project up into segments that can be completed in short spurts, and keep after them to maintain their schedule. Given the writing process we suggest in this chapter, most assignments can be completed in short concentrated sittings at the computer, with corrections and additions applied later to a final draft.

ALL KEYED UP!

There is a great debate over when kids should start learning how to use the keyboard. When working with a word processor, encourage very young children (up to age eight or so) to type at their own pace. Adults tend to become frustrated when watching kids type, but it is important not to show your anxieties. There is no need to introduce touch typing or home keys just yet. Instead, let kids figure out where the keys are and hunt and peck out the words they want to type. There will be plenty of time later in life—and larger hands that can reach the keyboard from the standard position—to learn touch typing. The most important thing is to transfer to the computer screen the words your kids just spoke with their voices or made up in their minds, in as natural a way as possible. With older kids, try to introduce a typing package (maybe the same one they are using at school) and find a way to encourage them to work at it a bit. Unfortunately, typing is one of those things that comes only with practice. If possible, refrain from relieving your child of the task of typing up a school project. Kids have to learn to plan ahead and leave time to create the final version. The writing method we suggest in chapters 1 and 2 should go a long way toward teaching kids how to organize their work to produce a final document—on time.

Voice Recognition

Some optimists predict that the keyboard is on its way out and will soon be an obsolescent tool. Someday we will be able to speak into our computers, and the words will appear as text directly on the computer screen. This is possible today on some computers, through a technique called *voice recognition.* The computer's microphone picks up your voice and matches the syllables it hears to a built-in database of spoken words. When it hears a match, it types the result on the screen. Apple Computer of Cupertino, California, and Articulate Systems of Cambridge, Massachusetts, today provide software that can respond to your voice and "take a letter." But voice recognition is not perfect yet; our kids will need to be able to use a keyboard for some time to come.

Using the Word Processor

Now it's time to get down to writing. Start by having your kids speak a sentence, type it, and then read it aloud from the computer screen. If it doesn't sound right, fix it. Kids should learn all the tools that the word processor provides for editing text to make it right. The easiest is inserting words. Kids often leave out words when they type. To insert a word, use the mouse to place the cursor exactly where you want the word to go, then type it from the keyboard.

To get rid of a word, click and drag the mouse across it so it becomes highlighted. Then press the delete key, or use the mouse to choose the Cut item from the Edit menu on the menu bar. Inserting and deleting are the basic tools for editing written work.

When you want to change the order of words or sentences, click and drag the mouse over the words you want to move until they are selected. Then use Cut from the Edit menu. Don't worry—the words will disappear, but they are not lost; they are waiting quietly in the computer's memory. Use the mouse to place the cursor where you want the invisible words to appear. Then select and click on Paste from the Edit menu to put the words where they belong.

Kids should be encouraged to cut, copy, and paste as much as they want so that the technique comes easily to them and they use it naturally. These tools will help your children arrange their sentences into paragraphs. Then they should read what they have written, aloud if that works best, to see how it reads (or hear how it sounds). When they think it makes sense, they are ready for the next step.

The First Draft

After cutting, pasting, inserting, reading aloud, and revising, your kids are ready to publish a first draft. The purpose of this early version is to get other people's reaction. Since the people they are dealing with are busy, the first draft should be easy to read and work with. Follow these simple steps:

Check Your Spelling.

Words are easier to read if they are spelled correctly. (It also leaves less work for the reviewer.) Up until this point, nothing has been said about the spelling of the words posted to the word processor. But before kids issue their work for public consumption, they should correct the spelling. In most word processors you can find the spelling checker under the Edit or Tools menu. Click on the button that reads "Check Spelling" or "Check Document." The spell checker will search your document for words not in its dictionary. When it finds such a word, it stops and displays the word in a window, along with a list of correctly spelled words that the computer reckons you had intended to type. It's up to you to decide

- if this highlighted word is indeed misspelled or is just an unusual word—a proper name or a place, perhaps—that's not listed in the word processor's dictionary. If it's the latter, you can add this word to the dictionary by clicking the "Learn" or "Add" button.

- if any of the words in the correct list is the one you really wanted. If so, just double-click the correct word, and it will replace the misspelled word in the paragraph.

◀ TO SPELL CHECK OR NOT TO SPELL CHECK ◀

Parents often ask teachers and computer educators about letting students use the spell check feature on their word processors: "How are they going to learn how to spell correctly on their own if they learn to depend on the computer?" Well, anyone who has used the spell check feature knows you have to be able to read and spell to use it in the first place. The computer is not a mind-reader

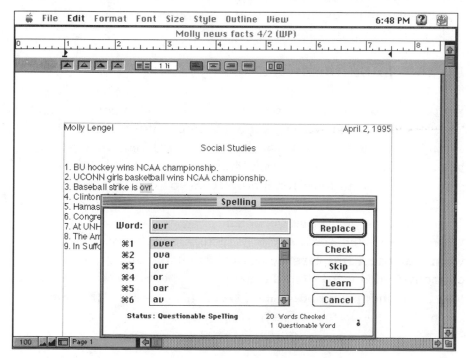

The spell checker is an important tool for young editors.

or a linguist. It does the best it can to match a correctly spelled word in its memory to whatever it has determined you may have spelled wrong. For example, if you type in "lisence" and ask the spell checker to look it over, it comes up with a list of words, including "lousiness," "loosens," "louseness," "license," "licensee" and "liaisons." The word I was looking for was "license," but I have to be able to read and spell to know it's not "licensee." The spell checker is not there as a crutch. It is a real-world tool that can help kids write better.

Save Your Work.

It's a good idea to make sure your child saves the project to the disk. Under the File menu, choose Save, then type in a name for the document. (On an Apple Macintosh you can type any name you wish, such as "CJ's Science Paper"; on a DOS/Windows computer the name can be no more than eight letters, such as "CJSCIPA.DOC.") You can save the document in two places: onto a floppy disk that you insert into the computer with your hand; or onto the hard disk built in to your computer. Work should be saved every ten minutes or so, just in case something goes wrong with the computer.

Saved by the Bell!

One of the most frustrating things that can happen to a child is losing work after spending a great deal of time on it. Remind kids to constantly save their work. The real forgetful types might benefit from a silent timer of some kind that will ring after ten or fifteen minutes reminding them to save their work. Also, keep it in mind as something to mention when you come in to check on their progress.

Format the First Draft

Because other people are going to read this paper, use the computer to make it as easy to read as possible. Here's how:

1. Use twelve-point type. Most people find that easiest to read. To change the size of the type, first select the entire text of the document, using Select All from the Edit menu. The text will highlight. Then choose the size you want from the Size or Font menu, and watch the letters change.

2. Use a serif *font*. Letters with little curlicues and feet on them are easier to read in a paper like this. Select the entire text, then choose a font like Times or Palatino on the Apple Macintosh, or in Windows try Times New Roman, or Courier, by selecting from the Font menu.

3. Narrow the margins. Set the margins so there are ten to twelve words on a line of text for readers who are adults or kids above fifth grade; or 8 to 10 words per line for younger kids. Under the Format or Document menu you will find the margin adjustment; make the margins larger until you end up with the right number of words on a line.

4. Increase line spacing. Select all of the text, then set the line spacing to 1.5 or 2. This will put enough white space between the lines to make the paper easy to read and mark up. The line spacing can be set from the Format menu or from the ruler at the top of the page.

5. Print two copies, one for yourself and one for your reader. Print more copies if you can find more readers.

font—the different kinds of lettering or typefaces available in a word-processing program.

Talk with Your Readers.

What kids want to learn from the people who read their draft is whether or not they got their ideas across. Ask readers to list the ideas they found in the paper. Ask them what they thought was the most provocative or interesting idea. Ask them if anything didn't make sense to them. Ask them if any ideas were missing. Listen to what they say and jot down their suggestions. Thank them for their help. By talking with your readers this way, kids can find out whether or not they communicated their ideas.

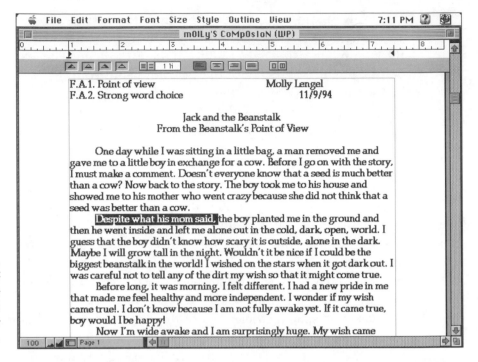

Kids should learn to use the cut and paste features of their word processor. First select the text to be moved by running the cursor over it and highlighting it.

Next open the Edit menu and choose Cut. The words will disappear, but they are not lost. The computer stores them until you are ready to insert them back into the text.

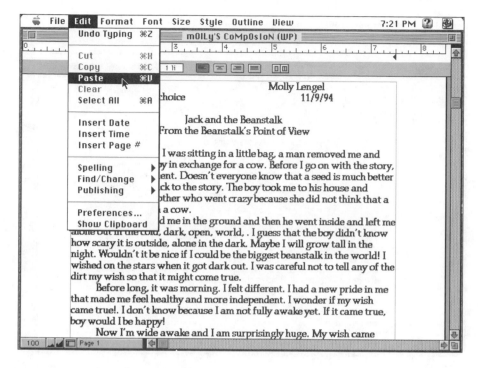

Put the blinking cursor where you want the words to go. Open the Edit menu and choose Paste. The words will be reappear at that spot on the page.

Back to the Computer.

Have kids take their notes and their marked-up draft and sit at the computer. They should open the file they've been working on and add sentences to fill in the ideas the readers suggested. Have them rewrite sentences that didn't seem clear. If readers had trouble making sense of a certain sentence, highlight it by clicking and dragging the mouse across it. Look at it. Read it aloud, twice. Does it make sense? Is its meaning absolutely clear? Ask the author to think of another way to express the same thought. Speak this new sentence aloud. Now type onto the keyboard what the author just spoke. The new sentence will replace the old.

This process of rewriting sentences is called *revision*. Tell kids it's just a second look at their work, a new view that's informed by the remarks of others. Revision is easier if you use the computer to help you along.

**revision—to rework
a project based on
comments, corrections,
and new thoughts on
the subject**

29

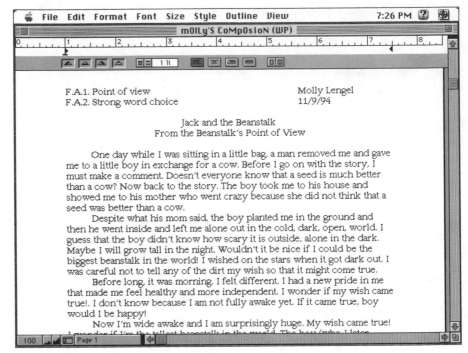

Before kids print their final
copy, remind them to check
their spelling one last time.
Their name and the date
should also appear.

Review Grammar and Style

The computer can also serve as a second reader for your child's paper. A program like Correct Grammar from SoftKey or Gram*Mat*Tik from WordPerfect can examine words and sentences, looking for phrases that might be improved. Such grammar and style checkers look for

- very long sentences
- subjects that don't seem to agree with their verbs
- missing capitals at the beginning of sentences
- missing periods at the end

They will also find oft-repeated words, and point out awkward word usage such as "but also" and "hopefully." Like the spelling checker, these programs do not "fix" your writing. They simply point out things you might want to change. Don't forget to remind kids to save their work after this grammar check.

Publish the Final Copy.

It's time to publish! Remind kids to check their spelling one last time, to catch any mistakes made in the act of revision. Check margins and type style again to make sure they fit the guidelines previously listed. Set the line spacing to 1.5. Put some nice paper into the printer. Print a copy. Read it over. Give it to someone else to read. If you find any flaws, fix them and then print another copy. This is the one that will be handed in to the teacher.

The Writing Process

The method we describe here for using the word processor parallels a proven technique for teaching writing—it's called the *process approach*, or the *writing process*. Many schools, and many successful writers, use these six steps to produce their writing:

1. Brainstorm ideas and words about your topic, then write them down.
2. Express the best of these brainstorms in written sentences.
3. Assemble these sentences into a first draft; read it and revise it.
4. Get other people to read your work and to talk with you about its ideas and meaning.
5. Rewrite your draft to take into account what you learned from other readers.
6. Format your work into an attractive, easy-to-read final publication.

Finding the Right Words for the Right Subject

Writing is one of the few skills that is used in every subject area. The general process of writing is the same in the various subjects, but the

Kids take great pride
in handing an
attractive project
to a teacher.

content is quite different. Following are some tips for you to hand on
to your kids for completing writing assignments.

Science

Science writing assignments include two main types: the research
report and the lab report. The computer can help with the research
report when you follow these steps:

1. Brainstorm about the topic you have chosen: list on the
   word processor a collection of ideas, questions, topics, and
   words connected with the topic.
2. Use the cut and paste capability of the word processor to
   arrange these brainstorms into logical groups.
3. Print a copy of this organized list and take it with you to the
   library or wherever else you conduct the research. Leave
   space for notes between each item. (In chapters 4 and 5, we
   show you how to conduct research right on your computer.)
4. Sit at the computer with your annotated list. Look at a topic
   and its attached notes. Speak a sentence about what you

have learned on that topic as a result of your research. Type that sentence into the word processor. Do this for each topic.

5. Reorganize these sentences into a report in the form assigned by the teacher. The cut, copy, and paste features of the word processor can help at this stage.

For the laboratory report or experimental observation, follow these steps:

1. Most lab reports must follow a certain form set forth by the teacher. This is usually an outline of topics that must be reported. Transfer this form to the word processor exactly as it comes from the teacher.

2. Save a copy of this blank form. You will use it later in the year for other lab reports.

3. Print a copy of the blank form. Take it with you to class or wherever you will actually observe the experiment. As you observe the experiment, jot down your notes in pencil right on the form.

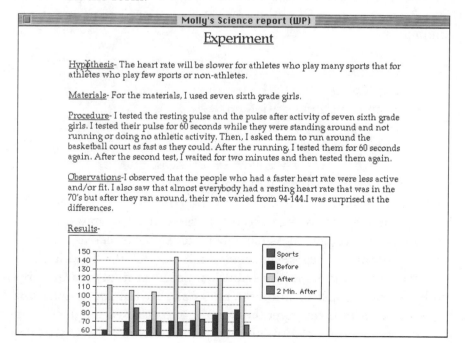

Clear and well organized science lab reports, complete with charts and graphs, are easy to put together on the computer.

4. Back at the computer, open the blank form with your word processor. Look at your handwritten notes. Describe with your voice exactly what you observed in the first note. Write your spoken sentence into the word processor. Repeat this look-speak-type process for each section of the form.

5. Read over your observations. Revise them right on the word processor until they make sense when read aloud.

6. For the conclusions or summary section of the report, follow a similar strategy: first voice your conclusions as a spoken sentence or two; then type into the word processor what you just said.

Social Studies

The computer comes in just as handy when tackling the social studies research report. To help the writing along, follow the steps previously described for composing a research report in science. Another approach, especially for assignments that are difficult to get started on, is to make a general outline on your word processor, with these headings:

- Questions
- Hypothesis
- Supporting information
- Opposing information
- Conclusion

Leave plenty of space between each heading. Before you conduct your research, fill out the Questions section by listing some questions about the assigned topic. These can be simple questions beginning with who, what, when, where, and why as well as more difficult questions of purpose and meaning. Then form a hypothesis by answering one of the questions you just posed. A final answer is not really necessary; just formulate a guess as to what the answer will turn out to be. Type this hypothesis right into that section of the outline. Before you print a copy, identify a dozen key words in what you have written by selecting them and changing them to boldface type. You can also follow this same procedure to research a historical or contemporary issue. Start by clearly stating the issue and two opposing viewpoints.

Print a copy of your partially completed outline. Take it with you when you go to the library. Use the boldface words to guide your information gathering: look up the words in the card catalog or use them as search words in electronic reference books. When you find information about your topic, don't just copy it down. Instead, write it into one of the blank spaces in your outline. If you find information that simply doesn't fit anywhere, write it on the back of the paper. If your topic is an issue. find three or more supporting or opposing arguments for each side.

When you get back home, sit at the word processor, open the partially completed outline, and type the notes from your paper copy into the spaces where they belong. You now have a fleshed-out outline of a decent social studies paper. Turn it into a composition by following the process, explained previously, of speaking aloud a sentence to describe each section of your notes, then typing what you just said. In this way, the computer helps you form the writing step by step.

Book Reports

Remember doing these when you were younger? Book reports are a staple of the reading and language arts curriculum in most schools. The best way to use a computer to help is to begin your writing *before* you read the book. With the word processor, type in this outline:

Title
    Author
    Character 1
        Name
        Sentence
        Action/Involvement
    Character 2
        Name

              Sentence
              Action/Involvement
        Character 3
              Name
              Sentence
              Action/Involvement
        (Add more characters as needed)
        Setting
              Place
              Mood
        An interesting sentence
        An interesting quotation
        A problem that needs to be solved
        How it gets solved

Save a blank copy of this outline. Print yourself a copy. Now you are ready to read the book. Fill out the outline as you read—whenever you come across a piece of information for the outline, write it down in the proper space. Fold the outline in half and keep it with the book, along with a pencil. Every time you pick up the book, it'll be easy to add items to the outline. When you are halfway through the book, take the outline to the computer. Open the blank form. Type into it what you have recorded in pencil. Print a copy of this document and use it to take notes from the rest of the book. When you've finished the book, you will have a rough draft of your book report right in your word processor. By turning your notes into sentences, using the read-speak-type method previously described, you will be most of the way to an interesting final product.

Foreign Languages

You don't need a special keyboard or a foreign word processor to compose papers in other languages. On the Apple Macintosh computer, you can use your standard word processor to produce all those special accent marks and characters that we don't see in English. Here's how:

To produce...	Press these keys:	Then press this key.
é	\<option\>+e	e
ñ	\<option\>+n	n
è	\<option\>+~	e
¿	\<option\>+shift+?	
ø	\<option\>+o	
ü	\<option\>+u	u
ç	\<option\>+c	
á	\<option\>+e	a

For a Windows machine, check your word processor's manual to see if you can follow a similar procedure.

In the not too distant future, kids will be carrying portable computers with them to school and to the library.

Assist kids in writing book reports by helping them create fill-in-the-blank book outlines on the computer before they even start reading.

Taking Notes

With the advent of smaller and less expensive portable computers and digital assistants (such as Apple's Newton), which sells for less than a full-packed Nintendo system, many students will be able to carry their computers with them to the science lab or the library. Students thus endowed should learn to take notes for their research or observations directly onto the computer. With a notebook computer such as the Apple PowerBook or the Compaq Contura, you can bring the word processor with you, typing your notes right into the document. With the much smaller Newton MessagePad, you don't type at all—you write your notes by hand with a pencillike stylus; when you get home, you can transfer the notes directly into your word processor by connecting a cable from the Newton to the desktop computer. Whichever device you use, the rules on taking notes are the same: write only key words; don't stop too long to write (you don't want to miss any of the action); review your notes and make additions immediately after the event is finished; don't worry about spelling. And if you can, don't be afraid to use diagrams in your notes.

Overcoming Writer's Block

Even at the computer, with all its features and tricks, there will come a time when the words don't seem to flow and the fingers don't seem to find their way to the keys. Here are some things you can do to break the spell:

- Go to the library, pick up a book, and read three sentences aloud. Use one of the words you read as the basis of a new sentence on the computer.
- Get up from the computer and find someone to talk to. Talk first about a topic not connected with your assignment. Then turn the conversation toward the topic at hand. Use one of the ideas from your discussion to spur some new writing back at the computer.
- Read the last three sentences you wrote out loud, in a dramatic voice. Go right on and speak the sentence that might naturally come next. Then type it into the word processor.
- Print out your brainstorm list. Put it on the refrigerator. Look at it every time you go by. Ask others to add to it. Next day, take the list with you to the word processor.
- Print out your brainstorm list. Next to each item write a synonym and then an antonym. Consult this new list as you prepare to enter each sentence into the word processor.

Other Schoolwork Ideas

A writing assignment doesn't have to look like a thesis. The modern word processor can format a student's work to look like a newspaper, a journal, an advertisement, a magazine, or a business report.

A report on a historical event or even a book report can be submitted as the front page of a contemporary newspaper. Use the Format menu on the word processor to create three columns. Create a header (also under the Format menu) to contain the seventy-two-point masthead. Type headlines in twenty-four-point bold, the body text in ten-point plain, justified left and right. Use the built-in graph-

Dark Ages Gazette

The Quarterly Newsletter of the Medieval Village   Fall 1292 Volume 1, Number 45

Robin Whittles a Boat

London, England — Even though he couldn't walk or run, Robin de Bureford has been able to learn the craft of wood-carving. His first product, completed today, was a scale model of a sailing ship. It made a successful voyage across the pond this afternoon.

Ever since seing this boat, the other children in the village have been wanting them. It is expected that Robin, now a successful carver, will become their teacher.

Reached today at his home in the monastery, Robin refused to comment

Not every homework assignment has to look the same! The computer can help kids create newspapers, journals, ads, magazines, and business reports.

ics if available to place hairline rules between the columns and under the masthead.

Submit your book report as an advertisement for the book. Use large type to capture attention and bullet points to communicate the main ideas. List the characters in their own column of text, line by line.

Describe a scientific discovery or historical event as a dialog, or a play. Use tabs and italics to separate the characters' names on the left side of the page, with their words on the right.

What to Look for in a Word Processor

· · · · · · · · · · · · · · · · · ·

This chapter has outlined many ways that a word processor can help in the task of a child's writing for schoolwork. When shopping for an adult word processor that you and your older (ten and up) children can use, look for these features:

- Built-in spell checker and thesaurus
- Ability to create automatic outlines
- Easy adjustment of the sizes and styles of margins and fonts
- Access to open and translate files from many different formats
- Easy and standard tools for cut, copy, and paste
- Ability to import and export text and graphics
- Built-in drawing and diagramming capability
- Facility for creating headers and footnotes and to number pages
- Opportunity to preview a page before printing
- Ability to move graphics easily on the page

Check the appendix for the specifics on a variety of word processing programs.

Next Steps

In chapter 3 we move from writer to publisher. We take the words and sentences that we have learned to compose with our word processor and format them so they are stunning in appearance and easy to read. We will learn to use the computer as a desktop publishing center for all sorts of school projects, from simple reports to flyers, brochures, newsletters, booklets, and broadsides. We'll learn how to lay out items on a page electronically and to print them with maximum effect.

chapter 3

Hit Them with Your Best Shot

Five hundred years ago, Johannes Gutenberg started a revolution. His invention of movable type and the printing press changed forever our expectations of how final printed words should look. Before Gutenberg everything was handwritten, copy by copy, so no two books were exactly the same. Books were expensive and hard to read and often took a lifetime to produce. Today we can buy attractive books to suit every audience. Inexpensive and colorful newspapers, magazines, books, and catalogs flood our homes.

The revolution that Gutenberg started continues today. The personal computer and printer sitting in your home has more printing and graphic power than Gutenberg imagined in his wildest dreams. In this chapter you and your child will learn to produce printed works that look every bit as good as books, magazines, or newspapers. This knowledge and the professional-looking documents that result can add to heightened self esteem and better grades.

We start by looking at a student project that uses a modern method to convey information required for a conventional homework assignment. From there we review the autobiography project introduced in the first two chapters and then discuss how to add some graphic highlights to a whole host of school projects in different curriculum areas. Along the way, we will show how to place different elements such as pictures, charts, maps, and titles on each of these schoolwork pages, with an eye for good design. We will consider the typography, the style and size of the letters we print, and how to use type to capture attention and organize text so it is a joy to read.

One advisory note: To illustrate our examples, we have tried within the confines of this chapter to refer mainly to resources that came off diskettes. We hope this will be useful to our readers who don't yet have access to CD-ROMs. Alternative CD-ROM resources are mentioned in this chapter, chapter 4, the appendix, and later chapters.

Before you continue with this chapter, pick up a good book. Find a hardback edition of a well-made volume. Open it up and look at the pages. See how attractive and appealing the page appears. Note the style of the type. Observe the amount of white space on the page. Study how titles and headlines appear. Read a few paragraphs. Notice how easy it is to read. We will copy many of the features of classic typography and print design as we work through this chapter. Follow this same procedure with your child before he or she starts working on any major report or project.

How Did He Do That?

Jacob, a middle school student, learned no more about Columbus than his classmates. They all covered the same material, read the same books, and confronted the same ideas. But Jacob's report communicated very well what he learned from his exposure to these ideas because he published it in an attractive and easy-to-read *format*. He used the computer to turn plain old text into a newsletter format. By doing this, Jacob increased his motivation to get the work done and took more pride in the final product. The computer makes it easy to publish a student's work in forms that are close to the kinds of communications we use in daily life—newspapers, brochures, books, and advertisements.

format—layout of the page

Jacob's first step was to gather information about his topic. He actually used some electronic research sources for this (we'll get into

Westward Ho!

The Quarterly Newsletter of the Amerigo Corporation   Fall 1994 Volume 1, Number 45

Columbus Finds Land

The long voyage is over. The Chief Executive Officer of Amerigo, Inc., has succeeded in his mission to discover new lands to the west. On March 13, sailing in Amerigo's three nautical exploration vessels, the Admiral and his crew sighted a low-lying island in what will someday be called the Caribbean Sea. "Land ho!" came the cry from the crow's nest. The men, all of whom are shareholders in Amerigo under the Employee Stock Ownership Plan, cheered the news and prepared to land. Columbus himself composed this message to the King and Queen of Spain:

New Territory for Spain

Hispaniola, New World — Admiral of the Ocean Sea Cristoforo Colon on March 13 claimed several new lands for the Kingdom of Spain. Included in the claim are several

I learned a lot about Columbus. But it didn't come across well as a plain old research paper. So I made it into a newsletter. This is what they might have published back in 1492, if they'd had a computer like mine. The teacher was not sure this kind of report would be okay, but she said to give it a try. She really liked the final result. Now all the kids want to make this kind of paper.

electronic research in the next chapter). Next, he composed and organized his written work in very much the same way that we outlined in chapter 2—brainstorming ideas, writing sentences, conferring with others, using the tools of the word processor—to prepare a document full of plain text about Columbus.

As he did this, Jacob considered the different forms in which he might publish his report. His social studies teacher from last year had students create brochures advertising the special qualities of a state of the United States they were responsible for researching. Jacob thought of using that same idea to create a brochure to advertise Columbus's second voyage; he sketched out what his project would look like as a kind of business report from Columbus to Queen Isabella; finally he settled on the newsletter format pictured above. At this point he also cleared the idea of trying this approach with his current social studies teacher.

From there Jacob moved to the word processor to create a new format to match his notions for a newsletter. First he set up the page to look like a newsletter. The margins were smaller, and he needed two columns instead of one. He wanted to attract immediate attention to what his report was about, so he constructed a masthead, the large graphic title at the top of the front page. The assignment sheet called for a paper at least three pages long, so he made room for page numbers to appear at the bottom of each page. By doing this, Jacob changed his word processor into an even more powerful desktop publishing program.

Desktop Publishing

It used to be that in order to be a publisher you needed to own a large printing press and complex typesetting equipment. Not anymore. The last decade has witnessed a revolution in the printing and publishing business. Most publications in the world today, from the school newsletter to *Time* magazine, are composed at a small personal computer on the top of someone's desk. Thus the term *desktop publishing*, or DTP. The computer has taken the place of type fonts, paste-up board, and Linotype machine. The laser printer has taken the place of the printing press. Today, almost anyone with a computer and printer can become a publisher. Watch out... that includes your children!

Once he'd set up the form of his page, Jacob brought in the graphic elements of his report. He had found a picture in a clip art collection (see the appendix for examples) that he placed into his computer's Clipboard. Next he pasted this onto the front page of the newsletter by using the Copy and Paste commands that appear on the menu bar of his word processor. Jacob used the mouse to drag the photo of Columbus to the lower left corner. Then he typed the headline COLUMBUS DISCOVERS NEW CONTINENT and changed it to twenty-four-point boldface type. He moved the headline into place at the top of the first column.

To keep the text from overwriting the graphic elements, Jacob selected the masthead, picture, and headline and applied the Text Wrap feature from the Options menu in his mom's word processor. (Text wrapping happens automatically in kids' word-processing packages such as the Student Writing Center.)

Pictures Worth a Thousand Words

As soon as kids move beyond the simple written report, they find a need for pictures and maps. These are very easy to get. The most efficient are the inexpensive clip art collections that are

- available in software stores
- accessible by mail order
- incorporated in software products such as ClarisWorks or Student Writing Center
- created in graphics programs such as Kid Pix.

The appendix offers a list of appropriate resources. These illustrations are already in electronic digital form and can be easily imported directly into the word processor or writing or drawing program. If you have a CD-ROM, even more images are available from such resources as Mindscape's *World Atlas*, Microsoft's *Art Gallery*, photo CDs or even by letting your kids take their own pictures and have them put on a photo CD. (More on photo CDs later in the book.) On the next level you can create or find images and use scanners, a digital camera, and even videotape to add another dimension to schoolwork; these are also taken up in parts 2 and 3 of this book.

After this, Jacob brought in the text. Instead of retyping it into the newsletter, he used the Insert command from the File menu to bring the document from his word processor right into the newsletter. The text automatically flowed around the pictures and from one column to the next. His work began to look like a real newspaper.

On the second page, Jacob created another headline, inserting it in the proper place between the paragraphs of text. He read over the text and saw that it referred to the geography of the Atlantic region. Off he went in search of a map to place onto this page. He found such a map in a clip art collection (see the appendix for some suggestions) and copied it from there, then went back to the newsletter and pasted the map onto page two. He applied the text wrap feature to this map and watched the words flow around the graphic. He used the mouse to shrink the map so that it fit neatly across the column, and the words again flowed around it to fill the column.

When the newsletter was complete, Jacob checked the spelling with the built-in spell checker, read through the entire work one more time, then printed a copy. Even the pictures printed well, with the grayscale capabilities of the laser printer that came with his computer. Several friends read the newsletter and suggested some improvements, which Jacob made before printing a final copy for school. Jacob had become a desktop publisher.

So You Don't Have a Color Printer?

There are some times in the life of a student when it would be nice to have access to a color printer. If you don't have one at home, see if your children can make arrangements to print out their color illustrations at school or at your (or a friend's) office. You can also add color to outline maps and photocopied pictures by using watercolor pencils available at any craft or toy store. Try to get the map or picture copied at a copy shop onto a slightly heavier paper that won't be affected by adding water to make the colors blend. Then color in the picture with the pencils and blend the colors with a little water. Voilà—colored artwork for an outstanding project.

Pick a Subject

Jacob produced a terrific project, one that his teacher rewarded with a good grade and that the other kids at school admired and perhaps vowed to use themselves the next time around. But just for a moment, let's go back to C.J., our student who had to write an autobiography. Her teacher wanted C.J.'s paper done in a more conventional way (one column, standard narrative) but C.J. still was able to add maps, pictures (she even modified some of her Kid Pix pictures from her brainstorming pages to fit her life story), a timeline, and a chart of her hobbies to her report. She basically followed the same procedures Jacob did in bringing in graphics and adding headings, but she only had one column to worry about in creating a stunning document.

This brings up a good point about the computer and schoolwork. Yes, your child can grind out attractive but traditional school reports on it, and that is the best way to start with kids. Single-column, straight narrative papers are what most teachers expect, and this chapter has practical suggestions on how you can help a student produce them. But we hope this book will inspire you and your favorite student to try some other, more creative versions of various kinds of schoolwork. Whether a writing assignment is short or long, a picture, map, diagram, chart, or other graphic can add immensely to the way it looks and the way people react to it. In the past, adding pictures and other graphics might have taken hours, but these additions can now be quickly devised on the computer. Jacob's approach also required him to think in a new way about the material he had gathered and studied, and he used a newsletter format that people are used to seeing every day. He took advantage of one of the great things that the computer can offer a student—the opportunity to convey information complete with graphics in a variety of interesting and compelling ways. Now and in the near future, this is going to become an even more important element in producing school assignments, as competition in the classroom—at every level—grows keener.

Just about every school subject can benefit from this kind of creative desktop publishing. A *science lab* report, for instance, can be clearly focused and easy to decipher when formatted and illustrated à la DTP (desktop publishing).

To create this kind of student report, set up two columns of unequal width on the page, a 1.5-inch column on the left and a 4.5-inch column on the right. Create a masthead or title as a graphic element and set the text to wrap around it. Next, type the section titles into the first column in eighteen-point bold type, leaving several

MAY I, PLEASE?

Most teachers are willing to allow kids to let their creative juices flow when it comes to assignments, but it is always better to ask before you do anything too different. C.J.'s teacher wanted all the autobiography projects to look very much alike. This was a beginning-of-the-year assignment, and she felt it would be better if all the papers conformed to the guidelines she had handed out; that way she could help any students who had trouble following them. On other projects later in the year, she agreed to let C.J. experiment with novel approaches. If your child is going to produce documents using the computer, it's important, in this transition time when some homes have computers and others don't, to find out what each teacher will allow the computer to be used for. Can your child do a variation on the assignment, or does it have to be done in a more traditional recitative style? Can your child use the computer for everything, or do rough drafts, for example, have to be handwritten? Can all final products be done on the computer? If not, will guidelines be issued for each project, letting the students know what the restrictions are? Very few schools or teachers, at this point, have laid down these kinds of guidelines. So avoid disappointment and misunderstanding by having your child check with his or her teacher first about how to proceed with a project if the computer is going to be used for any part of it.

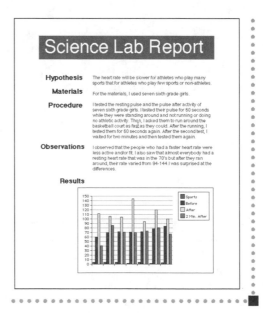

It is easy to format and illustrate a science lab report on the computer.

blank lines between each one. Insert a page break at the bottom of the first column. In the second column, type the body of the text for each section. Insert illustrations into the second column, such as a chart of data developed in the spreadsheet program or a photo or clip art of an experiment, and make the text wrap around them. When the second column is complete, go back to the first column and adjust the space between the section titles to match the body text in column two.

Get the Picture

Try one of these two basic methods to insert a picture or graphic into a desktop publishing document: paste it from the clipboard or import it from a disk file.

To use the copy/paste method, go to the source of the image you want, get the image on the screen, and use Copy from the Edit menu to copy it. (If the software doesn't include a Copy command, use a utility like Flash-It, described in the appendix, to make the copy.) The picture is now on the Clipboard of either your Macintosh or Windows machine. Now in your word processor or desktop publishing program, paste the image from the Clipboard onto the page in your project where you want it. If you are using a Macintosh computer, you can also paste the image into the Scrapbook found under the Apple menu. Once it's in the Scrapbook it will be saved on the hard disk and can later be pasted into any other program. (See chapter 4 for more about the Scrapbook feature.)

To import a picture from a file on the disk, first save the picture as a PICT file on the Macintosh. On a Windows computer, save the picture as a .PCX, .BMP, or .WMF file. This can be accomplished by getting the image you want on the screen, then using the Save As or Export command from the File menu. If given a choice, save or export the picture as a PICT file. Save it to the desktop or even a separate disk so you can find it easily later. Now, back in your desktop publishing program, use the Import, Insert, or Place command to get the picture onto the page. You will have to tell the computer exactly which file you want to import and where it was saved.

Little Women

Here's the Story
The four girls in the March family grow up while their father is off tending to wounded soldiers in the Civil War. Mother and older sister work outside the home to make ends meet. It isn't an easy life, but it's full of family tales and adventures. Meeting Laurie, the next door neighbor; sending Jo off to stay with the old Aunt; dealing with the death of a loved one; all make the book flow along quickly.

The Setting
Little Women takes place in a town in New England, during the 1860's.

Main Characters
Marmee: Mrs. March, the hard-working mother of the girls, manages to keep the family together while working all day.
Meg: The oldest sister, often must act as mother when Marmee is gone to work.
Jo: The main character, is a tomboy who learns how to grow up.
Beth: The sweet, frail, and shy sister who uses music to communicate.
Amy: The prissy sister who tries to use big words.

Louisa May Alcott
The author of this book grew up in a place very much like what she writes about in this story. Some people say that the character Jo represents Louisa May Alcott.

Book Review
The book is sometimes hard to read, because the author uses big words and long sentences, but once you get into the story it is very involving. You really get to know the March family and the differences between the sisters.

Book report by
Cario Inlet, 5th grade

An advertising brochure is an appealing alternative as a book report for summing up the high points of a book.

In *English and the language arts,* a book report can be presented as a brochure advertising the book. One panel can show the plot, another the main characters, another the reporter's opinion, and so forth.

Follow these steps to publish a brochure:

1. Collect all the elements of the brochure in a folder on your hard disk. Include the text for each section, pictures, diagrams, and so forth.
2. Open your word processor or desktop publishing program. Create a new document with margins set to one-half inch all around.
3. Adjust the page setup from vertical (portrait mode) to horizontal (landscape mode) by accessing Page Setup in the File menu.
4. Create three columns of equal width, with three-quarters of an inch between columns. Columns are usually adjusted under the Format menu or as an option when setting up a new page.
5. Place all the graphic elements on the page: pictures, maps, diagrams, photos, and so forth. (See the sidebar "Get the Picture.")
6. Create titles and headlines as graphic elements, and place them where you want them.

7. Apply the Text Wrap feature to all these graphic elements. Text Wrap is often found under the Options in the Drawing or Painting menu. (Text wrapping occurs automatically in many of the kids' word processors.)

8. Bring in the text of the brochure by importing it from a word processing file or by typing it directly into the page. Watch it flow in around the illustrations.

9. Adjust the size and placement of the illustrations so the text just exactly fills the columns of the brochure.

10. Check the spelling, print a copy, and show it to some friends for comment.

11. Revise the brochure as necessary and publish the final copy. To get the two sides to match up, print page one first, then place it back into the printer upside down and print page two. If you did it right, the columns should line up when you fold the brochure in thirds.

Typography and You

All those fonts that came with your computer are not just for show. Certain kinds of type are better suited to different purposes. You can make your works easier to read by using the best type for the job.

- Titles and headlines should be set in a sans serif font such as Helvetica on the Macintosh or Arial in Windows plain styles that are more legible for this purpose. Obviously titles and headlines should be set in larger type than the main body of the text.

- Set the body of the text—the paragraphs that people will read several sentences at a time—in a serif font such as Times or Palatino on the Macintosh (Times New Roman or Courier in Windows). This embellished type is easier to read in a block of text.

- Use no more than two different fonts on a single page.

- Use the fonts that are built in to your printer. This will give better, faster results. And always use scalable fonts (TrueType

(continued)

Typography and You *(continued)*

or ATM), never use bitmapped fonts (fonts formed of dots in a particular arrangement), which tend to distort at customized sizes.

Typography is an art form with hundreds of years of history and much research on what kinds of fonts are easiest to read. By choosing the right type, and laying out the page correctly, your child will produce better-looking papers.

For the *social studies* curriculum, the newsletter format (the kind Jacob used for his report on Columbus), is a good way to capture the spirit of the age that your child is studying. Pick a day in history; find out what kinds of things were happening, what was on people's minds in those days. (Use the electronic encyclopedia for this; see chapter 4.) Then write five articles that might have appeared in a newspaper of that date. Import or draw three or four illustrations for the newspaper. Format the document for three columns, create a masthead, flow in the pictures and text, then lay in hairlines between the columns.

Why not try doing a newsletter on a particular day in history? It's a great way to make history come "alive."

Modifying and Creating Art

If your favorite students can't find the exact clip art they want or if a little doctoring will make a piece more useful, don't be afraid to slip the clip art into an art or drawing program and make some adjustments. Add arrows to draw attention to something in particular or change the colors of an object if it fits better with the text. Color in maps or apply rubber stamps from a program such as Kid Pix to show different special features, and label them in a map key. If all else fails, try drawing a picture! If drawing freehand doesn't work, you can always trace something onto the computer by placing a thin-paper tracing of the piece over the monitor and then copying it onto the screen.

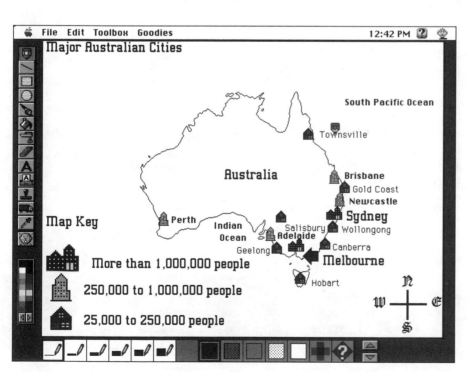

It's fun to use the stamp feature of Kid Pix to create maps and map keys.

Computers and Education Standards

All over the country, schools are setting higher standards for students. At the national level, groups like the National Council of Teachers of Mathematics (NCTM) have proposed very specific standards for what students should know and how they should learn it. The mathematics standards call for, among other things, learning through practical problem solving rather than rote drill. They also expect every child to use the modern tools of mathematics, including calculators, graphing calculators, and computers, from the earliest grades.

The Problem   You have 15 meters of fence with which to build a rectangular enclosure for a small dog. What is the largest area that you can enclose with this much fence? What are the lengths of the sides of this largest enclosure?

The Solution

1. The facts   The enclosure must be a rectangle.
The perimeter must equal 15 meters.
The sum of the lengths of the four sides must equal 15.
The area will equal one side multiplied by another.

2. A Diagram

3. Steps   1. We know that side A + side A + side B + side B = 15

If your child is having problems visualizing a math problem, try diagramming it on the computer.

A *math* problem, especially of the sort suggested in the national curriculum standards from the National Council of Teachers of Mathematics, lends itself to publication on the computer. Students can use the same format described for the science lab report, setting forth the steps in solving the problem on the left column and an explanation of each step on the right. Diagrams can be created in the drawing program, then imported into the desktop publishing program.

By constructing an *advertisement,* kids can practice their skills and create works that show the principles of design they are learning in art class. Help them by first looking together for interesting advertisements in magazines, then use the desktop publishing program to duplicate the style on the computer screen.

Out of this world.

Galactica

The new Galactica 5000
takes you beyond earthly
experience. Speed. Smooth
shifting. Tight turning.
Galactica has it all. Test
drive the Galactica 5000 at
you dealer today, for a
truly out-of-this world
experience.

How about creating an
ad for a product of the
future on the computer?

Left axis

Right axis

Offset axis

Center axis

Page Design Principles

A well-designed page is easy to look at and inviting to read. Browse through a quality magazine with your child, and, by studying several good-looking pages, you will pick up some of the principles of good design:

- *Contrast.* Titles should be much bigger than the body text. Dark areas of the page should be quite a bit blacker than the light areas. Large graphic elements should clearly overwhelm small ones. Contrast helps your eye determine what is what on the page.
- *Balance.* The top of the page should somehow be balanced by the bottom and the left to the right. Dark and light on the page should somehow work out evenly. Pictures in one corner should have another element to balance them somewhere else on the page.
- *Axis.* Build your work around a single axis—an invisible line around which the elements line up. In most DTP documents, the axis will be on the left, on the right, or in the center. Your eye can follow the words better if they follow a single axis.
- *White space.* A page is easier to read if there is ample blank area around the text. Do not crowd text up to lines or pictures or margins. Leave space. A good document includes almost equal areas of black (masthead, photos, headlines), gray (body text in columns), and white (margins, gutters, other blank space). White space is your friend.

By following these four principles, the student's work will be easier to read and more attractive to look at.

No Matter What the Subject

No matter the subject or which desktop publishing program you have available, the steps in constructing a good-looking assignment are the same:

1. *Plan the piece*. Decide what form it will take (illustrated research report, newsletter, brochure, and so on); what elements it will include (text articles, pictures, graphics, and the like); and how many pages it will run. At this stage you may want to help your child get a rough idea of what the document will look like by sketching out the page(s) on paper and drafting a list of elements. If your child is planning anything other than what is usually expected by the teacher who assigned the work, make sure he or she gets it cleared with them beforehand.

2. *Develop each element*. No matter how creative a project your child has planned, composing the right words is important. Follow the process in chapters 1 and 2 to develop a good piece of written work. Remind kids to check their spelling, and let another person read it. Diagrams and art work can be drawn with your drawing program and saved. Your child may need some help finding pictures and artwork. Use the sources described in this chapter and the appendix. Edit them as necessary, and get them ready as files on the disk. It is important that you create each element carefully with the most appropriate software tool, *before* you open the page layout document.

3. *Lay out the page*. Create a new document with the desktop publishing program you have available. Set the margins and the number of columns, and choose the *orientation* of the page. The sketch that was made in step one should be your guide at this point.

4. *Place each element* on the page, beginning with the graphics. Set the text to wrap around each graphic. (This will happen automatically in a children's publishing program such as

orientation—direction in which the type runs, vertically or horizontally across the page.

59

Student Writing Center.) Set the masthead and headlines as graphic elements with text wrapping. When all the graphic elements are in place, it's time to import the text articles and watch them flow into the columns. When the text is placed, you may need to adjust the size of the type and the size of the graphic elements until the text fills the columns.

5. *Print a draft copy* and review it with friends. Other people will find flaws that you didn't see and often give you good ideas that will improve your work. Revise the content and layout as necessary before printing the final copies.

Desktop Publishing: Hints and Tips

These "how to" instructions use ClarisWorks as an example. Other programs will use similar commands.

How to...

Create a Multicolumn Layout

Select Columns from the Format menu. Enter the number of columns you want. Adjust the "space between columns" setting—which is set automatically by the computer—only if you want a special effect. When you click OK, you will see the column guides in your document.

Create a Masthead

A masthead should be a graphic element, not a text element, if you want it to span several columns or to appear in reverse type. A masthead appears only on the first page of a newsletter or report. It is different from a header (see below), which appears at the top of every page.

Create a Header

A header appears at the top of every page of your work. It is usually the document title and perhaps a page number and can

(Continued)

Desktop Publishing: Hints and Tips *(continued)*

span the width of the page regardless of the number of columns. The same text must appear in the header on every page. To create a header, use Insert Header in the Format menu. Your header will appear on the page; type into it the text you want. Align it with the alignment buttons as necessary. (To make a title that appears only on the cover page, create a graphic masthead rather than a header.)

Create a Footer

A footer appears at the bottom of every page, just like a header. This is usually where the page numbers appear and sometimes the name of the article and the author. The computer will automatically number the pages consecutively if you open Insert Page # from the Edit menu. To create a footer, use Insert Footer in the Format menu. The footer will appear on the page; type into it the text you want. You can also align it with the alignment buttons.

Create Reverse (White-on-Black) Text

Create two graphic elements, a black rectangle and some transparent white text, and then place the text over the rectangle.

To make a black rectangle, use the rectangle tool, available from the graphic toolbox, which you get by pressing the icon at the bottom left of the ClarisWorks window. Choose the rectangle tool. Click and drag to draw a rectangle of the size you want. To fill in the rectangle with color, use the color tool under the paint bucket.

Next, create some white text as a graphic element. Type your text in the Notepad. Select and copy it. Back in ClarisWorks, select the paintbrush tool. Paste the text onto the page. It will appear as a graphic element with handles. Use the handles to stretch the text box to fit the place you want the text to appear.

The text box will be opaque when you create it; to make it transparent, use the pattern tool under the paint bucket and select the transparency square.

(Continued)

Desktop Publishing: Hints and Tips *(continued)*

Next, choose the text tool (A). Select the text in the box you just made by clicking and dragging over it. Now you can use the Font, Size, and Style menus to adjust the text. To make the text white, select it, then use the Text Color item from the Style menu to set it to white. You should have white text on a black background.

To Create Headlines

You will have more flexibility if you create headlines as graphic elements and then place them exactly where you want them *after* the body text is formatted. It's best to keep the body text all of the same point size so it lines up properly column to column. As you set the body text, leave out the headlines but use returns to allow enough blank space for the headlines.

To Tweak the Location of Graphic Elements

Use the arrow tool to select the graphic so its handles are showing. On the keyboard, use the arrow keys to move the graphic up, down, left, or right one pixel at a time.

To Align (Justify) Text

Select the text you want to align. Use the alignment buttons on the ruler to align left, center, right, or force-justify to both margins.

To Make Text Wrap Around a Graphic Element

Use the arrow tool to select the graphic element. Choose Text Wrap from the Options menu. Choose the type of text wrapping you want. Now the body text will wrap around the graphic element no matter where you move it.

To Adjust Line Space (Leading)

Select the text you want to adjust. Choose Paragraph from the
(Continued)

Desktop Publishing: Hints and Tips *(continued)*

Format menu. Change the unit from lines (li) to points (pt) using the pop-up button.

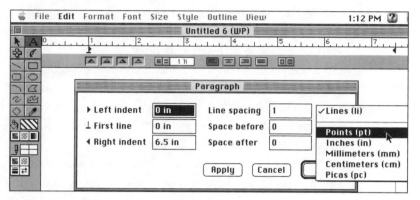

Then set the line spacing to the point value you desire. (If you are using 12-point text, for instance, normal line spacing would be 14 points, or 20 percent more than the height of the letters. For more leading, use a line spacing of 50 percent more than the text size.)

Desktop Publishing Programs

Software programs for desktop publishing allow you:

- To design and lay out a page of text and graphics in just about any format you wish.
- Provide for multiple columns of text and a way to adjust the "gutter" of white space between the columns.
- Align the text in each column flush left, flush right, centered, or justified.
- Bring in pictures and diagrams and then to stretch, shrink, crop, or move them on the page.
- Create mastheads, titles, and headlines, as well as borders, lines, and boxes.

ClarisWorks

ClarisWorks from the Claris Corporation is an "integrated software package." That means it's one program that does many things. It's a word processor, a drawing and painting program, a spreadsheet, and a database all rolled into one. It comes with an outlining feature and tools to help you create presentations. It can even connect with a modem for telecommunication. Most new computers come with an integrated software package like ClarisWorks already installed: Microsoft Works is a similar program.

ClarisWorks has lots of parts, but they all work together. When you want to create a word-processing document, choose it and you get an appropriate menu. When you want to draw with ClarisWorks, create a drawing document; the tools and menu bar change to include all the things you need for drawing. You can even incorporate drawings right in your word-processing document, so that when you click on the drawing, you get the drawing tools to use. Much of the basic schoolwork described in this book can be accomplished with an integrated software package like ClarisWorks.

■ ■ ■ ■ ■ ■ ■ ■ ■ ■ ■ ■ ■ ■

For kids' schoolwork projects, there are three kinds of programs for desktop publishing:

1. *Word processors*—The "adult" word processors with the best page layout features include ClarisWorks, WordPerfect, and Microsoft Word. Any of these will allow a child in fourth grade or above to publish the kind of work that Jacob showed us earlier in the chapter. In many homes, one of these programs is already on the computer, so this is a good place to begin. By adjusting the margins, columns, and orientation of these programs, you can produce the kinds of research reports, newsletters, brochures, and advertisements described in this chapter. Make sure the program you choose has been fully and properly installed on your computer. Desktop publishing calls on many of

the optional features of the word processor, such as spelling dictionaries and file translators, that are usually included as extra files that get installed on your hard disk.

2. *Children's word processor programs*—Some young students may find the "adult" word processors a bit daunting with their long ribbons of menus and complex features. Programs like Student Writing Center from The Learning Company have almost all the same features as an "adult" word processor but are set up with features such as a Type Preview window that lets you see what a particular font is going to look like in terms of size, color and individual letters before you use it. One other neat feature about them is that it's a lot easier to move graphics around on a page. Text automatically wraps around pictures and other graphics in these programs, but that sometimes means that you have to do a bit of adjustment with the placement of the type. These programs are simpler, easier to use, and designed to anticipate the kinds of desktop publishing projects students might do in school. Most have preset forms for building newsletters, reports, and brochures. Many include extensive libraries of school-related clip art. The Amazing Writing Machine from Brøderbund even comes with brainstorming ideas built right in. Most children younger than high school age will work better and faster with these programs than with adult word processors.

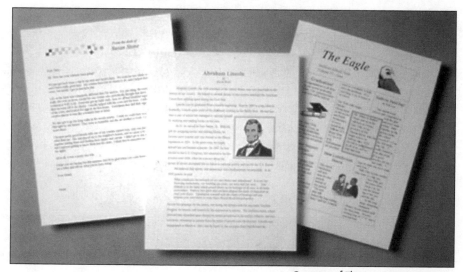

Courtesy of The Learning Company

Many kids benefit from the special school project features of a word processor such as the Student Writing Center.

Courtesy of Brøderbund

It is hard to suffer from writer's block with a program like the Amazing Writing Machine on your hard drive.

3. *Desktop publishing programs*—Of this variety you will find two types: expensive, full-featured programs such as PageMaker or QuarkXPress, which are used professionally but cost more than $500; and less expensive "junior" programs such as Aldus Home Publisher and Microsoft Publisher that are still fully capable of producing the kinds of documents students need for school. One of these programs may be a good choice for older children, especially those who want to try some unique formats. It's easier and more efficient to produce a quality piece of work with one of these programs than with a standard word processor.

Just a Word about Paper

Make sure you have good quality paper that is suited to your printer so that when it comes to printing out a final project, your child is ready to publish in style. You might also point out to the young publisher that a variety of preprinted papers are available that can add to the looks and style of a particular project. For example, a weather report might look great on blue paper with the hint of white cumulous clouds printed on it. Maps of the eighteenth-century settlement of the American colonies could be enhanced by using a parchmentlike paper. Newsletters, brochures, and advertisements can also receive a boost from paper with a preprinted border on it. Papers like these can be bought at business and art supply stores or through the mail from a company called Paper Direct at (1-800-A-PAPERS).

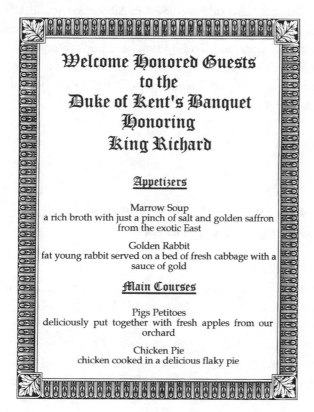

The right paper can make a special project a stand out!

67

Storybook Creation Programs

In addition to the standard kinds of word processor and DTP packages available for young students, there are also storybook creation programs that would be useful for creating documents or creative writing exercises. In these programs, backgrounds, characters, objects, and the like are available for students to arrange in scenes. Kids then use the built-in word-processing capability to write what is happening in that particular scene. Two outstanding examples are Imagination Express from Edmark and Storybook Weaver from MECC. In one theme pack of Imagination Express, for example, kids are able to create medieval castle scenes complete with characters representing royalty, servants, jugglers, knights, ladies-in-waiting, and more. They also can add appropriate props, animals, and furniture. If they are viewing their production on the computer screen, kids can also add medieval music tracks, sound effects, or their own voice. After they type out what is happening in each scene, they can print out their story and bind it to make a book. Storybook Weaver is a more generic story creation program that allows kids to create their own scenes from a variety of environments; it includes a host of multicultural characters and props to create tales from any culture.

What to Look for in Desktop Publishing Programs

Regardless of which program you choose, some features are absolutely necessary to a student's desktop publishing:

- the ability to adjust the number of columns on the page, the space between them, and the margins
- the ability to easily import files of various types, including

(at a minimum) text files from your favorite word processor and pictures in the standard Macintosh PICT format (.PCX or .BMP in Windows PCs)

- the ability to move, stretch, and shrink graphics once they have been placed on the page
- standard cut, copy, and paste features for both text and graphics
- text that can automatically wrap around pictures and graphics
- a built-in spelling checker

Other features add to the convenience of producing DTP works:

- the ability to create headers and footers that can appear on every page
- automatic page-numbering and dating capability
- translators that allow you to import files in a wide variety of formats
- a built-in collection of subject-related clip art
- preformatted templates for newsletters, brochures, reports, and advertisements

What's Next

Gutenberg's revolution is finding its way into homes and classrooms throughout the land. Students are learning to be publishers of beautiful typeset documents. You will find that they take an increased pride and sense of responsibility in their work when the papers they turn in reflect the best electronic page layout and illustrations possible.

Meanwhile, another technological revolution is redefining the world as we know it: we are shifting the way that we get information, from books and papers to electronic data. The next chapter will show you how to engage your child in this revolution, by using the computer to seek out ideas and information that can help compose the content of their work.

part

2

. . . .

Becoming a Knowledge Navigator

chapter 4

The Library That Never Closes

I can remember wishing that I could get locked in overnight, all alone, at the local public library. The library was such a special place, full of old books on quiet shelves from which it seemed I could learn just about anything I wanted to know. I dreamed about having an endless amount of time to poke around the place on my own.

When I got a bit older and busier and *had* to spend more time in the library, I didn't always feel quite the same way. Sometimes, all I wanted to do was find what I was looking for and get it down on paper to complete an assignment due the next day. I was lucky, though. My early wanderings in the stacks paid off, as I usually knew where to find the information I was looking for. But it still took time, attention to detail, and some plain dumb luck to find everything I needed.

For today's students, the scenario is a bit different. Much of the library that used to occupy a large room or an entire building can now be contained on a short bookshelf of CD-ROMs. Information that used to take hours to find can be located in an instant with the help of a computerized index. The information-finding skills that could be learned and practiced only in the library can now be developed and used every day on the computer in your own home. A sin-

CD-ROM—stands for compact disk read-only memory and looks like the kind of disk you use in your stereo; a compact disk on which a large amount of digitized read-only data can be stored.

gle CD-ROM can contain information from about five hundred books. That's a bookshelf as tall as you are and as wide as you can stretch your arms. A stack of CD-ROMs about a foot high can reproduce the resources of the typical school library. And it's so much easier to find that needle of information in the haystack of data when it's in fully indexed electronic form.

Give the young researchers at your house a head start in school by building an electronic library for your home computer. A few well-chosen general references can provide your children with a variety of sources suitable for completing homework assignments and for educating themselves in the process. This chapter will show how these electronic references can best be used for schoolwork, with examples from many subject areas. Along the way, we will review all the basic types of reference works: encyclopedias, dictionaries, image collections, text references, atlases, and more. We will also offer some hints and tips for using these resources creatively and efficiently.

As you work your way through this chapter, remember that the electronic versions of familiar reference works need not be used in exactly the same ways as the printed versions. In fact, some of us may need to unlearn some of the tried-and-true rules of thumb for finding information in books, in order to take full advantage of the new indexing and navigation tools available in the electronic editions. You'll be surprised at how much more your children—and you—can learn if you all open your minds to new ways of finding information with the computer.

This chapter also introduces an addition to your computer that makes electronic information accessible: the CD-ROM drive. Without a CD-ROM, you and your child will not be able to take advantage of the best electronic sources for schoolwork. Most of the computers sold for use in the home today come equipped with a CD-ROM drive built in. If you need to add either an internal or an external CD-ROM drive, kits are available for less than $400. Make sure you buy at least a 2x (double-speed) CD-ROM that is "photo CD access ready" (can read photo CDs off a photo CD disk—See chapter 8 for details).

How Did He Do That?

▪ ▪ ▪ ▪ ▪ ▪ ▪ ▪ ▪ ▪

Danny turned a typical school research assignment into an exploration of the world of electronic information. He surprised himself, as well as his teacher and his parents, with the enormous amount of

The Rain Forest

by Danny J.

Yeah, I had heard something about the rain forest, but it seemed like just another dumb assignment. But once I got into it, it was amazing. It's nothing like the forests I've been to. Some of the animals there are really weird. Look at this picture of the tree frog—this little guy is less than an inch long! And did you know that we get medicine from the rain forest? Look on page four and you'll see a list of the diseases that can be cured by these medicines. I found this list in the electronic encyclopedia as I was looking for some pictures of rain forest flowers. There are forests in Brazil, in Africa, on some islands in the Pacific, and they are all different.

I found lots of different information on the rain forest. Some of it I found in the school library, but most of it I found with the computer at home. I used the encyclopedia, of course, which is real easy to find things with. But I also found some good stuff in the CD-ROM with all the maps. I collected a zillion different things into the scrapbook on the computer, and I ended up with so much I couldn't use it all in my report. Did you know that rain forests are disappearing?

The teacher was surprised at how much different stuff I found. But she made me organize it—she wouldn't accept it until I had put it in order and explained the ideas that I had learned. She said it wasn't enough just to collect all that information—she wanted me to make some sense out of it all.

75

information he could find with his computer at home. No report will ever be the same for Danny—he will exploit this new-found resource for all his future assignments. Danny is taking advantage of the world of electronic reference works now available for the home computer, most published on CD-ROM and easy enough to be used by anyone eight or older. Using his computer to find and wade through a sea of relevant information at home, Danny was able to prepare a fully researched and truly interesting report.

CD-ROM

Compact disc read-only memory. That's quite a mouthful. CD-ROM (really just a fancy name for a plastic computer disk) is simply an inexpensive way to store lots of computer information in a small space. Using the same technology as music CDs, the CD-ROM enables a publisher to code the entire contents of an encyclopedia, or a room-size collection of maps, in a format that can be reproduced easily, shipped quickly, and "read" by any computer. Instead of using the magnetic material of floppy disks, the CD-ROM records its information with pulses of laser light that etch a pattern of holes in a piece of aluminum foil sandwiched between two disks of clear plastic. A small laser inside the computer bounces light off the foil, thus re-creating the pattern of holes, and the original information, in the computer's memory. The read-only memory part of the title means that at this point you are only able to read information off the disk (the technology to record onto a CD using a home computer hasn't yet been perfected).

Let's follow Danny through the progress of his information finding. First, after he was given a rather vague but typical assignment—a report on the rainforest—he began a search on the topic at the school library. As did many of his colleagues, Danny began his work at the school library. In forty-five minutes he managed to locate four references in the card catalog (the "R" drawer was busy, since most of his classmates were there for the same purpose, so he pulled out the "F" and looked up "Forest"), only one of which was actually on the shelf. That's all he had time for. And that book turned out to have more pictures than words, which limited its value as a project resource.

That was all Danny had time for that day, but back home, Danny continued his search for information. His mother had been using Microsoft *Bookshelf*, and it was still in the CD-ROM drive. *Bookshelf* is a set of seven common reference works on a single CD-ROM that can be searched by key words. So Danny looked up "rain forest": he went to the Find section, typed in "rain forest," then clicked on the Find button. In a few seconds, the computer returned a list of fifty-five places where rain forest appeared, including citations in the dictionary, encyclopedia, almanac, quotations, and chronology of events.

Key Word Search

Just about every electronic reference work allows you to search its content by key words: you type in a word, and the program looks through the entire text for that word. The list of instances of the word, or *hits*, is presented to you in a list. Click on any item in the list, and you are switched to the place in the text where the word was found. In most cases key word searching is the best way to find information and ideas in these references. Doing key word searches is very different from using an index or a table of contents and often yields more extensive results. Students growing up in the computer age, and adults who want to survive in the world of electronic information should learn the ins and outs of key word searching.

Danny clicked on the first citation, the dictionary definition of rain forest. From this he learned exactly what a rain forest is and viewed a picture of a typical rain forest.

He highlighted, copied, and pasted what he found into a new page in his word processor for future reference.

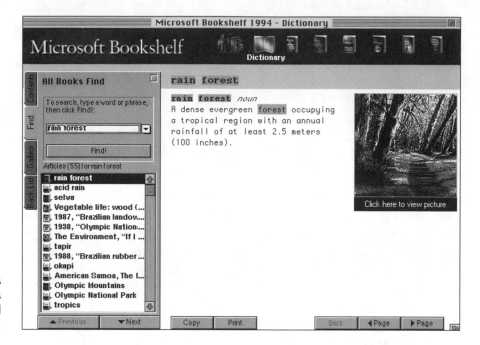

The seven different resources contained in Microsoft's Bookshelf make it a powerful research tool.

Another next citation on the list was an unfamiliar word, "selva." He clicked on it and found that in Brazil, the rain forest is called "selva." This too he placed with his notes in his word processor. Secretly Danny hoped that his teacher would not know this word and that his report might teach her something as well.

The next item Danny found in the list of electronic references was a brief story in the chronology resource about the burning of eighty thousand acres of rain forest in Brazil so that the land could be used for farming. Another article, this time from the encyclopedia, introduced him to the tapir, a small mammal that dwells in the rain forest and whose habitat is endangered. This made sense to Danny in light of the destruction of eighty thousand acres. He didn't know how to pronounce "tapir," so he clicked on the speaker to hear a human voice speak the word (it rhymes with "paper.")

This information gathering took Danny less than ten minutes. Already he had gathered more information and learned more ideas than he did in his forty-five minutes at the school library. And he was well on his way to learning more.

Scrapbook

As you browse through reference materials on a Macintosh computer, you can also take notes by placing copies of what you find into the Scrapbook. The Scrapbook, which can be found under the Apple menu, is like a pile of electronic notecards. Whenever you paste something into the Scrapbook, a new card is created. The items in the Scrapbook are automatically saved to the hard disk inside the computer, which means they can be retrieved later even if the computer has been turned off in the meantime. Whatever is in the Scrapbook can be in like manner copied and pasted into other places, such as the word processor or a drawing program. With the Scrapbook, information from a variety of electronic sources can be set aside for future review and may eventually find its way into the final report. It's faster to use the Scrapbook.

Unfortunately, Windows platform computers have no facility like Scrapbook; instead, cut and paste your snippets of text and graphics onto a page or set of pages and save the whole as a file in your word processor.

In the list of rain forest citations from the *Bookshelf,* he sees a long list of countries, most of them in Africa and South America. After reading one or two of the articles, which explain that these countries all have rain forests, he locates two or three of these places in the electronic atlas that's part of *Bookshelf.* Next, he double-clicks on "tropical," an unfamiliar word on the list, and reads along to find that most rain forests are in tropical areas and that tropical areas are warm and humid and near the equator. He even finds two rain forests in the United States, one at Olympia National Park in Oregon and another in Puerto Rico. Oregon seems a bit far north to have a rain forest, so Danny makes a mental note to check it out later.

Danny's brain, and the page of notes in his word processor, are now full of ideas and facts about the rain forest. His brief foray into the universe of electronic information has, of course, provided him with basic knowledge, but more important, it has fired his imagination and caused him to think. He has come across the "big ideas" of endangered species, human impact on the environment, and the effects of climate. He has also found specific facts about plants, animals, and locations of the rain forests of the world. And he's used only one program!

Before gathering more ideas, Danny called up his word processor document, made some additional notes and jotted down a few of the "big ideas" he found. He also set forth some questions that his search so far has led him to think about: "What good are rain forests to anyone but the animals who live there?" and "What's more important, farming for Brazilians or forests for tapirs?" (This last question comes from a quotation uncovered by the multireference electronic *Bookshelf:* "If I were a Brazilian without land or money or the means to feed my children, I would be burning the rain forest too." the *International Herald Tribune*, April 14, 1989 attributed to the rock singer Sting.)

Even though Sting is not an "authoritative source" for this kind of information, and would not be listed in the school library, he nonetheless caused Danny to think. Finding the most important aspect of dealing with information is nowhere near as important as *thinking* about it. As your young researcher opens up the world of information on the computer, make sure he or she reflects on what he is finding. Encourage him or her to talk about what he or she sees, to ask questions, to wonder about what it means, to check out unexpected and unfamiliar words and ideas. The electronic versions of classic references make it much easier to do this kind of free-form cross-referencing and to put ideas aside for future investigation. An almost playful attitude toward information is essential for effective learning in an electronic context. Danny was not after "the right answer" in his search; if he were, he might never have uncovered the most promising ideas. He was instead on a search for new ideas, for a way of looking at the rain forest that was interesting to him and perhaps even novel for his teacher.

During supper some of Danny's ideas formed the basis for family discussion. His mother and father got to arguing about the farmers vs. tapirs in Brazil. His older sister refused to believe that there was a rain forest so far north. Danny wondered whether the "sylvania" part of Pennsylvania (his home state) was in any way related to "selva," the new word he had learned. After supper he went back to the computer to continue his research.

He removed *Bookshelf* from the computer's CD-ROM and replaced it with *The Grolier Multimedia Encyclopedia*. With a key word search on rain and forest (in the same paragraph), Danny uncovered several dozen hits, articles that contained both of those words. From one of them, a long article about "rain forest and jungle," he learned that a number of the medicines we use come from plants found in the rain forests of the world; he copied pictures of some of these plants to his word-processing document on the computer.

This kind of interesting, "second-tier" information, which enhanced Danny's core collection, was obtained by using a technique called *hypertext*. Whenever Danny encountered an interesting word, he selected it, then chose the Hyperlink option from the Search menu. Immediately the computer took him to the section of the encyclopedia that discussed that word.

hypertext—a means of
connecting references
about particular
words, terms, or
phrases.

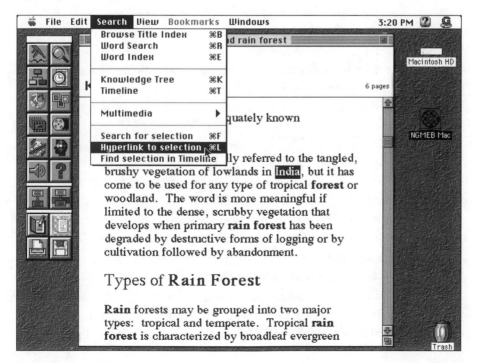

Be sure your child knows
how to use the hypertext
option in your electronic
encyclopedia.

So when Danny selected "India" in that one article about rain forests and the jungle, the Hyperlink option took him directly to an article about India. Later he selected the word "vegetation" and then chose Search for Selection from the Search menu. This found, within a second, all the articles in which the word vegetation occurs. It was through this hypertext searching that he encountered the connection of rain forest plants to medicine.

Hypertext

It sounds like "reading that makes you nervous." But it isn't. Hypertext is a serious technique for navigating through textual information. It's used by leading computer-based librarians and scholars around the world. The World Wide Web* collection of resources on the Internet* was set up to be hypertext efficient. And products such as *The Grolier Multimedia Encyclopedia* and *Bookshelf*, which are geared for school-age students, were designed with extensive hypertext capability. Like key word searching, hypertext cross-referencing is a skill that most of today's adults did not learn in school. You click on a word, and the computer helps you find connections to that word: illustrations, definitions, similar occurrences, and whatever links the author has set up for you. Some hypertext systems even let you define your own links.

Danny wanted to consolidate some of what he found, so he went to the electronic *World Atlas* from Mindscape and copied out a map of the world. He pasted it into the KidPix drawing program and then used the paintbrush to draw green spots where the rain forests were. He labeled the countries, and saved this new map as a PICT file on the desktop (on Windows PCs the file format would be .PCX or .BMP). He was surprised at the number of places he'd marked. Next

---

* See the appendix Kids, Homework, and the Internet.

he browsed through some of the material he'd collected in his notes on his word processor. He found the tapir from the selva, along with pictures of several other animals. His curiosity piqued, Danny put *The Animals!* CD-ROM (Mindscape) into the computer, and found more information on some of the rain forest animals. This information, and the accompanying photographs, were far richer and more provocative than what he'd seen before. He was almost ready to side with the tapir against the Brazilian farmer!

The next day Danny came home with a new CD-ROM called *Art Gallery* (Microsoft) that he'd borrowed from the school library. An electronic version of the London National Gallery of Art, it offered all the museum's paintings and sculptures with explanations and annotations. He wandered in the gallery for a while, looking at paintings and listening to the guide's oral commentary. One painting of a dark forest led him to wonder whether there was anything in the gallery about the rain forest. He used the Find feature to uncover two paintings relevant to his research project, and read about when and why they were painted.

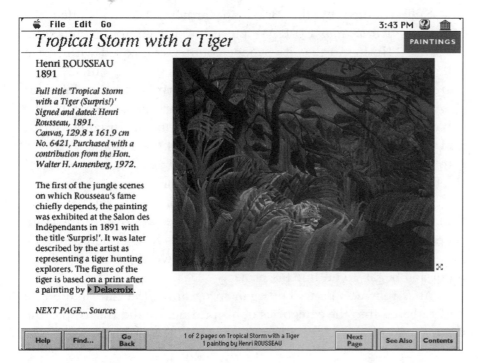

Microsoft's Art Gallery CD-ROM opens the world of art to kids in a whole new way.

Messing Around

Good news! When using electronic reference resources, you're better off *not* going straight to the task at hand. Mess around a bit and begin your work by browsing through what's there. Learn to use the search tools in a relaxed, informal way, and find out how they work by playing around with them.

When approaching a new resource on the computer, young students should be encouraged to play first and work later. This helps set up a positive attitude toward information, and offers a more effective way of learning to use the program. Most information CDs are inherently interesting, and just about any kid will find a picture or paragraph on a favorite subject. A few moments of playing around now will pay off later when the serious referencing needs to be done.

Still troubled by the Brazilian farmers, Danny located the Mindscape *World Atlas* CD-ROM, put it into the computer, and studied Brazil. He found that it's a poor country compared with North America and Europe and that its population is growing quickly. After copying out a map that showed how little farmland is available for Brazil's people and how much of the country is taken up by the Amazon rain forest, he zoomed in to see pictures of Brazilian farms and cities and close-ups of the people. Some of these found their way into his notes on his word processor. Danny was back on the side of the forest-burning farmers—at least for a while.

Danny had gathered quite a bit of information, and the first draft of his report was due the next day, so he sat down at the computer to get it done. First he reviewed the items he'd gathered and the notes he had taken. Then he created a new word-processing document and began to outline his project

After that was done, he began to organize the information he had gathered into the categories of his outline. He did this by pasting the text and pictures from his note page (in the word processor) into

```
Danny's Rain Forest Report: Outline

  I. What is a Rain Forest?
 II. Where are they located?
III. What good are they?
        I. habitat for animals and plants
        B. source of medicine for humans
 IV. What problems arise?
        A. acid rain destroys the forest
        B. farmers destroy the forest
        C. animals are endangered
        D. the climate changes
  V. Tapirs vs. Farmers in Brazil
 VI. Conclusion
        A. no easy answer
        B. humans vs. nature: who wins?
```

the appropriate places on the outline. This caused the outline to expand to several pages. Then he went back, adding new paragraphs of his own composition, editing text, removing redundant pictures, and moving items around. He printed an early draft and showed it to his sister and parents for their reaction, then made a few revisions before printing a draft to take with him to school.

Essentials for the Electronic Library

. . . .

You don't need a roomful of references to create an electronic library. Most of Danny's work came from four carefully selected CD-ROMs. Here are the basic types, along with some examples and what to look for in each.

Encyclopedias

All of these are electronic versions of printed brand-name encyclopedias that have been in homes and libraries for many years. In fact, these days more encyclopedias are sold in CD-ROM format than in paper. All contain numerous text articles, interactive timelines, maps, pictures, sound and video clips, animations, and tools for conducting key word searches. *Compton's Interactive Encyclopedia*, derived from the print work of the same name, is designed for children in grades three to eight. *Encarta* from Microsoft contains the Funk and Wagnall's text embellished with extensive photos, interactive charts and graphs, and lots of sound and video footage targeted for the older elementary school child on up. *The Grolier Multimedia Encyclopedia*, aimed at students from fifth grade through high school, contains text from the *Academic American* encyclopedia (print), and offers more information on scientific matters. Grolier's CD-ROM also has the best hypertext search tools. Many computer retailers include one of these encyclopedias in the package of software that accompanies the purchase of a home computer. Any of them will serve the purposes described here for Danny's work. Each of them also allows the user to access a word processor for note taking.

The most important feature of an electronic encyclopedia is the breadth and depth of information it contains and its suitability to your student's age and interests. The next most important criterion is its ability to search quickly and to cross-reference easily. Examine the quality of the text itself. An encyclopedia's text is more important to your child's success than its multimedia sparkle and flash. (Don't assume you have to duplicate the one they have at school; buy the one that fits your needs.)

Electronic Encyclopedias: Hints and Tips

Searching for information in an electronic encyclopedia can be both interesting and rewarding. For best results, follow these guidelines as you work:

- *Don't use the index.* For most people and most school projects, it's best to begin with a key word search. You will find many things relevant to your topic that don't show up in the index or the list of articles.
- *Don't print.* Most students tend to race through their search task—they find one article on their topic and then print it.

This gets you nowhere and wastes paper besides. A better strategy is to find many articles on the topic, skim or read each one, then copy relevant sections into the encyclopedia's Notebook or onto a word-processing document for later reference. (On the Macintosh you can also use the Scrapbook feature under the Apple menu.)

- *Search and link.* Start your research by taking the topic in different directions. Do a key word search on the topic, then use the Hyperlink option to seek out other related articles. Look for new ideas relating to your topic that others might not have thought of.

- *Mess around.* Take some time just to explore ideas and information with the encyclopedia before you get down to serious searching. This breeds familiarity with the search tools and helps develop a positive attitude toward information.

- *Search words, not phrases.* The search engines work better, and you get more hits, if you search one word at a time. In looking for information on the rain forest, you will get more interesting and varied results if you look for "rain" and "forest" in the same article, than if you search for "rain forest."

- *Try again.* If you get very little by searching under "forests," try "forest" instead. If a search on "endanger" yields nothing, try using "endangered." Think of a synonym for your search word and try that. If your yield is too rich, narrow the search by adding a second search term: "rain" alone results in hundreds of citations; adding "forest" brings it down to a reasonable (and more relevant) selection.

Electronic Dictionaries and General Reference Works

Electronic dictionaries are useful for the student who needs to find out quickly what a word means, how it's spelled, how it's pronounced, and where it came from. In the course of research, students will encounter unfamiliar words; the electronic dictionary is the fastest way to understand what the word means. All the electronic dictionaries provide words, meanings, and symbolic pronunciations; the better ones also provide photographic illustrations and oral pronunciation. (See the appendix for specific titles.) Like the electronic encyclopedias, the dictionaries are versions of previously printed works. Many home computer software packages include one of these dictionaries, and any of them will do the job for students. (The *Encarta* and *Compton's* encyclopedias also include dictionaries.)

Some disks combine several reference works into one CD-ROM, such as Microsoft's *Bookshelf* or Future Vision's *Infopedia*. A desk reference encyclopedia, thesaurus, dictionary, atlas, almanac, book of quotes, timelines, and grammar usage reference all come on one disk and are cross-referenced. These easy-to-use resources are where Danny started his investigation and formed an inexpensive core for an electronic library.

Image Collections

This form of CD–ROM-based research information is growing by leaps and bounds. All of the popular electronic encyclopedias include a large collection of images, so for many students additional collections are unnecessary. Some of the most useful collections include

1. Titles from Microsoft's Home Collection, such as
    *   *Ancient Lands,* an up close and personal look at the lives of soldiers, servants, and nobility from ancient Egypt to the fall of Rome
    *   *Dinosaurs,* a database of facts and theories about prehistoric creatures
    *   *Musical Instruments,* a look at the instruments that make up the modern orchestra
    *   *Dangerous Creatures*, 250 extraordinary creatures from land, sea, and air
    *   *Art Gallery,* treasures from the National Gallery in London

2. *World View* from Aris, a collection of images of planet Earth from space that also includes a fine collection of sounds and video clips

Microsoft's Home Collection contains titles of interest to the whole family.

Courtesy of Microsoft

3. Mindscape's *The Animals!*, a photographic and text database of animals from all over the world

4. *Revolutionary War Gallery of Images* from Fife & Drum Software, a collection of engravings from the National Archives

5. National Geographic's *Picture Atlas of the World* and *Earth's Endangered Environments—Picture Show*, collections of some of those famous pictures from all over the world that National Geographic is known for

6. *Space—A Visual History of Manned Spaceflight*, *Ancient Cities* (including Crete, Petra, Pompeii, and Teotihuacán), *Wild Africa*, *Ocean Life Volumes 1–5* (explorations of undersea life in the world's oceans and seas) and *Exploring the Lost Maya* from Sumeria.

When purchasing an image collection, make sure it offers copy and paste or save capability and provides a text description of each image and tools for key word searching. Also make sure that the images are stored in the standard PICT format for the Macintosh (.PCX, .BMP, or .WMF for Windows), so that they can easily be transferred to other programs. The appendix lists some additional titles.

Text Collections

For less than $40, you can own the five thousand classic works of world literature; or the complete works of Shakespeare; or the Monarch Notes from every book you or your child is ever likely to read. Searchable by key words, and programmed with copy and paste capabilities, these make an excellent addition to the home software library. They are a great source of literary allusions and quotations for reports and can help to link literature with science and social studies topics. Even though Shakespeare, Milton, and Cicero never entered a rain forest, all refer to the forest in their written works. In a moment you can find that forests appear in literature as mysterious places, groves of solitude, and unnavigable confusions of trees. A search through classic literature seldom results in "the right answer" but often provides an interesting insight into the topic at hand. (See the appendix for specific titles.)

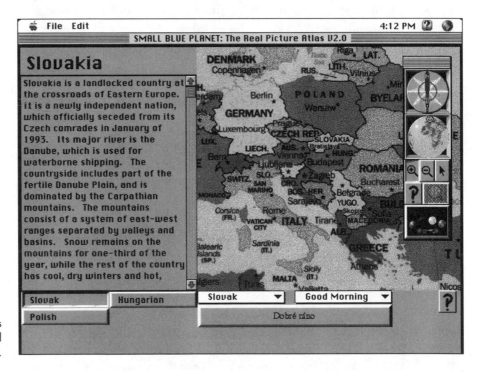

Electronic atlases give kids an up-close and personal view of the world.

Atlases

In electronic form, these are quite different from their printed cousins. Start with index maps of the entire world or the U.S. From the index maps, zoom down to the continent or country or state you're interested in.

Most electronic atlases include topographical as well as political maps, along with statistical information on each country or state. Some include photographs, spoken language, and national anthems. Most include key word searches for places to complement the zooming visual indexes. Here are some examples:

- *World Atlas* from Mindscape is included in many of the home computer software packages. It is a fast and easy-to-use reference work with photos, facts, and easy copying and pasting. The same publisher also sells a U.S. Atlas with similar features.
- *Small Blue Planet* from Now What Software consists of a complete political atlas with text about each country and live language examples—you can learn to say "hello" and a dozen other phrases no matter where you visit. The unique features of this reference work are the satellite images of planet earth that zoom down from continent to city level in amazing detail, and the provide links with political maps.
- *Picture Atlas of the World* from National Geographic provides maps, movies, dazzling photographs, sound clips, and animations that students can use to liven up a report or create a travelogue.
- *3-D World Atlas* from Electronic Arts doesn't have as many clip and copy features but allows kids to "mess around" as they take a 3-D flight over the globe and look at case studies on topics ranging from habitat loss to the urbanization of Cairo, Egypt.
- *Maps and Facts* from Brøderbund lets students customize maps by adding or deleting map labels; changing text size, color, and position; and displaying or hiding city symbols.

- The popular encyclopedias, as well as the multireference volumes, include concise collections of maps that provide sufficient information for student reports.

Other Useful Reference Works

The field of CD-ROM references for the home computer is exploding. Check the appendix for other titles of interest and add these references to your library as they pertain to your interests and as your budget allows. In the meantime, for help with homework or for just "messing around,"consider these additional items:

- *Time magazine,* through Compact/SoftKey Publishing has created the *Time Almanac Reference Edition* and *Time Almanac of the Twentieth Century*, with articles from past *Time* magazines, fact sheets, videos, and all kinds of data. Compact/SoftKey also publishes *CNN Global View* with lots of maps, videos and fact sheets.
- Dorling Kindersley Multimedia publishes a whole set of interactive reference tools, taken from book titles of the same name, aimed at kids ages eight and up but sure to please the whole family. *The Way Things Work* looks at machines from A to Z. Text, animations, biographies of inventors, and a look at relevant scientific principles add to the exploration of why things work. Other titles include *The Ultimate Human Body* and *Eyewitness Encyclopedia of Science*.

Don't Be a Copycat!

The new electronic media makes it easier than ever to turn in someone else's work as your own. Just think, in ten minutes at the computer you can locate several different sources, copy and paste them into your "research paper," print it, and hand it over to the teacher—a task that used to take a week of tedious hunting and copying and rewriting in the library. So it's more impor-

(Continued)

Don't Be a Copycat! *(continued)*

tant than ever to acknowledge sources of information and set clear standards for citing quotations. If your child's school does not have a clear published standard, consider these:

- Acknowledging all the sources you used. Insert a note at the end of your final publication. Even if you just browsed through a source and picked up an idea, you should mention it.
- List the source of each picture or map or diagram right next to it in the caption.
- Put each quotation from any text source in italics, with the citation immediately after it (for example: *The Grolier Multimedia Encyclopedia*, 1995).
- It is not necessary to cite page numbers (since there are no pages per se in most electronic references), but it is important to list the exact source and version or year of the publication (such as: *Time Almanac Reference Edition*, Version 4.0, 1995).
- During your research, as you save items to your word processor or to files on the disk, keep a record of exactly where the item came from. Some references, like the Microsoft *Art Gallery*, automatically stamp each item that's copied from them; others will require you to keep your own record.

Resources for All Subjects

A good library is useful in all subjects. The same is true for the electronic library—and a comprehensive home setup, available at a moment's notice, twenty-four hours a day, is an invaluable resource. Successful students will learn to turn to the computer as their first source of information whenever they get a new assignment. Just about any subject can be understood better by working your way through the electronic references as just described.

- For the *English, reading, and language arts class*, students can use multireference disks or the encyclopedia to help them brainstorm ideas for their essays and compositions. Take a key word from the topic at hand, search for it, read a few of the references, then use the hypertext features to find further references. You'll be surprised at how many new ideas you will turn up. These same references can provide quotations and examples to spice up your writing, and even pictures to illustrate it. Rather than helping you simply find the answers and the facts, electronic references can be more valuable if they are used to uncover new ideas and to relate one topic with another.

Even a book report can be improved with electronic references, by reading about the author's life and times, exploring others who have written books on similar topics, or learning more about the setting in which the book takes place. And current CD-ROM collections of literature, annotated inventively with hypertext links and valuable

Authors' biographies, available at a keystroke, can give kids insight into their writings.

commentary, enable any student to easily understand the various allusions, metaphors, and cross references that make literature fully enjoyable and understandable.

- Danny's foray into the electronic sea of information showed how easy it is to relate one idea to another and to see the interdependencies among the parts of the world. This understanding is essential to the *social studies* curriculum. Social studies teachers tend to assign the most research projects, so it is likely that for work in this subject, the electronic library will be highly useful. Far beyond providing students with facts, the computer can help them think about what they find, ask questions, and discover new relationships.

Having immediate access to multireference or to encyclopedia titles makes reading history more meaningful. In seconds you can look up words and events you don't understand (or forgot.) You can call up a map or a photograph of the place you are studying, to help you visualize what really happened. Your reports can be peppered with little known facts and cross-references to happenings in other locations that even the teacher was unaware of. Students spend less

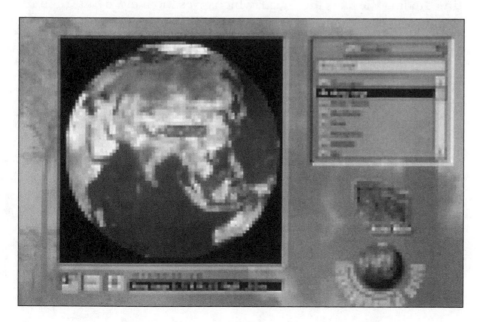

Resources like Electronic Arts 3-D World Atlas give kids a birds-eye view of the globe.

Courtesy of Electronic Arts

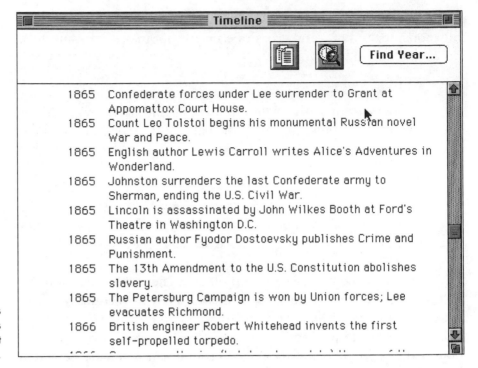

An electronic timeline lets kids quickly compare events that happened in different places at the same time.

time finding the facts they need, which gives them more time to think about what they mean.

- It is in the *sciences* that the information explosion booms the loudest. An accessible set of electronic references can:
  1. act as a reading companion, allowing quick look-up and illustration of unfamiliar terms and science vocabulary
  2. provide a source for tying science theories to the practical world, by uncovering the applications of the chemicals and laws and processes not mentioned in the textbook
  3. serve as a source of illustrations, diagrams, and photographs to embellish science reports and projects
  4. provide information on the history of scientific inventions and discoveries that are not included in the textbooks, information that adds a human touch to even the most technical topics

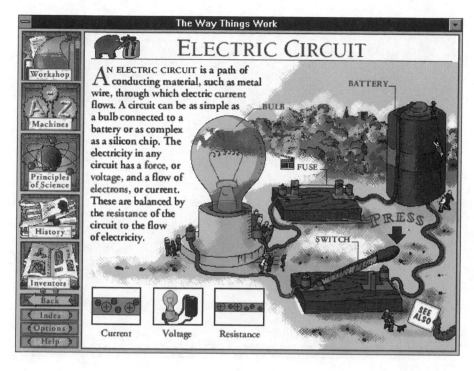

Ever wondered how an electric circuit works or about the principles behind a vacuum cleaner? Resources like Dorling Kindersley's The Way Things Work can help with animations and other graphic examples.

Courtesy of Dorling Kindersley Multimedia

- Few research papers are assigned in *math* class, but that doesn't mean the electronic library is inapplicable. Every mathematical concept has a history, and every one has some practical application in the everyday world. By conducting key word searches in the standard reference works, it's easy to find who invented a particular type of math and where it is applied in the real world. Some of the encyclopedias provide diagrams to illustrate key math concepts.

Building Your Digital Library

The Basic Collection

The exact nature of a home electronic library depends on the age and interests of the students in your family and the capabilities of your

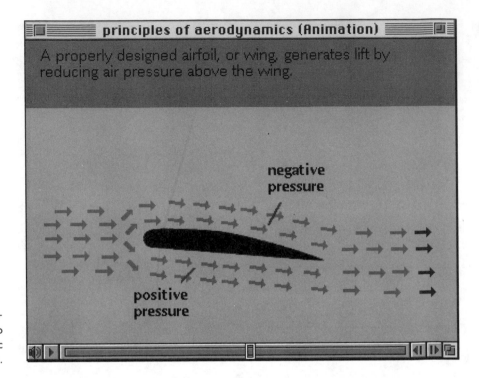

principles of aerodynamics (Animation)

A properly designed airfoil, or wing, generates lift by reducing air pressure above the wing.

negative pressure

positive pressure

All of the electronic encyclopedias use animations to demonstrate various scientific principles.

computer. But for most families, the following resources, in the order listed below, will provide a good basis for success in schoolwork:

1. **Multireference disk**—Microsoft's *Bookshelf* contains a concise dictionary, encyclopedia, atlas, thesaurus, book of quotations, and chronology on a single CD-ROM. A good place to start, a multireference disk like this one will find small bits of information on almost any topic.

2. **Encyclopedia**—*The Grolier Multimedia Encyclopedia* is our choice because it covers all age levels with excellent hypertext searching tools and many illustrations. The level of information is deeper than the multireference disk *Bookshelf*, and it's easy to make connections among ideas.

3. **Image Collections**—Most homework research projects are assigned in history or social studies classes. This means you need a collection of maps that can be modified such as those in the atlases mentioned in this chapter. Next you need a set

of either pictures or clip art to fit the kinds of historical topics your student is studying in school. (Keep your ears open
and when a project is first assigned try to find some
resources that might be helpful—it's no fun to be looking
frantically for illustrations the night before the project is
due.) Some sources to try include

- titles from National Geographic: *Mammals: A Multimedia
  Encyclopedia; Picture Atlas of the World; The Presidents: A
  Picture History of Our Nation*
- photo collections from Corel: disks are available on different countries, animals, parks, important cities, and a
  variety of other topics
- Media Clip's *Worldview:* an art gallery of images from all
  over the world

Beyond those, try to find resources that fit the age and interests of the students at your house. The Microsoft Home
Collection has many wonderful titles that appeal to the
whole family. (See the appendix for more titles.) Also look
ahead to Part 3 of the book for information on how to create
your image collections using photo CD.

4. **Other resource**s—A news summary or annual almanac,
such as the *Time Almanac Reference Edition*, is useful for
finding contemporary (and connections to even historical
topics). A discovery disk like *The Way Things Work*, that surveys the world of machines, is a treat for any family to poke
its way through. Talk to other parents and to the librarian at
your child's school to find other disks that might tickle your
student's fancy. (See the appendix for additional titles.)

Most of these titles are available for less than the cost of a CD-
ROM computer game, and all can be applied to a wide variety of school
assignments and student interests. Many come as part of an introductory computer hardware and software package. They may also be purchased from stores or mail-order catalogs that sell computer software.
Watch for bundles that give you two disks for the price of one.

The Digital Revolution

Why the sudden plethora of books and movies and pictures on CD-ROM? One reason is the explosion of home computers, which has provided an active marketplace for such products. But behind all this are some new technologies that turn *analog* information—what we see and hear and read with our ears and eyes—into *digital* information—what the computer can understand with its processors and disks. Only recently have we learned how to convert from *analog* to *digital* information—that is, to convert a book to a text file, or a movie to a digital video file, and then to publish it inexpensively on CD-ROM, and then finally to turn it back again from digital to analog so we can read it or listen to it. This new ability has fomented the "digital revolution" we hear so much about.

Organizing the Collection

Most of the reference works mentioned in this chapter will not work properly until you install certain files from the CD-ROM onto your computer's internal hard drive. As soon as you get the CD-ROM home, install it according to the manufacturer's directions. The installation process will create a new icon or a folder (or a directory in Windows) on your hard drive. Group all the new icons and folders from your reference CD-ROMs into a single folder (or directory) called "Digital Library"; this will make it easy to find the software when it comes time to do the research. Then locate a small wooden or metal rack for the CD-ROMs themselves near the computer, and keep them there in their plastic cases, ready for instant use. Also register your disk: be sure you either fill out the registration card or call the number that sometimes appears on the first screen of a program. This will entitle you to free or reduced cost updates, especially in the case of the encyclopedias.

A New Attitude toward Information

. . . .

More important than the CD-ROMs or even the information stored within them is your child's *attitude* toward finding information and seeking new ideas. Introduce the volumes in your digital library not as schoolbooks, but as collections of provocative information. Start students off by letting them browse through the information, exploring the areas they find interesting. You, too, can access the electronic references, looking up ideas and terms used in family conversation and showing off new topics that you discover as you wander through the text and pictures and maps. Make sure your child knows how to make hypertext links between a word in one article and an idea in another, and that he or she is not afraid to try alternative ways of searching through the information. Encourage open exploration early on, and you will find later research will be more efficient and more creative. Most important, *talk with your child* about what she is finding, about what it means and why it might be interesting. Encourage your child to report bits of information that you might not be aware of. "Dad, did you know that..." is a healthy way to start a dinner table conversation.

What? No More Books?

Will the CD-ROM ever replace the book? Will we find ourselves one day curled up on the couch with a laptop computer instead of a good book? Probably not. It's easier, less expensive, and less cumbersome to read a novel from the pages of a bound volume than from the screen of a computer. I can't (not yet, anyway) put a computer in my pocket and read it on the way to work or in the school bus or at the beach. But in this chapter we are talking not about novels and stories, but about reference works. When's the last time you took the twenty-one volumes of the Academic American Encyclopedia to the beach? And it is indeed easier, cheaper, and less cumbersome to publish and use an encyclopedia (or dictionary or atlas) on CD-ROM and computer. So for reference works the revolution is over; computerized versions have won. But for novels, biographies, and mysteries, the paper-printed book remains the preferred form.

What's Next?

■ ■ ■ ■ ■ ■ ■ ■ ■ ■ ■ ■ ■

This chapter has stuck pretty much to home, to the information resources available on CD-ROMs that reside with the computer at your house. The next chapter moves beyond the walls, to the world of on-line information, and shows how the networks of cyberspace can be harnessed to help a student with schoolwork. Many of the information-finding and browsing techniques that we learned with CD-ROM can be applied to on-line reference works, especially our newfound attitude toward information. So get your modem ready and turn the page.

chapter 5

Driver's Ed. for the Information Highway

I recently went to a party at the house of a friend of a friend. The party theme was a spoof on the information superhighway and particularly the Internet. When we got to the house we had to walk through a big "net" that had been placed on the porch. Pretty cool, I thought. There was a short line at the front door as the hostess asked each guest whether they were on the Internet. Everyone in front of us responded "No" and were each given a bunny sticker to indicate their "novice" standing. When we got to the front of the line, my friend introduced me, and the hostess posed her question once again. Truthfully I said, "Yes, I'm on the Internet."

Well, remember those old E. F. Hutton commercials where everybody stops everything to listen when E. F. Hutton talks? That's just what happened. People in the front hall stopped to look back at me. People stopped eating in the dining room. It was only for a second, but it felt like an eternity. Quickly my friend jumped in to explain that I "work with computers."

The point of this story is that everyone talks about the information superhighway, but few have gone for a ride on it. Dreamers from the telephone companies, TV, and the government advertise the potential of this fiber-optic link to change our lives—everything from the way we buy our groceries to how we watch movies to the way our kids do their homework. But for most people, the information highway remains a distant dream.

This chapter shows how to make at least part of that dream come true for your kids. It shows how to open up a part of the information highway that already exists and to travel along it to places that will help students improve their schoolwork. The trip requires neither fiber-optic cables in the living room nor satellite dishes on the roof. Your vehicle for taking the drive is the personal computer on your desk, along with an inexpensive modem.

By tapping into the information stored on other people's computers, students can acquire valuable information and ideas to fulfill and improve their school assignments. Using these sources of on-line information is similar to using the CD-ROM products we learned about in chapter 4. First you locate the appropriate information source, then you use your computer to search within it for the data you need. Of course, you need permission to search the contents of someone else's computer in this fashion. This chapter explains how to gain this permission in the form of a subscription to one of the public information services growing quickly as the first "country roads" of the information superhighway system.

This chapter will acquaint you and your child with the plethora of heavily marketed on-line options and help you select those that are most valuable for schoolwork. We'll show you how to get connected, and once you're connected we'll point you toward those areas most useful for math, history, science, literature, and the arts.

How Did She Do It?

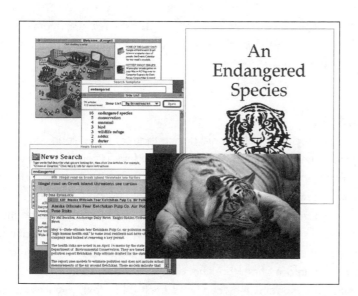

My dad says it's a "politically correc"t assignment. All I know is I put it off till the last minute and all of a sudden it was 7 P.M. on Thursday and it was due Friday morning. Mr. Kowalski wanted a report on endangered species—you know, animals that are dying out. The town library closed at 6, so I had no place to go. But the new computer we got for Christmas came with this eWorld program already on it with a picture of a library. My mother helped me get the program running, and I'm glad she did. I found all the information I needed for my report: words, maps, pictures, and lots of other things.

It took me a while to learn to use this library on the computer. Some of the stuff I found was really boring. A lot of it made no sense to me. And once, my sister started dialing the phone in the kitchen while I was working and messed it all up. It was really fun to watch the picture of the white tiger come onto the screen. I got that tiger from the Software Library at the Reference Desk. Some other kids told me to look there. Not kids from my class—kids I met on-line. There's this place called Youth Central where we can talk with each other (actually we type to each other) and share information. You can learn a lot from other people.

I gathered a lot of information that Thursday night. But that wasn't enough. I had to get up an hour early on Friday morning to put it all into a report. The computer does not automatically write your report! Even though you can find lots of information quickly with it, you still have to put it together into something that makes sense. And that Mr. Kowalski will accept. So I spent an hour cutting and pasting and reorganizing the things I found into a report.

Molly took her first cruise on the information highway as she struggled with her last-minute report making. She didn't know it, but she connected herself to more than a dozen computer information banks all over the world, in less than an hour. From her living room. For less than $3.

Her cyberspace journey was not for fun, nor was it in vain. She was seeking not to entertain herself, but to get her homework done. She used the computer and a readily available on-line information service to gather hard facts and colorful photos for an everyday assignment from school. She learned some new skills, and she had fun.

Modem

A modem is a small electronic device that connects your computer to the telephone line. The computer uses the modem to send signals through the telephone wire to another computer at the other end of the line. The word *modem* comes from *modulate–demo*dulate, which is what the modem does: it changes the pitch (modulates) of a continuous beep on the phone line. Ever listen to a conversation between one modem and another? All you really hear is a kind of high-pitched squiggly beep. The squiggles represent the information that the computers are sending to each other. Through the modems they can send each other text, pictures, sound, and even video. An average modem costs about $100; many retailers include the modem as part of the system for a home computer setup.

Each on-line service has a set of screens that guide your entry to the service. This electronic village is the opening screen shot for eWorld.

On-Line Services

Public on-line information services aimed at families with computers began in the 1980s as CompuServe migrated from a business computer time-sharing network to a computer hobbyist's "information broker." CompuServe bought information from companies such as Reuters News and Grolier Publishing and placed it on a huge mainframe computer in Ohio. It set up a bank of phone lines and modems so that anyone with a computer and modem at home could connect to this mainframe full of information. For about $6 an hour, you could connect and search through the information. You could also send electronic mail to fellow CompuServe users: the message you typed on your keyboard was saved as a file on CompuServe's mainframe, tagged with the name of your intended recipient. Next time your correspondent logged on to CompuServe, she was able to download this file to her computer and read it on her screen.

Today CompuServe is but one of half a dozen national on-line services. Molly connected herself to one of the newest, eWorld, which is sponsored by Apple Computer and packaged with every Apple Macintosh computer that comes off the assembly line. The fastest-growing service is America Online, an independent company with over one million subscribers; the largest is Prodigy, which is controlled by Sears and IBM. These and others are competing to provide the best collections of information, in the form that's easiest to use, to families in the United States and around the world. Subscriptions cost just under $10 a month, with the providers supplying special software for Windows, Macintosh, or DOS computers.

download—to copy a file from a distant computer to your own. The file, which might contain words, pictures, or even sound and video, travels *down* the wire from them to you. When you reverse the process and send one of your files to the distant computer, it's called an *upload*.

Like many others, Molly's family computer came equipped with a modem and a subscription to an on-line information service. Up until last Thursday night, only her father had used that part of the computer (and he'd used it to get a recipe for pasta sauce). Molly used the on-line service, called eWorld, to locate and *download* information and ideas for her assignment on endangered species.

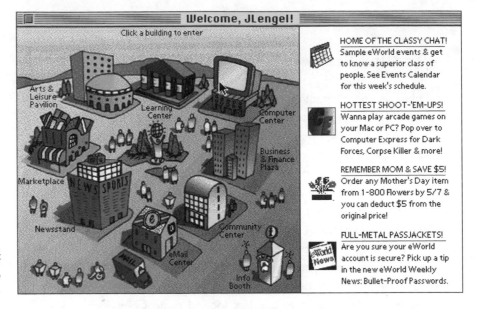

Once you are connected, you can click on any one of the buildings in eWorld to get more information.

Let's follow Molly's progress as she worked. She double-clicked on the eWorld icon on her computer to start the program that would connect her up. She typed in her family's password and clicked on the Connect button.

The computer told the modem to dial eWorld's number. It rang twice, then the modem at the other end picked up and emitted a steady beep. Molly's modem, upon hearing the beep, beeped back with a coded message saying "Connect us to eWorld, please." This message found its way through the national telephone network to the Apple Online Services computers in Napa, California. The eWorld computer checked its subscriber list, verified that Molly's family subscription was paid up, and let her into eWorld. What Molly sees at this point is a picture on her computer screen that looks like a little village.

This is where Molly sees the picture of the library, which she clicks on in order to begin researching her report. The clicking takes her to the Learning Center, where she clicks on the Reference icon. Here she finds an icon for *Grolier's Encyclopedia*, clicks it, and searches for the word "endangered." In less than five seconds she has a list of over 100 places where the word occurs in this reference. Molly chooses one and reads a lengthy article on "endangered species."

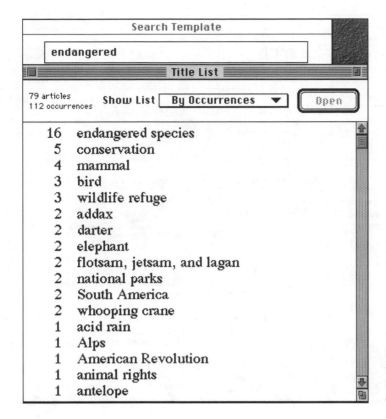

Key word searches are
the best way to start your
research in the electronic
on-line encyclopedias.

Skimming the article for things she doesn't already know, she finds that pollution is a common source of endangerment, and that both chimpanzees and tigers are on the list of animals soon to be extinct. She copies some information about wildlife refuges to a word-processing document. She finds the reading level a bit high for her, but she plows ahead nonetheless. While browsing through other reference sources, she finds a few items on the Time Machine, then finds her way to the Reuters News Service icon. She selects "News of the Environment." Her key word search on "endangered" garners her a news article about trading in animal skins, which she reads and excerpts of which she copies into her word-processing document. She makes sure to copy the source and the date, so it can be cited properly in her report. Later in her cruise through eWorld she finds United Press International, with articles about pollution in Peru, the earth winds balloon, logging in Cambodia, and a man attacked by a

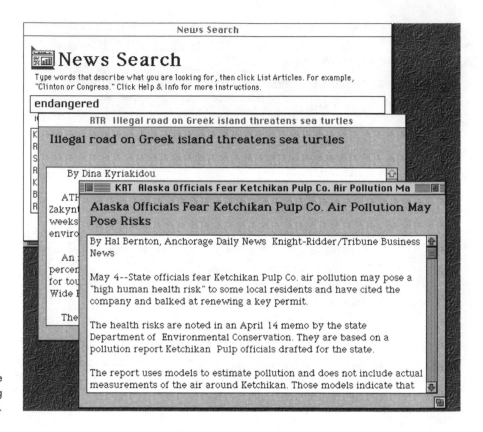

News Search

News Search

Type words that describe what you are looking for, then click List Articles. For example, "Clinton or Congress." Click Help & Info for more instructions.

endangered

RTR Illegal road on Greek island threatens sea turtles

Illegal road on Greek island threatens sea turtles

By Dina Kyriakidou

KRT Alaska Officials Fear Ketchikan Pulp Co. Air Pollution Ma

Alaska Officials Fear Ketchikan Pulp Co. Air Pollution May Pose Risks

By Hal Bernton, Anchorage Daily News Knight-Ridder/Tribune Business News

May 4--State officials fear Ketchikan Pulp Co. air pollution may pose a "high human health risk" to some local residents and have cited the company and balked at renewing a key permit.

The health risks are noted in an April 14 memo by the state Department of Environmental Conservation. They are based on a pollution report Ketchikan Pulp officials drafted for the state.

The report uses models to estimate pollution and does not include actual measurements of the air around Ketchikan. Those models indicate that

Topical news stories are easy to search for using the on-line services.

FAIR USE

Can students freely copy what they find at the on-line services and reprint them in school assignments? Yes, just as they can quote from a newspaper or magazine or book. The law specifically allows students to use copyrighted material for student school assignments. Most schools will expect the student to acknowledge the source of anything copied into a report, whether it's a single sentence, a whole page, a picture, or even an idea. *Even if the student ignores this rule, most teachers are canny enough to detect when a student has constructed a report simply by assembling pieces of copied work. If Mr. Kowalski spots a suspect phrase—a string of words he doubts Molly composed herself—he can use that phrase as a key word to search the electronic library and quickly find the source of her words.

* Check with the teachers at your school on how to credit electronic sources.

deer in Canada. All are relevant to her topic. Among the news stories she notes is "China Executes Panda Skin Seller," which causes her to think seriously about the subject of her report.

While browsing on-line at eWorld, Molly encounters Youth Central, an electronic street corner for kids. She engages in live on-line conversation—through words entered from the keyboard—with other students around the world. In the midst of comparing ages and schools and opinions about music, Molly learns from a student in Minnesota (known on-line as C607, but in reality named Bonnie Montoya, age twelve) that some great pictures can, downloaded at America Online, in the Reference Desk.

Molly walks across the street to the home of her friend Emily, whose mother subscribes to America Online so she can get daily stock market quotes. With Emily as her guide, she finds her way to the Reference Desk and the Software Library. She searches "endangered" but finds nothing. So she searches for a typical endangered animal, the tiger, and finds sixty-five items with "tiger" in the title. Most are irrelevant (items about the Detroit baseball team and contributions from the Tiger Software Company), but many are useful. She finds one file described as a "life-size color poster of a Bengal tiger." As she begins to download it, Emily points out that the file is so large it will take forty-one minutes to transfer it from the America Online computer to hers. They don't have time for that now, so they cancel the download and find a smaller drawing that comes across the wire in less than a minute.

Another picture, this one of a rare white tiger, will take twenty-one minutes to get, so they instruct the computer to download it later. Next morning, Emily brings (on a floppy disk) a full-screen detailed photo of an endangered tiger for Molly to use in her report. But before she left Emily's America Online, Molly found quite a bit for her report:

- a short article on wildlife conservation from *Compton's Encyclopedia* (from the Reference Desk)
- ninety-six short articles that mention the tiger, also from Compton's
- an article from *Scientific American* about the manatee as an endangered species, with an African folk tale about the ori-

gin of this unique animal; from the same magazine, articles about ridley turtles in India (from the Searchable Index section of the Reference Desk)

- from today's *New York Times*, an article about congressional Democrats' power base being endangered (from the Reference Desk)

- from the on-line TV listings, notice of a show to be aired Sunday evening at eight: "Corbett: In Search of the Disappearing Tiger" (Molly watched the show on her computer screen and clipped several frames to use as still pictures in a subsequent report.)

- from an archive of the last year of stories from *Time* magazine, sixty-eight references to tigers, including a cover story, "Tigers on the Brink" (from the Reference Desk at America Online)

- also from *Time,* an article called "Tiger Poacher," which helped Molly better understand the morbid fate of the Chinese panda-skin thief

- the names of at least 150 books on endangered species that sit on the shelves of university libraries in five states (gathered through a Gopher search at America Online's Internet Connection)

- a long paper on the endangered red-legged frog, which included references to Mark Twain's "The Notorious Jumping Frog of Calaveras County" as well as interesting scientific information (found in *Newsweek* archives, available via Gopher at America Online's Internet Connection).

Skimming

It was one of the things they taught in "study skills" class: how to skim a book for information. This skill is absolutely essential to survival in the online universe. Molly uncovered hundreds of articles and pictures in her eWorld and America Online searches. Without the ability quickly to peruse a list of hits to identify those that might be relevant, or to scroll through a long article for fresh ideas and information, Molly would never have completed her report. You can't read everything that comes across the electronic desktop. Nor should you. To read every word on the information highway would be like inspecting each pebble on the pavement as you drove down the street. It's safe and interesting, but you don't get there on time. Skimming has always been a key to literacy; its importance multiplies when you're on-line.

information server—a computer set up to serve information over a network. Any computer can be turned into a server with the right software. By connecting my computer to a server, I can download any files I find there.

Molly's report found its way to Mr. Kowalski's desk on Friday morning. It wasn't bad. Molly wished she'd had more time to think about all the information she'd gathered on-line—it was too bad she'd waited until the last minute. It's not enough simply to gather information, pictures, facts, and ideas. People need time to compare one with another, to look at the problem from several points of view, to put the found items in some sort of order, and most important to come up with an overarching concept or "angle" around which to build a report. Molly's angle was that we ourselves are the cause of much endangerment of animals, that there's no one to blame but us: we demand to see pandas in our zoos, we think that the ground-up

The Internet

Of all the hours Molly spent on-line Thursday night, most frustrating was her time on the Internet. The Internet is a collection of university and government computers that are connected so they can share information. Many of these institutions set up *information servers* on the Internet, which anyone can tap into and explore. Setting up (and later maintaining) such a server is purely voluntary, and the practice is common among colleges and independent research groups. Through her connection to America Online, Molly browsed through a list of these Internet servers, looking for material on endangered species. Most of what she found was irrelevant, no longer connected (someone shut the server off or changed its name), or useless to her at the moment (such as the list of books in the East Wisconsin State University Library). Because the Internet is voluntary, decentralized, and unindexed, it's not an easy place to find what you are looking for in a short time. But because some of the leading researchers in science, history, and literature are publishing new ideas to Internet servers every day, and because they don't charge you to read them, the Internet is a lush garden of ever-changing unpredictable information. Don't start your child with the Internet in its raw form; begin with one of the family on-line services, where information is indexed and organized. As kids become adept at this kind of online work, they may wish to move up to the Internet. (See the appendix for a list of suitable Internet sites for kids.)

bones of tigers will heal our sore ankles, we like to wear jewelry made of elephant tusks, and we want the cheapest lumber to build our houses, even if it comes at the expense of an owl's habitat. She arrived at these rather sophisticated ideas by reading many of the on-line sources, which tend to be more up-to-date and less afraid of controversy than her school textbooks.

Her report included quotations from several of the articles, a map of tiger habitats in the world, and a photo of a white tiger. On the cover was an enlarged tiger face surrounding the title. Not bad for two hours' work!

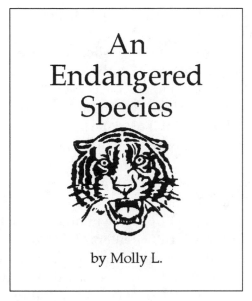

An Endangered Species

by Molly L.

Using On-Line Information

. . . .

Most families new to the world of on-line information gain the best introduction by subscribing to one of the public information services. For far less than the cost of cable TV, any one of these services will provide students with plenty of valuable references, provocative ideas, and relevant facts. Any student who makes serious use of such a resource will no doubt succeed in school.

The on-line services provide a variety of features that are useful for schoolwork:

- *Reference works*—Encyclopedias, magazine and newspaper current editions and archives, and image collections, all searchable by key word, and with copy and paste capabilities. These can be useful in almost any subject, to gather background information and uncover new ideas. Most are well indexed and fast, so that searching and finding is almost instantaneous. Magazines available on-line range from those of general interest to specialty titles in sports, health, hobbies, technical subjects, cooking, home repair, consumer information, and technology.

- *Scholarly organizations*—Collections from the National Geographic Society, the Smithsonian Institution, NASA, and others for students to use in their work. Many provide subsections on school curriculum areas such as science, geography, and history, full of materials useful for students.

- *Educational publishers*—Works by Scholastic, Random House, and others. Students will find excerpts from books, collections of stories, and image libraries that they can incorporate into their reports and research projects.

- *News and weather*—Up-to-the minute dispatches and feature articles from AP, UPI, Reuters, *USA Today*, *The New York Times*, and others. Many are posted to these services as soon as they're filed and often before they're printed. All are searchable by key word, so you can find the story you need from the thousands of articles stored in these electronic news files. You can also get weather reports from all over the world.

- *Discussion groups*—Homework helper advice, live student-to-student conversations, a chance to question politicians, authors, and celebrities, and topical discussion areas. These can be useful sources of new ideas, reactions from peers, and pointers to new sources of information. You will recall that Molly used one of these discussion groups to help her find some of the material for her report on endangered species.

- *Curriculum projects*—Easy access to the results of studies conducted by groups of students and teachers from disparate locations. Survey responses, discrete data, and author reports are compiled at home, then sent to a central location through the on-line service. Apple Global Education, for instance, on eWorld, links schools from several dozen countries who study topics of student interest and produce a weekly global student on-line newspaper. National Geographic's Kids Network, available on America Online, enables thousands of students to gather information on the pH of their raindrops, then share it electronically.

- *Electronic Mail*—The ability to send messages to other folks on-line. You can send a message to anyone who subscribes to one of these services or has an account on the Internet. Your correspondents might be fellow students working on similar projects or scientists at leading research centers.

The Commercial On-line Services

Most of the on-line services offer many more types of information: stock market quotations, airline schedules, and home shopping, for instance, that are not immediately useful for schoolwork but add to the value of the service as a family resource. Here is a brief summary of the five leading services, with suggestions on where to go to find help with schoolwork. All of them work with both Macintosh and IBM and compatible machines that run Windows.

America Online

With over 1.5 million members, America Online (AOL) is the fastest growing of the services and among the easiest to use. Its reference

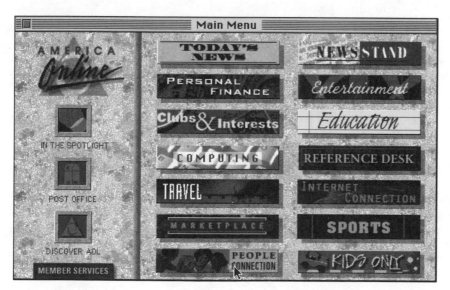

There is a whole world of information to explore on America Online

117

works include the text of *Compton's Encyclopedia*; an archive of articles from *Scientific American*; the *National Geographic* magazine and many others, all organized in the Reference Desk, visible as an icon on the America Online main menu. AOL is easy for beginners to use and has an index so you can find what you need from the huge array of information.

For the news, you can find Reuters, *Time* magazine, UPI, and *The New York Times* on America Online, along with many other magazines. In addition, America Online hosts

- the Academic Assistance Center, designed to help kids connect with teachers for additional reinforcement of what they are learning, help with homework, or help with skills that have become rusty
- an active education area, including a forum called Kids Only On Line (KOOL) and a Parents' Information Network
- Barron's Book Notes, an on-line set of book notes on classic writings
- the Scholastic Network, an area designed especially for teachers and children in school
- resources from the Library of Congress
- guides to CNN, the Discovery Channel, and the Learning Channel
- SAT preparation guides
- bulletin boards for the National Education Association, the Association for Supervision and Curriculum Development, the National Geographic Society, and other scholarly organizations
- an Internet gateway that allows key word searching of a selected set of Internet servers.

eWorld

This is the newest of the family-oriented on-line services, a part of Apple Computer, Inc., and installed inside every new Macintosh computer. eWorld does not offer all the information services that America

Online does, but it is easier to use and better organized. eWorld offers the text of *Grolier's Encyclopedia*; Reuters and UPI news; and a timeline of historical events, all organized into the Reference area in the eWorld Learning Center. On your computer screen, eWorld opens with the Town Square, a place with several buildings: the Learning Center, which looks like a library; a news building; a business and finance edifice; and an Arts & Leisure Pavilion. You click on a building to go inside and find the information you need. Like the other services, eWorld has electronic mail, stock quotes, and on-line shopping. It also has lots of technical information from Apple Computer that can help you upgrade or troubleshoot your home computer.

eWorld has several areas particularly useful for schoolwork:

- the Educator Connection in the Learning Center, with information for parents, students, and teachers on home schooling, software reviews, a software "Dear Abby" to help find programs of interest, and lots more
- the Family Focus section, with templates for projects using standard kids' software packages, stories, interactive mystery games, and book reviews
- the Apple Global Education Forum in the Learning Center, with ongoing curriculum projects for students around the world
- the Multimedia and Education Forum, with examples of multimedia school reports done by real students, all downloadable for fresh ideas
- the Arts & Leisure Pavilion's Hollywood Online section, with QuickTime clips of current movies that can be used in student projects

Prodigy

Prodigy has more than a 1.5 million subscribers, almost all home users. Prodigy sports the *Academic American Encyclopedia*, with a feature that links current events to the encyclopedia, and the AP online news services. In Prodigy, you choose your information sources from a series of menus on the screen. The screens are colorful, but they draw slowly on the screen compared with America Online or eWorld. On most screens, Prodigy includes advertisements from airlines, book companies, and food vendors. In addition to the usual list of services useful for schoolwork, Prodigy includes

- the Homework Helper on-line research service, where kids can type in questions that send the service searching through hundreds of sources to come up with pertinent on-line articles and graphics and creating a list in order of relevance
- an index of news photos that can be clipped and copied
- a Political Profile section, which contains information about members of Congress, including short bios, voting records, ratings by political organizations, special-interest contributors, and committee assignments; you can also send an electronic letter to any member you look up
- the White House Memo, an in-depth look at the president, his staff, and their daily agendas of speeches and public memos
- in-depth travel guides
- a special feature from National Geographic that lets kids take an on-line trip to the seven continents and even outer space

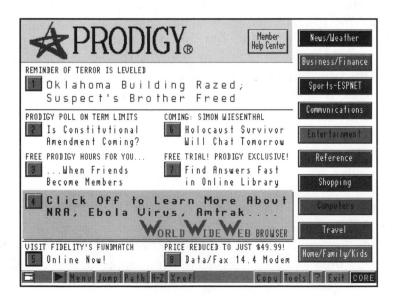

Prodigy's Homework Helper on-line research service has received high marks from kids and teachers alike.

CompuServe

The oldest and largest of the services, CompuServe includes a huge variety of information sources, many of which are technical and wide-ranging. Its encyclopedia is Grolier's *Academic American Encyclopedia*; its news services include the Associated Press and Newsgrid, a combination of domestic and international news services. In addition, the following areas on CompuServe can be quite useful in completing school assignments:

- the Reference Library, with an up-to-date listing of *Books in Print* for both the United States and United Kingdom, the *American Heritage Dictionary*, a variety of resources from the United States Census Bureau, Information USA (a listing of all the free and nearly free government publications) and *Marquis Who's Who*
- an extensive Newspaper Library, whose articles are listed by subject
- Forums for a great variety of hobby groups, issue-centered groups, and professions, each with a bulletin board where novices can ask questions

CompuServe offers several different user interfaces. Make sure you get the one best suited to your computer's configuration. These interfaces work well for a student, but compared with eWorld or America Online, it's not as easy to point and click your way around.

The Microsoft Network

Sometime late in 1995, the Microsoft Network is scheduled to come on-line at the same time Windows '95 is shipped. It will offer many of the same services as the other on-line services plus a number of extended services all its own.

What to Look for

As you choose an on-line information service, look for the following features:

Ease of Use

Students must be able to get their information without difficulty or confusion. First, connecting with the on-line service should be simple (with most services this is automatic). Next, it should be obvious to the student where the information is and how to get it. Equally important, the service should allow key word searches to help students find the data that's most relevant to their assignment—and to find it quickly (pointing and clicking at a picture or menu item is easier for kids than typing in commands with the keyboard).

Useful Information

Not all on-line services are equally useful when it comes to schoolwork. It is important to choose a service that offers the right mix of information for kids. Make sure your child has no trouble reading the encyclopedias. Make sure the reference works are not limited to *Hydrodynamics Abtracts* and *Digest of Pork-Belly Futures Prices,* but extend to works that are useful to children. Look for strong collections of information on literature, history, science, and geography; avoid services that focus on business, finance, sports, and entertainment.

Easy Navigation

It should be so easy, a child could do it! It shouldn't take more than two or three mouse clicks to find the encyclopedia or the newswire. Look for lots of Find or Search buttons on most of the information screens, to help students find what they need quickly. A student should be able to browse through the service, looking for new sources of information, without getting lost.

Fast Local Access

Make sure that the on-line service you choose maintains a phone number that's a local call for you. If at all possible, choose the service that offers the fastest access, which today is 9,600 or 14,400 baud. Find a neighbor who subscribes to one of the services or ask if your child's school subscribes, and see how fast it is: click on a piece of information and see how long it takes to view it on the screen.

How On-line Access Works

When you launch your on-line service software, the first thing it does is tell the modem to dial up the local number of the service. You can usually hear the modem pick up the phone line, beep in the touch tones, and ring the number. This call will be answered by a modem down at the local phone company building. The two modems beep back and forth to establish a conversation. Then the modem in the phone building connects itself to the information service's computer through a set of special shared telephone lines. Now your computer is talking directly to the "host" computer at America Online or eWorld or Prodigy. When you click on a picture, for instance, the location of the click goes through the phone lines to the host computer, which sends back the information that you asked for so it shows up in a window on your computer. Your computer carries on a digital conversation with the computer at your favorite information service. Sometime early in the conversation, the host computer asks you for your password, so that it can make sure you're a subscriber. All the while you are talking, the information service is keeping track of the time, so your account can be billed accordingly. When you sign off or disconnect from the service, the billing clock stops and the modem hangs up the telephone.

Cost

The various on-line information services compete with each other to sign up subscribers, so the subscription prices are comparable no matter which service you choose. At the time of this writing, the going rate for a full subscription is about $9 per month, which includes three to five hours of connect time. Most families will not use more than five hours each month—a project like the one Molly did at the beginning of this chapter used up about an hour of connect time. Additional hours cost $3 to $5.

What You Need to Get Started

. . . .

To begin using one of the on-line services, you need

baud—the speed at which a bit of data is transmitted per second. The higher the baud, the faster you will get the information.

- A Macintosh or Windows personal computer.
- A standard modem of at least 2,400 baud. 9,600 works much better and is well worth the additional cost.
- A telephone line. You can use your regular telephone line: just plug the modem into it as you would attach an extension phone. If someone calls while you're using the modem, they will get a busy signal.
- Special software. Each of the information services provides its own software that you must run on your computer.

How to Subscribe

. . . .

If the software for one of the on-line information services came already installed on your computer, simply double-click on the software, and follow the instructions. With most setups, the software will connect you to the service, where you will be asked for your name and address. Then it will establish a way for you to pay your subscription fee; in most cases you will type in your credit card number. Then you're in. Each month your credit card will be billed for your monthly subscription fee and any extra hours that you use beyond the minimum.

If your computer came without software for one of the services, you need to obtain a "starter kit": a floppy disk and a set of instructions that you can purchase from your local computer store, from a mail-order software catalog, or by calling the information service directly. These kits cost $15 to $30 and usually include ten hours of free connect time. You copy the software from the floppy disk to your hard drive and from there follow the steps in the previous paragraph to establish an account with the information service. Check the appendix for a list of 800 numbers for the various services.

On-line Services Closer to Home

How would you like to have twenty-four-hour access to PTA notices, permission slips, and homework assignments and a place where you can exchange notes with your child's teacher or principal? To accomplish this and to connect with the community, many schools are creating their own BBSs (bulletin board systems). All you need to start your own BBS is a computer with a hard drive, a modem, a telephone line, and some special setup software available for purchase through mail-order catalogs or your local computer store. Besides fostering better communications in the school community, the software can be used by members of the larger community (such as local nursing homes, retirement communities, or grandparents). Children and older citizens can then communicate and compare notes about their lives, past and present.

Next Steps

In the next chapter, we take a side road on the information highway and look at what a student's life might be like as we come of age in the information era. We'll move from fact gathering to idea creating, using the home computer as a tool for linking and thinking.

chapter 6

Making All the Right Connections

None of us grew up with the kinds of information tools that we explored in chapters 4 and 5. References available on CD-ROM and on-line represent a whole new world of instant information for students and parents to probe and examine. In turn, the availability of these references is going to transform the way homework is conceived, plotted out, completed, and rewarded.

Chapter 6 outlines the new skills that students and their parents need to take full advantage of this latest information revolution. It shows how the CD-ROMs, atlases, and on-line references that we learned about in chapters 4 and 5 can be combined and linked to establish a rich environment for study and learning. It provides examples, hints, and tips on how to conduct effective key word searches, a common feature of most of the information sources mentioned in Chapters 4 and 5. It demonstrates how to use copy-and-paste and hypertext features to quickly grab an idea and follow it up in a variety of sources. It suggests methods for deciding which kinds of sources are best for various types of student projects.

Beyond these details, this chapter points up the value of an open, almost playful attitude toward information and ideas. This new attitude, coupled with the power of computerized information, can turn the task of completing a homework assignment into an opportunity for exploring, thinking, and learning.

You and your child will learn the value of uncovering interesting bits of information and anecdotes that spice up a school project or homework assignment. You will learn how to use the computer to capture and save certain excerpts from their electronic sources as you navigate through them, so that the words and pictures and ideas can become part of the finished product. The purpose of all this is to help your child approach even a simple report as a voyage of discovery— and to help your child grow into the role of *knowledge navigator.*

How Did He Do That?

The Beatles said it: "There's gonna be a revolution." And they're not the only ones. It all started in history class. We were studying the American Revolution—you know, 1776, George Washington and Bunker Hill, and all that—when some of the kids were grossed out by all the shooting, stabbing, and blood. Then the teacher asked, "Did we really have to have a war to get independence from England? Could we have had a revolution without a war?" Well, that got us all to thinking. So the teacher gives us a special homework assignment—we have a week to finish it—to write an essay on revolution and war.

I used my computer at home to get information on this topic, and boy, was I surprised. I found out all sorts of things about revolutions that I never knew. And that my parents and my teacher didn't know, either. Did you know about the Industrial Revolution? It happened in the 1800s, but there was no war, no army, no guns. And see these two guys on the computer? One's Thomas Jefferson, the other Mao Ze-dong (they used to spell it Mao Tse-tung, but they changed it, as I learned from my computer). Both of these guys were revolutionaries, but in two very different revolutions. I learned a lot while searching through the information with my computer, and my essay turned out to be an illustrated report that I showed to the class on the computer at school. I would have gotten an A instead of B+ if I had spelled "scientific" correctly.

Let's follow Alex's progress in his work to complete an essay assignment on revolution for his history teacher. It's interesting to note how, in the process of finding information, thinking about it, and making connections to even more resources, he learned new skills and reflected on his attitude toward his assignment.

It all started at the end of a typical school day. Alex came in the door from school, banging his backpack down on the kitchen table. The history book fell out onto the floor and spilled loose papers and notes all over the linoleum. His father spotted one, over by the refrigerator, with "homework" scrawled across the top. "What's this?" he asked. Alex looked at it and explained that they'd gotten a new assignment that day about revolution. If they did a good job on the essay, he added, they wouldn't have to take the unit exam next week. Alex's father hummed, "there's gonna be a revolution, oh oh," part of a Beatles tune recalled from his misspent youth. Alex asked, "What's that you're singing?" and learned from his father about the "revolutions" of the 1960s. This made no sense to Alex, who was born in the 1980s; rolling his eyes, he went off to begin work on his assignment.

First into his CD-ROM drive was the electronic encyclopedia. A search for the key words "revolution" and "war" appearing in the same paragraph uncovered several dozen hits.

As expected, there was a long article on the American Revolution. Alex browsed the article, then highlighted, copied and clipped a sentence that included the phrase "struggle to ensure freedom"; this, he pasted into his word processor which he accessed through the encyclopedia. From there he went on to find a photo of Thomas Jefferson. Could a man with a ponytail be a revolutionary?

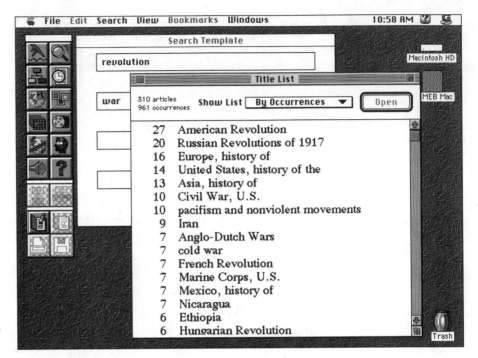

Start your research using an
electronic encyclopedia by
doing a key word search.

Jefferson's name appeared many times in the article as a key revolutionary. Alex didn't think he looked like much of one. Neither did
Benjamin Franklin, a bald, paunchy fellow. He checked out their
biographies (which were available as captions to the photos) and
found that both were scientists, writers, and diplomats, but neither
was a military man. He saved their pictures to his word processor.

Back at the article on the American Revolution, he encountered
the phrase, "anticolonial movement." He wasn't sure what that
meant, so he instructed the computer to do another key word search
for that phrase wherever it appeared. Up came many references to
African countries and leaders. He followed up the references to
uncover Kenya's movement for independence from England in the
1960s, Kenneth Kaunda, and Nelson Mandela. These gray-haired
leaders' pictures were saved into his word processor along with
Jefferson and Franklin. Alex wondered about the parallels between
Africa of the 1960s and America of the 1770s. He called up a map of
Africa from the CD-ROM to find Kenya and South Africa. He noted

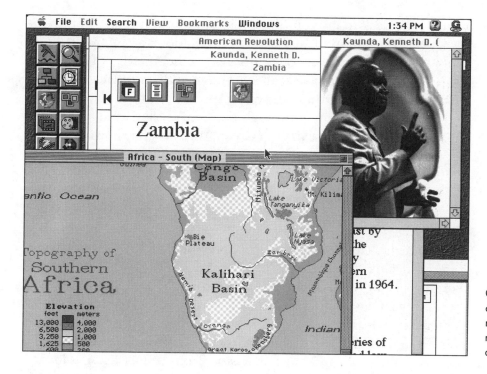

Opening multiple windows
on your computer lets you
move quickly from text, to
maps, to pictures, and back
again.

in his mind that they were even farther from England than the American colonies were.

Looking through his original search results, he found many revolutions listed, all violent: France, Russia, China, Cuba. He hyperlinked to China, and discovered yet another revolutionary, Mao Zedong. The photograph revealed a tired-looking man with thinning hair and a chubby torso: another face to save to his word processor. Checking in Microsoft's *Bookshelf* CD-ROM, Alex found the name spelled Mao Tse-tung. Curious, he uncovered a brief explanation of the shift to the pinyin spelling system for Chinese names in the early 1980s. Just at that moment Alex's mother looked over his shoulder and asked what he was working on. She didn't see the connection between Chairman Mao and the American Revolution, so Alex explained to her the train of references that got him to where he was. Alex realized he'd gotten a bit off the track, so he took a snack break, then went on his bicycle to the town library. There he browsed through some big picture books on the American Revolution. He went to the desk to take out the book, but found it didn't fit into his backpack. The librarian suggested he take a look at a new CD-ROM that just came in, a collection of images on the American Revolution from the National Archives called *The Revolutionary War Gallery of Images* from Fife & Drum Software. Alex checked out the CD-ROM and took it home. Leafing through the images, he found an engraving of the massacre at Lexington Green, then several showing British tax collectors getting tarred and feathered. These images from the 1770s were both amusing and scary. The next image showed a mock hanging of a British official by angry colonists. Alex's natural abhorrence to and curiosity about violence rose to the surface as he saved these images to his word processor. Who started the violence? Was it the colonists' hate for the British oppressors? Or was it the trigger-happy redcoats at Lexington? Alex jotted down these questions in the word processor on his computer, so he could look at them later.

The next day Alex took the CD-ROM of images to school to show his teacher, but first he visited the school library; there the librarian pointed him to the computer in the corner and suggested he call up a program called *Point of View: U.S. History* from Scholastic. Alex looked through the menus to figure out how to do a key word search in this program, which was one he'd never used before. He chose the Find menu and entered "revolution" in the text box. After almost a minute of searching, the program listed several dozen hits, including many of the same topics he'd seen before. But there was a new listing: "Industrial Revolution." Alex clicked on the phrase and found a concise summary of the economic changes of the nineteenth century. He copied part of this text to a disk he had with him, for later reference. He found a picture of a factory and an excerpt from a factory worker's journal. Alex had uncovered a revolution that hadn't required a war.

Back home in the evening, Alex was intent on finding more warless revolutions. At the computer he used the modem to connect to the Prodigy on-line information service his family subscribed to. In the News area, he did a key-word search for "revolution." He found only one reference to a violent rebellion, that of rebels in Kashmir, but many references to news articles on telephone, computer, and TV broadcasting companies. Curious, he brought up the articles on the computer screen and skimmed through them. The first was a press

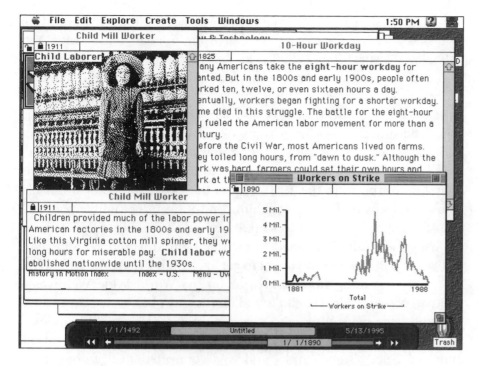

Programs like Point of View: U.S. History let kids browse through history peeking at pictures, journals, charts and graphs, and text.

release from Intel, boasting about the "revolutionary 0.6 micron manufacturing technology" used in its latest computer chip. Another was a news article reporting the merger of a film company and a cable TV company to form what the reporter described as "a revolution in the delivery of entertainment to U.S. homes." Alex had uncovered yet another form of revolution—the technological revolution spurred by scientific discovery and invention. He filled the page of notes in his word processor with relevant excerpts from these news articles.

On his way to the News area, Alex could not help but notice Prodigy's advertisements of its "Web browser." Alex had been studying spiders in school, so he wondered whether he might find some interesting information on this electronic web. After he downloaded the Web browser software he found it had nothing to do with arachnids but was some kind of Internet connection. He ran the browser and found that he was connected to the World Wide Web, a part of the Internet that linked information on several thousand computers across the globe.

The music from the living room was getting louder. Both Mom and Dad were singing along: "We don't want to change the world. You talk about destruction, well, you know you can count me out. There's gonna be a revolution. Shoo be doo, all right!" Alex asked them to cool it, but was fascinated by the song, which was full of references to "changing the Constitution," "Chairman Mao," and "revolution." The song ended as he and his parents discussed what a revolution was. Mom and Dad were impressed with Alex's understanding of the concept but disappointed that he hadn't learned of the social revolutions they lived through in the 1960s. From the closet they pulled out old photographs from that era, including one of his father with a ponytail. Alex took one of the pictures so that he could scan it into the computer using the *scanner* at school, which he figured would keep his parents happy. But he really wanted to get back onto the World Wide Web.

The first thing Alex looked for on the World Wide Web was a method of searching. He had found, in his short but varied experience of knowledge navigating with the computer, that searchable indexes were the key to quickly finding what you wanted. So he clicked on the button labeled "Net Search" and was connected to a computer at Carnegie-Mellon University in Pittsburgh. This connection was made automatically by the Web browser software program. Now the computer at Carnegie-Mellon presented Alex with a blank space into which he could enter his search words. (Next to the space Alex saw a picture of a spider, along with the Lycos and CMU logotype. The spider was apparently an *iconic* reference to the World Wide Web.)

scanner—is a device, almost like a photo-copier, that allows you to digitize picture and text from books and other documents to use in the computer.

iconic—a symbolic or pictorial representation

The World Wide Web

A few years ago, a group of scientists in Switzerland wanted to develop a system so that they could share their scientific papers with each other over a computer network. Their papers were in word-processing files already, and each of their universities or institutes had a computer network that linked them together. So each scientist set up one computer as a public information server by putting all of his or her articles onto its hard drive, along with an annotated directory of what each article was about. Then each computer was connected to the Internet. Now the other scientists could "log on" to that server and browse through the articles, thus keeping up with the growth of scientific knowledge. This idea captured the interest of scientists around the world; over the next several years most scientific groups—and many other kinds of folks—set up a public computer "site" on the Internet. A group at the University of Illinois then created a new software program that would allow people to more easily connect to and browse the information on these servers. As more and more of the sites began using this same software to organize and search their works, the network became known as the World Wide Web. Today the Web is the fastest-growing part of the Internet, and the easiest to use. To tap into the resources of the World Wide Web, you need a full connection to the Internet as well as a Web browser software program on your computer. (See the appendix for more information on connecting to the Internet.) Mosaic and Netscape are two popular (and inexpensive) Web browsers. Some of the on-line information services offer a Web browser as part of their package of services.

Alex entered "revolution" and "war." The Lycos spider searched the Web. In a matter of seconds, it returned to Alex's computer a list of several Web sites that had information on this topic. He clicked on the first item in the list, which happened to be a book collector's site. The collector had for sale an original copy of a book by Thomas Jefferson, printed in Virginia during the American Revolution. The bookseller included a lengthy excerpt from the book, concerning Jefferson's views on how Americans should treat British sympathizers in the colonies. He was against tarring and feathering. Alex copied part of this excerpt to his word processor, making careful note of its source. He was sure this was one item his teacher had never seen.

After returning to the Web browser, Alex found a listing called "Web Directory." Clicking on this phrase connected him to Stanford University, which maintains an orderly directory of many of the sites on the World Wide Web. He clicked on the News directory and from there found his way to the *Newsweek* magazine listing. He searched here by the key word "revolution" and found an article about the

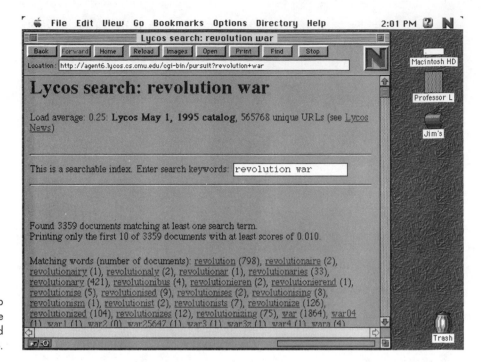

Lycos search: revolution war

Back | Forward | Home | Reload | Images | Open | Print | Find | Stop

Location: http://agent6.lycos.cs.cmu.edu/cgi-bin/pursuit?revolution+war

Lycos search: revolution war

Load average: 0.25: **Lycos May 1, 1995 catalog,** 565768 unique URLs (see Lycos News)

This is a searchable index. Enter search keywords: `revolution war`

Found 3359 documents matching at least one search term.
Printing only the first 10 of 3359 documents with at least scores of 0.010.

Matching words (number of documents): revolution (798), revolutionaire (2), revolutionairy (1), revolutionaly (2), revolutionar (1), revolutionaries (33), revolutionary (421), revolutionibus (4), revolutionieren (2), revolutionierend (1), revolutionise (5), revolutionised (9), revolutionises (2), revolutionising (8), revolutionism (1), revolutionist (2), revolutionists (7), revolutionize (126), revolutionized (104), revolutionizes (12), revolutionizing (75), war (1864), war04 (1), war1 (1), war2 (1), war25647 (1), war3 (1), war3z (1), war4 (1), wara (4)

Macintosh HD

Professor L

Jim's

Trash

Search programs help users find things more quickly on the World Wide Web.

Widening the Web

The World Wide Web uses a system of hypertext links among its documents and sites. Click on a highlighted phrase in one document, and it takes you to another document at another site, and so forth, so everything is linked to everything else. The authors of the documents embed the links in their works, using a common system called the hypertext markup language, or HTML, to identify their documents. The Web browser software on your computer can interpret and automatically interlink any HTML document on any other computer in the Web. *Hypertext cross-referencing, searching, and backtracking are new skills that students must learn to navigate successfully in today's interlinked webs of electronic information.*

rebels in Chiapas, Mexico, along with a photograph of one of their mountain guerrilla camps. It reminded Alex of the picture of Valley Forge in his history book. He copied and saved the article and picture to his notes for later reference.

Alex had navigated well, but he had not yet reached his destination. All this electronic information would be of no use unless he could find meaning in it and express that meaning to others. So he continued, no longer searching for new information, but thinking about what he had.

Alex browsed through his pages of notes, and as he did he jotted down a list, "Revolutions with War," adding five entries: French, American, Cuban, Chinese, and Russian. The "Revolutions without War" list included headings titled industrial, scientific, and technological. When he saw the pictures of Jefferson and Franklin, he typed "revolutionary warriors" and "revolutionary thinkers." He began placing his pictures under the appropriate column. Franklin was a thinker, so was Jefferson; Washington was a warrior, as is Fidel Castro. But he wasn't sure as where Mao Ze-dong should go. And he didn't know enough about Kaunda or Mandela to place them properly. To the list of revolutionary thinkers he added Einstein and Galileo, whom they had learned about in school last year.

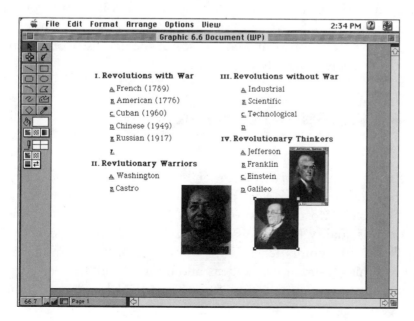

The computer can help students quickly pull their thoughts together using both pictures and words.

Now he had an idea. Up at the top of his word-processing document, Alex typed, in big letters "WHAT IS A REVOLUTION?" This, he thought, would be a good organizing scheme for his essay. He began writing, "Some say a revolution is political rebellion and protest," and went on to describe anti-British actions in colonial America and rebels in present-day Mexico. He illustrated each of these with a photograph and a quotation. The next section began, "Some say a revolution is a change in the type of government," then went on to describe Jefferson's ideas and included a reference to Mandela in South Africa. Each of these was also represented by a photograph. Alex's third section opened, "Yet others refer to scientific revolutions, such as Einstein's theory or the invention of the computer," followed by an explanation of three examples, with quotations and pictures. "Finally," wrote Alex, "you can have an industrial revolution," and described that event and why it was called a revolution. In this part he made use of data indicating a rise in manufacturing wages by means of a graph produced with the Point of View program at his school.

Alex now got to the thesis of his essay. "Not all of these revolutions involve war. Some are completely nonviolent." From here he discussed many of the ideas he had found in his searches, from Jefferson's writings about the British to the anticolonial movements in Africa. Alex concluded with the idea that all revolutions have one thing in common: something changes. But the necessity of violence, in Alex's essay, was open to question.

The Knowledge Navigator

That's not a bad report from an eighth-grader. It's full not only of specific historical examples, but of quotations, photographs, and graphs as well. Most of us would be happy if our children produced work of this quality. But Alex is not an exceptional child, except in the way he uses the computer. It is the assistance of his computer, coupled with his attitude toward ideas and information, that led Alex to produce this interesting report out of a typical homework assignment. The sources of information that Alex used are all available publicly today, at less cost than cable TV, to any home or school in the United States. The difference lies in the way that Alex employed these resources.

In completing his homework assignment for history, Alex played the role of knowledge navigator. He sailed through a sea of information, in a variety of forms, from many sources. He seemed an old hand at using the computer and connecting to all the CD-ROMs and on-line services that we learned about in chapters 4 and 5. But he exercised more skill, engaged in more thinking, and made more connections as he did his work. The successful navigator knows not just how to find her way, but also how to reflect upon where she is, to be looking constantly for new passages and connections, and to take note of the sights along the way. Most of all, the knowledge navigator *thinks*.

The computer alone cannot develop this thinking capability. Parents and teachers must help it develop in the student. If Alex had simply collected all that information, without thinking about it and relating one piece to the next, he would never have been able to assemble such an interesting piece of work. As a wise librarian once told me, "It's not how many books you have, but how well you read them." The new computerized information sources can also be "read well"—when used as the tools they're meant to be, cultivating and encouraging *independent thought*.

Developing Thinking Skills

What can parents and teachers do to encourage the kind of knowledge navigation required in today's "infotech" environment? There's no magic formula, but this set of suggestions may help.

- Talk with students about their work. When they seem absorbed in the computer, look over their shoulder, ask them what it's about, ask questions about the topic at hand, have them explain to you how they found what's on the screen. By explaining what they are working on, children often consolidate their thinking.

- Maintain a playful attitude toward information. Reward your child for uncovering a little-known fact or bringing home an interesting historical tidbit. When you don't know something, look it up on the computer. Be surprised when you learn things you didn't know. For some adults, this is not easy. But it's important to show that curiosity and finding out are positive activities.

- Ask questions that you can't answer. Then let your child (or student) impress you by finding information that helps answer the question. Encourage them to use the computer to perform this feat, and it can become a healthy game that all can learn from.

- Ask questions that have no right answer. You don't have to be much of a knowledge navigator to find the population of West Virginia on the computer. While it may be an important fact, it does not exercise the child's mind or the computer's capabilities. Open-ended questions are better. Questions that begin with "why" or "how" are usually more interesting to pursue than simple "what" or "where" questions. Open questions lend themselves to thinking.

- Delve beneath the facts. Do not accept a piece of work from your child that consists simply of reporting the facts she has found, regardless of how many there are or how many pictures and graphs accompany them. Expect students to relate the facts to some larger concept, idea, or aspect. Encourage them to have an opinion about what the facts mean. Even at a young age, children are capable of more thinking than we give them credit for.

Navigating through Information

What do you need to nurture knowledge navigators in your midst? What conditions are necessary for the kind of process and work that Alex accomplished at the beginning of this chapter?

New Tools

You need to equip your child with a new set of tools. The information-gathering tools that most of us grew up with are no longer appropriate for Alex's world. Your home computer needs a shelf of CD-ROM–based reference works that fit the needs of the growing child. Microsoft *Bookshelf*, *The Grolier's Multimedia Encyclopedia*, and an atlas can form a good beginning. That's all Alex needed to get him started. In addition, connection to an on-line information service provides new places to go in search of ideas. For clipping and excerpting whatever he found, Alex also needed software tools, such as his word-processing program or the Scrapbook on the Macintosh. He needed a computer powerful enough to do two things at once, like be connected to the on-line service while pasting items into the word processor. For most computers, this requires at least 4 megabytes of random access memory, and preferably 8.

The Electronic Art of Juggling

My children can listen to music, play the clarinet, carry on a conversation, and do their homework, all at the same time. They can *multitask*. Today's computers can do the same thing: they can run several programs simultaneously. The word processor can be open in one window while you search the encyclopedia in another. This capability allows you quickly to bring information from your references right onto your workspace. Current versions of the Macintosh and Windows operating systems allow this multitasking, but they require adequate memory to do it well, because each program that's running must take its place in the computer's internal memory bank, or RAM. The more RAM you have, the more programs you can run at once. On a Macintosh, 4 megabytes of RAM will allow you to run the operating system (1.7 megabytes), an integrated tool package that includes a word processor such as ClarisWorks (0.8 megabytes), and the on-line service eWorld (1.2 megabytes) at the same time. But just barely. Windows programs take up proportionally more RAM, so you'll need even more memory to multitask with Windows. To encourage experimentation and active knowledge navigation by your child, try to arrange an upgrade to 8 megabytes of RAM.

New Attitudes

The old guidelines—narrow your topic, use the index, locate the relevant section, and copy out the citation—are less useful to the knowledge navigator. New attitudes toward information have been evolving: use references to brainstorm novel ideas, connect to related material, ask questions about search results, and compile all significant data. This change denotes a different attitude toward learning and using reference works.

What's Out	**What's In**
Narrow your topic before beginning your research.	Use the computer to brainstorm your topic.
Use the contents and index to home in on your topic.	Hyperlink to related materials and sources.
Locate the relevant paragraphs and sentences.	Ask questions about what you find.
Copy out useful citations to note cards.	Clip, save, and compile all relevant materials.

Tools for researching have changed, the order of events is different, and effective strategies have been altered. In some ways the digitization of information liberates us from restrictions on how we locate and use information. At the same time, the freedom carries with it new responsibilities to use information wisely and meaningfully.

New Skills

More information is available to our children, it's easier to find, and it comes much more quickly to hand. But by itself that is not an advance in learning. New technologies must be coupled with new skills that make sense out of the information and turn it into knowledge.

First we need to ask good questions, questions that demand research from a variety of sources, questions for which there are no easy answers, questions that provoke a child to seek new information. Teachers, parents, and kids need to ask questions this way if they are to take full advantage of the new information technologies.

Snot

A good science teacher began the sixth-grade curriculum with this set of questions:

What is snot?

Where does it come from?

Why do we have it?

It may not seem like it, but this seemingly crass and tasteless sequence was carefully thought through and crafted to fit the curiosities of adolescents and the needs of the curriculum. These are questions that inherently interest the audience; the answers to them are wide-ranging, requiring considerable research and thought; and in the process of answering them, the students will learn quite a bit about the life sciences. Questions like these provoke a good start to the process of computerized navigating through knowledge. They take the student in many different directions, along many different paths on the information highway. And the concepts the students uncover are certainly worth knowing, extending far beyond the immediate topic.

A good question and an active exploration, though, are not enough. A successful knowledge navigator knows when to expand the search and when to narrow it; when to seek out new sources of information and when to go back to the ones that started it off. These are skills developed only through practice. The student must "mess around" with information, make some mistakes, and waste some time. Otherwise no learning occurs.

As students wander along the information highway, they will find it helpful take notes: jotting down in the Notepad or in a blank word-processing document each place they visit, each source they browse. Keeping a good record of where they've been builds organizational skill and helps them guide the next search.

When searching is done, yet another skill comes into play: organizing and thinking. Suggest students lay out on the table (actually, onto the computer screen) all the things they've found: ideas, words, pictures, tidbits of data. Have them look for commonalities and contrasts—ferret out key ideas, look for items that fall into a natural order. Alex practiced this skill when he sat down to compose his report. Having done it several times before, he could do it easily this time. But organization is a skill that requires teaching and practice.

New Expectations

Going to the library was once the generally accepted research method in completing a school assignment, and a simple report on the results was all that was expected of today's parents. I remember being asked in high school to find and compile the agricultural output of each of the states in 1840. It took several trips to two libraries, a shelf full of books, many note cards, and most of a month. In the end, even though my report consisted simply of a table of facts, it earned a good grade. Today, however, a student knowledge navigator could find that same information with her computer in a few moments. These days, facts alone are not enough for a good report. Instead, students must think about what the facts *mean*, compare data across decades, relate agricultural data to population figures, and draw some conclusions about how these numbers relate to the course of history. We can move beyond fact finding, toward thinking and analysis. Consequently, intellectual expectations become greater. These day both the nature of the assignment and expectations for the quality of the results have changed.

Constructivism—A Political Movement for Cement Workers?

No, no such luck. Constructivism is a view of how children learn and how education should take place. It says that in order for a student to understand an idea, she must build that idea in her own mind. It is not enough for the teacher or the book (or the computer) to explain the idea; the student must actively construct the concept for herself from its raw materials. We can look at the knowledge navigator as a student who is constructing her own path through the sea of information and from what she encounters slowly building up a map of the oceans. Not that this construction is random and unguided and without a plan; in most cases it is best accomplished under the tutelage of good teachers and parents. These guides ask questions, suggest new paths, and sometimes provide charts of unknown waters. But they let the child sail the boat. The computer can be like a set of power tools for constructivist learning.

The New Navigators

Where is the school for knowledge navigators? As in fifteenth-century Portugal, where Columbus and Vasco da Gama learned their trade, our society offers no central training authority for navigators. You learn through apprenticeships, by joining the crew and sailing with a master, by learning how the compass works, by sailing your own skiff in a protected bay. The process is the same with the computer. Your child needs to find older students who can navigate well, especially those who have been to a college that supports electronic research. Let your child watch them at work. Outfit your home computer with the right navigational tools: an encyclopedia and an on-line information service. Encourage your child to make short forays into the sea of information. Talk with your child as this happens, help him reflect on the kinds of information that rise to the surface. Make sure your child knows how to use the Scrapbook and Notepad on the Macintosh and the Notepad in Windows and/or how to save pictures and take notes in a word processor and how to multitask. Upgrade your random access memory to make this possible. Establish an environment that nourishes the budding knowledge navigator.

▶ SAFETY ON THE INFORMATION HIGHWAY ◀

There has been a lot in the press about kids and some of the unsavory characters and materials they have encountered on-line. The on-line services, just like network television, cable TV, the movies, Nintendo and Sega, music CDs and tapes, and school, can expose your children to different people with different points of view and some ideas and materials that are not always suitable for them. But these encounters are few and far between unless you intentionally seek them out—and frankly, this is all part of the challenge of being a parent in a technological age. When we advocate that the young student at your house should have time and room to "mess around" with information on the various on-line services and the Internet, we assume that you, as a parent, will be checking in now and then to make sure your child hasn't wandered too far off the path of research. The benefits from being exposed to this vast resource of information far outweigh the risks. In addition, be sure to explain that real-world safety rules about dealing with strangers apply to on-line encounters as well. Remind your children not to give their full name, address, or phone number to anyone on-line without first getting your permission. They should also never agree to meet someone they have met on-line or send that person money or their picture with-out checking with you first. You may also want to get to know their cyberspace friends just as you do their "real-world" friends. Obviously you can't always supervise your children's on-line time (and you shouldn't need to). But be sure to ask them what they have been looking at and explain that on-line services are part of the adult world and as such can be a dangerous place—just like school, the mall, and other places where you can't be with them all the time. An excellent free brochure (*Child Safety on the Information Highway*) is available from the National Center for Missing and Exploited Children, 800-THE-LOST.

From Data to Wisdom

Megabytes of facts do not a wise man make. In fact, some of the world's most famous fools are full of information but empty of ideas. Computers make more data available more quickly, but do they make us wise? Long before they had computers in classrooms, a memorable teacher once made a pyramid on the chalkboard:

Wisdom
– – Understanding – –
– – – Knowledge – – –
– – – – Information – – – –
– – – – – Data – – – – –

Data, of which there is a lot at the bottom of the pyramid (and even more today with the advent of computers), is nothing but facts, numbers, simple observations. Important, but meaningless as it sits, *data* is necessary to support the rest of the structure but insufficient to reach the top.

The human mind can absorb data and, over time, learn to relate one bit of it to another. When data are combined in our minds, the result is *information,* the second level on the pyramid. Information is useful as it builds toward knowledge but has little value in and of itself.

By combining pieces of information carefully through thinking, we can come to *know* an idea or a thing. We can distinguish it from other ideas, and we can remember it when we encounter it again. This is called *knowledge.* We can't build knowledge without information. But knowledge is not enough.

After knowing many things, we begin to realize how they are related and how the world works. With experience we confront the world with our knowledge and we find out what makes sense and what doesn't. We begin to *understand.* We can't understand without knowledge.

A few people live long enough to realize that they don't really understand anything, that the world and the people in it are more complex than they seem, and that what passes for understanding is at best tentative hypothesis. These people are wise. *Wisdom* comes only after we have a chance to stand back and reflect on how our limited human understanding meshes with the universe.

The computer is less and less useful as you move up the pyramid. But it's great at building a strong and rich foundation at the lower levels and for encouraging the spirit of mental combination and reflection that can lead us upward.

part

3

. . . .

It's Multimedia Showtime!

chapter 7

Quiet on the Set! Organizing a Simple Slide Production

At my house, "computer" has come to be something of a dirty word. Every time my daughter has a project assigned at school and it comes up in discussion at the dinner table, I always volunteer some way in which I think the computer can be helpful. She sighs and rolls her eyes (just for a moment I think she wishes she could turn in a standard report like everybody else), but in the end she is always pleased with her work. Usually, my suggestions encourage her to add a new twist to some standard project assignment—from creating maps of Australia on the computer to producing a slide show on the creation of colonial baskets. In the end she gets lots of praise for her efforts and really learns something in the process.

Since the advent of the school project, the most successful students are those who can find the requisite information, exercise the skills to summarize it quickly, and present the result in a clear and interesting way. So far in this book we have looked at how to research using the computer, how to brainstorm and organize information, and how to create a written report, newsletter, or brochure. But the computer can help in other ways too—ways that can make that final presentation a real knockout. With a little guidance and information about how to get started, your children can take advantage of some of these alternative presentation methods. That's what this section is all about. In this chapter we look at how Sarah, a sixth-grader, enhances a standard oral report project using her computer and some readily available software that her family already had (or could have easily and inexpensively acquired). She uses her computer to find information; analyze, organize, and summarize it; and create a slide show that really wows 'em in the aisles.

How Did She Do That?

Most sculptures were made out of plaster, bronze, or marble.

When I presented my slide show, I was nervous at first in front of all the other kids, but that wore off as soon as I saw that they were looking at the screen and not at me. It took me a long time to put the slide show together, but it was worth it. All the kids paid attention, and they even asked questions.

The teacher had never seen a slide show like this done by a sixth-grader like me. It had pictures of statues, buildings, sculptures, masks, and busts. Some of the statues had parts missing. One of them had no clothes on, but I decided not to use that one in my slide show. Did you know that they used different kinds of marble for different types of statues? If you look at the slide show in order, you will see that the sculpture got better over time—see, this one here on slide three is pretty crude compared with this one on slide eight. Those Greeks were pretty good artists, for two thousand years ago.

After I presented the slide show, I had to turn in a written report as well. But this was easy. Once I had prepared all the stuff for the slide show, it was already organized. All I did was take what was on my note cards and reformat it into a regular report on the word processor. I even used the pictures from the presentation as illustrations in my report.

Note from Mrs. Sullivan:
Sarah earned an A+ with this presentation. In all my years of teaching sixth grade, I had never seen a student presentation demand such attention from the other students—and from me. Frankly, I learned some new ideas about Greek art from this presentation! I had never seen most of the pictures that Sarah used, and the way she organized them was fascinating. I never knew the computers here at school could do this kind of thing. And I was surprised that kids at home could do this kind of work on the computer. What Sarah did was more than just a flashy gimmick. She actually learned more about Greek art than the other students who did their reports the old-fashioned way. I guess it's time I learned how these computers really work.

Everyone groaned when Mrs. Sullivan assigned the oral reports along with a written paper on ancient Greece. Sarah found that her topic, the art of ancient Greece, was best understood through pictures. As she conducted her research—using many of the electronic sources we learned about in chapters 4–6—Sarah came across many striking photographs of sculptures and buildings. She wanted to use these pictures in her report, and she found that the best way was to arrange them as a slide show. This she did with her home computer, saving the result along with some explanatory text on a floppy disk. At school, she popped the disk into the department's computer (which was connected to a large television monitor), and presented her slide show to the entire class.

Sarah's slide show turned out to be the best of all the oral reports delivered that week. The students watched the screen and listened to her explanations. The teacher was impressed both with the effectiveness of the presentation and the amount that Sarah learned about the topic at hand. Sarah herself grew in self-confidence, learning not only about Greek art, but about the art of presenting ideas to others. And she became a more competent computer user in the process.

How did Sarah accomplish this? Let's analyze the process she went through, step by step, and see how the computer served as the essential tool for learning at each step. In completing this very typical assignment in social studies, Sarah followed a six-step process:

1. Research

Sarah knew very little about Greek art when she started. Her text-book offered less than a paragraph of text on the topic, with a small black-and-white picture of the Parthenon up in the corner. So she followed in the footsteps of Danny (chapter 4), Molly (chapter 5), and Alex (chapter 6), using her family's computer as a tool for gathering information and learning new ideas about Greek art. She started off by exploring the topic, reading and looking at as much information as she could find, to immerse herself in the subject and get a feel for what it was all about.

She started with the electronic encyclopedias, one on CD-ROM at home and the other on the on-line information service her family

Multimedia

After much discussion and debate, we have decided, for this section only, to use examples of kids creating multimedia using the Macintosh as our base computer. This is because, at this time, there are too many individual variables (such as sound cards and monitors with varying capabilities) with machines that use Microsoft Windows to be able to troubleshoot all the "for instances" you may encounter in the limited amount of space we have. If you have recently bought a Windows machine with built-in multimedia capability, you will find it easier to do many of the projects we suggest than if you have an older machine which will be difficult to upgrade. The software products we use as examples in the chapters all run on both platforms (or equivalent software titles are named) and can be used to create the same kinds of end products, but only you the user know what adjustments you will need to make. The process of researching, organizing, and even creating a multimedia presentation remains the same for both platforms, so follow in our footsteps but take a different path when you need to. We hope the examples in these chapters will inspire you to find out what you need to know about your individual machine to be able to replicate them.

subscribes to. Here she learned that sculpture, architecture, and vase paintings seemed to be the chief examples of Greek art. She also gathered half a dozen pictures into the Scrapbook on her Macintosh computer. From an atlas on CD-ROM she copied a map of Greece. From the on-line service's Internet browser, she discovered that Yale University Press had published a CD-ROM called *The Perseus Project*, which included much information about ancient Greece, in both picture and text form, in both Greek and English. With the help of the school librarian and an interlibrary loan, Sarah managed to borrow a copy of the *Perseus* CD-ROM, and from it she uncovered a wealth of information and examples of Greek art, including hundreds of *high-resolution* photographs.

Browsing this CD-ROM enabled Sarah to learn many other ideas about the Greeks and earned her some new friends: the other kids found out that her CD-ROM could help them with their reports as well, so several of them ended up at her house after school that week to do their own research on Sarah's computer.

**high resolution —
images that contain a
large number of pixels
(the dots the computer
reads) and are there-
fore sharp.**

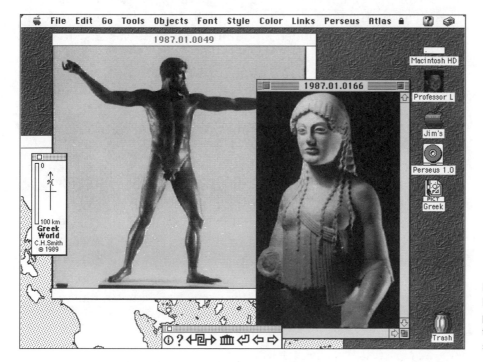

Reference CD-ROMs like The Perseus Project, filled with pictures, music, movies and text, add new dimensions to student research.

As she conducted this research, Sarah gathered many excerpts from text and copies of pictures and maps. She also confronted quite a few new ideas, which she jotted down on her computer's Notepad. She was not simply looking for an answer; instead she was exploring a wide array of information on her topic, in order to learn as much as possible about it. Because of this attitude toward information, Sarah was able to form and organize ideas of her own, the basis for independent thought.

2. Organize

It was around these ideas that Sarah began to organize her project. Using the word processor, she typed in words to represent key ideas she had found: "types of sculpture," "purposes of sculpture," "materials used," and "artistic style." Then, under each heading she jotted down the examples she had gathered. Under "types of sculpture" she listed "bust, frieze, animal, warrior, gods." Under "materials" she listed "marble, plaster, limestone, bronze, pottery." Under "marble" she listed "Parian, Hymettian, island, and plain." Since her family's word-processing program included an outline feature, it was easy to build and modify such a list.

Next Sarah printed the outline, then sat down with it and marked it up with a pencil. She moved the section on style to the end and on materials to the beginning, by drawing arrows on the outline. Then back at the computer she simply moved the words around on the screen to reorder the outline of her project.

Now she was ready to make a storyboard of her presentation. Again using her word processor, she created one page for each element of her outline. On each page she typed a key word or two to represent the point she wanted to make. This resulted in a seventeen-page document, which she saved to the hard disk in her computer. Sarah ran through the seventeen pages quickly, to see if they made sense. To improve the flow she moved one page to the end, deleted one page, and added a new one. Her pages were labeled like this:

Sculpture in Ancient Greece

Ancient Greece
Types of Sculpture
Bust
Animals
Warriors
Gods
Frieze
Purposes of Sculpture
Sculpture Materials
Plaster
Marble
Bronze
Limestone
Artistic Style
Other Greek Arts
The End

The basic organization of her project was complete. She had her key ideas, in order, on the computer. Along the way, she had many opportunities to think about her topic, to consider in her mind the ideas she had learned, and to formulate ways of explaining each idea. She also had a good storyboard, which would form the basis of her final slide show.

3. Illustrate

To make her slide show interesting to the audience, and to help them understand the main ideas, Sarah included pictures wherever she could. She looked through the images in her Macintosh Scrapbook to get a good idea of what she had collected. On each page of her outline in her word processor in ClarisWorks, she pasted an appropriate picture. A map of Greece went on page two, a bust of Pallas on page four, a statue of Achilles on page six, and so forth. The illustrations were chosen carefully to convey the topic in each case.

The Power of Images

The American Flag. The Statue of Liberty. The Mona Lisa. When you read or hear these words, the picture of the thing pops immediately into your mind. And that image leads inevitably to the key ideas the image stands for: patriotism, freedom, beauty. Image making is an ancient art. One of our earliest forms of communication was the images we painted on the walls of our caves in prehistoric times. Images are powerful and lasting representations of ideas. The computer enables students to bring these kinds of images into their schoolwork, in ways never possible before. In this chapter, and more so in the two that follow, we learn how to bring powerful pictures to bear on typical school assignments.

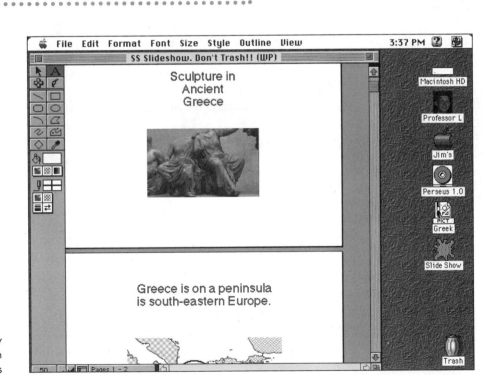

Sarah was able to quickly assemble her slide show in ClarisWorks

After working with four slides, a problem occurred: the computer was out of memory! A message appeared on the screen as Sarah was pasting in a picture on slide five: "Not enough memory to complete this operation." Sarah clicked OK to close the dialogue box, but slide five remained blank. What to do?

Sarah needed to bring more memory to bear on the situation. She recalled that she could view the memory setup by looking under the Apple menu, using the About this Macintosh item. Here she found that ClarisWorks was set to use only 800 kilobytes of memory, while her computer had more than 2 megabytes of memory left over. So, she saved her slide show, quit ClarisWorks, and increased the amount of memory allocated to the program by using the Get Info command from the File menu. She set ClarisWorks to use 2,500 kilobytes (2.5 megabytes) of random access memory. Then she opened up her slide show again and went back to work. (Check the software manual for similar problems in the Microsoft Windows environment.)

At this point Sarah began to format her slide show, first by setting the pages into a horizontal orientation, using the Page Setup item under the File menu. Because the screen of the computer is wider than it is high, this horizontal plan better fit the shape of the screen. Looking at each page, Sarah stretched and shrank the pic-

Dialogue boxes help guide the creation of a slide show in ClarisWorks.

tures by clicking on the frame around them and adjusting the size of the text so that it could be seen from a distance. She found that sixty-point type was large enough to see from far away, but small enough to allow all the words to fit on the screen.

Each page of her word-processing document had become a slide in her slide show. Sarah was now ready to run the show to see how it looked. From the View menu, she chose Slide Show and from there followed the dialogue boxes to customize her work.

For the overall "look" of the presentation, she chose a light yellow background with a dark yellow border. She set the program to advance from slide to slide each time she clicked the mouse, and she directed the computer to fade in and out of each slide. When she was finished setting it up, she clicked OK to start the slide show.

Her first viewing was pretty successful. The slides seemed to make sense, and most of them looked good. Sarah made notes as she watched: the picture in slide five needed to be centered; the illustration of the mask needed to be bigger; and the text might look better in a color other than black. Sarah stopped the slide show, went back to the word-processing document, and made the improvements she'd noted. When she viewed the slide show a second time, with its dark red text and carefully placed pictures, it seemed just right. As she watched this time, she mulled over in her mind what she might say as she showed each slide to the class.

4. Explain

Sarah was not yet ready to deliver her oral report to the class. While she had a fine show of slides on her topic, that was not enough. She needed to plan carefully what she would say as each slide appeared. At the word-processor once again, she brought up a copy of her original twelve-page outline, without the pictures. For each page, she searched her Scrapbook and Notepad for items she had written or clipped that applied to that page's topic. She read each one and thought about it. On some pages she pasted her quotations directly onto the page. For others she included only an excerpt. For some she wrote a new sentence summarizing what she had learned. By the time she was through, she had short written notes for each page.

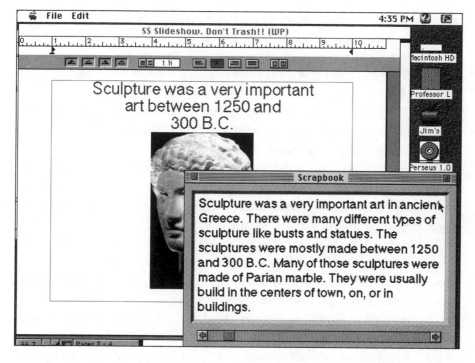

For each slide in her presentation Sarah created a notecard on the computer.

Sarah consolidated her notes onto three pages and printed a copy on paper. Then she sat with the notes in her hand as she clicked through the slide show with pictures. She looked at each note and then at the slide and decided what she would actually say as each slide appeared. It took three passes to get this right. Then she went back to the notes document, made a few revisions, adjusted the size of the type and the margins, and printed out a final set of notes for herself. This time she used heavier paper, which she trimmed down to the size of note cards. With oral explanations for each picture, Sarah now had a fully illustrated lecture with slide show, ready for the sixth-grade audience.

5. Practice

It's not easy to get up and speak in front of your peers. So Sarah spent some time rehearsing. In fact, this was one of the reasons her presentation was so successful: the time she spent practicing. Over and over she clicked through the slide show and spoke the words of explanation. After a while she didn't really need to look at the note cards. Since she knew the topic pretty well after several repetitions, the words came naturally to mind when she saw the pictures on the screen. And she used the words on the slides to remind her of what she was supposed to say.

At first Sarah practiced by herself. Then she asked her dad to watch and listen as she went through the show. He suggested that she not use "and then..." between every slide, simply pause and take a deep breath as the pictures faded from one to the next. This new technique worked well for Sarah. Her next audience included her sister and her mother, who challenged her by asking some tough questions about the topic. Finally Sarah was ready.

The day before the oral report, Sarah went down to the computer room at school to talk with Mrs. Mercer, the computer teacher. Mrs. Mercer showed her how to hook up the computer to the big TV monitor. She also made sure that the computer was equipped with a copy of the ClarisWorks program. The night before she was scheduled to deliver her report, Sarah practiced one more time at home. Before she went to bed, she saved a copy of her program onto a floppy disk and placed it along with her note cards into her book bag.

6. Present

At last the big day was at hand. During morning recess, Sarah went down to the computer room to set things up. Into the drive went her floppy disk. Up on the screen came the icon of her slide show. Her heart beat faster. She double-clicked on the disk icon. The computer beeped. Onto the screen came a dialogue box: "Not enough memory to complete this operation." Sarah's heart was racing now. She tried again. Same message. She was cooked!

Overhearing Sarah's cries of frustration, Mrs. Mercer looked over at the screen, then suggested that Sarah increase the memory for ClarisWorks. Suddenly, Sarah remembered: this had happened at home! She recalled the solution from last time and increased the memory for ClarisWorks. Again she double-clicked, and there on the screen she saw the words "Sculpture in Ancient Greece." Off to the slide show!

Standing at the front of the class a few minutes before the bell, Sarah ran through the show one more time, clicking along without incident. Everything worked, and it all looked great up there on the big TV. Then she heard the students coming in from the hall. They saw the TV and the title of the show, and they took their seats. Sarah clicked once and started talking.

By now Sarah's note cards were well-thumbed and wrinkly. But she hardly needed them as she clicked her way along. The kids, she found, were looking at the screen most of the time, not at her—except for Jimmy, who seemed fascinated by what she was doing. All of a sudden Jimmy raised his hand. Sarah looked at Mrs. Sullivan. She nodded toward Jimmy. Sarah said, "Yes, Jimmy?" and he asked what the statues are made out of. Sarah answered by clicking to the next slide, which showed the various types of marble the Greeks used. Jimmy was in awe, and couldn't take his eyes off Sarah for the rest of the presentation.

The end was near. Sarah saw from their faces that the other kids liked her presentation. She stood a little straighter as she delivered her concluding remarks. Some of the kids actually clapped. (In the entire history of Beechwood Middle School, no one had ever asked a question or clapped during the sixth-grade oral report.)

Sarah would be the first to admit that you never really understand a topic until you have to teach it to someone else. By going through the process of researching, thinking, and presenting ideas about sculpture in ancient Greece, Sarah became master of the subject matter. She also developed a keener understanding of how to communicate ideas to other people. Her computer provided the set of tools that made this all possible, and she increased her knowledge about how her computer works.

Steps in Preparing a Presentation

Follow these steps to prepare and deliver a computer-based presentation for a school assignment:

1. *Research*—Gather information and illustrations. Look for ideas as well as facts. Investigate a variety of sources on CD-ROM and on-line.
2. *Organize*—Set forth your ideas on paper. Use the outline feature of your word processor. Identify your key ideas. Reorder your ideas into a storyboard.
3. *Illustrate*—Add pictures for each key idea. Compose a few words that capture each idea. Use words and pictures that will provoke the audience to think.
4. *Explain*—Develop an oral commentary for your slides. If your research notes are already in the computer, print them out as comments onto note cards.
5. *Practice*—Rehearse your slide show alone with the computer, then with family members. Go through it several times.
6. *Present*—Prepare the equipment you will use. Arrange the audience for good visibility. Look them straight in the eye and present your ideas.

Tools for Organizing and Presenting

To complete her assignment, Sarah used many different software programs and services on her computer. But her chief tool for building and delivering the presentation was ClarisWorks, the integrated software package that comes with many of the Apple Macintosh computers and is also available for Windows computers. The capabilities of ClarisWorks made it easy for her to organize her information and present her ideas.

Sarah could have used other programs to get this work done: Brøderbund's Kid Pix, Aldus Persuasion, Microsoft's Fine Artist or PowerPoint, Pierian Springs' Digital Chisel, Davidson's Multimedia Workshop, or ClarisImpact could have served her needs just as well. All of these programs to some extent can help a student like Sarah develop an effective presentation. Let's look at how ClarisWorks helps the process along at each stage.

- In the gathering of information, ClarisWorks' word-processing function makes it easy to jot down notes and ideas as you go along. And because ClarisWorks takes up relatively little memory in this mode, you often have room to keep several programs open at once, including your electronic encyclopedia and your on-line service, with ClarisWorks waiting patiently in the background.
- To help organize information, ClarisWorks includes a built-in outline builder that is easy to use and modify. This allows the student to move ideas around organize and integrate information as it comes in.
- When it comes time to illustrate the pages, ClarisWorks can take images that have been cut and copied from a variety of sources and temporarily placed either into the Clipboard in Microsoft Windows or in the Macintosh Scrapbook. ClarisWorks can also import pictures that have been saved as files on the disk, by using the Insert function under the File menu. The translators that come with ClarisWorks allow the program to import pictures from just about any file format.
- The Slide Show function of ClarisWorks, found under the View menu, makes it easy to turn your pages from the word processor into attractive slides on the screen. You can adjust background colors, borders, timing, fades between slides, and other elements of the show. It's easy to reorder pages and also later to add sound and movies to your slides.

If she were a little younger or if it were all she had available to her, Sarah might have used Kid Pix to compose her slide show. Kid Pix is a drawing program (available for both Macintosh and

Windows machines) that can also enter words and photos on each slide. Sarah would follow the same basic steps as she completes her assignment, and Kid Pix would help her along the way.

- While gathering information, Kid Pix slides created one by one in the drawing portion of the program can serve as repositories of information, recording the student's own typed words as well as words and pictures pasted in from other sources. It can also record the student's voice or use canned sounds from within the program.
- To help organize information, each slide can be individually brought into the Slide Show feature of the program. Using the Kid Pix Slide Show viewer, students can display up to ninety-nine slides in order and move them around simply by clicking and dragging. Numerous special effects can be used to smooth the transition between slides.
- Each slide can be illustrated in Kid Pix by pasting in pictures from other sources, using the Clipboard (or the Scrapbook

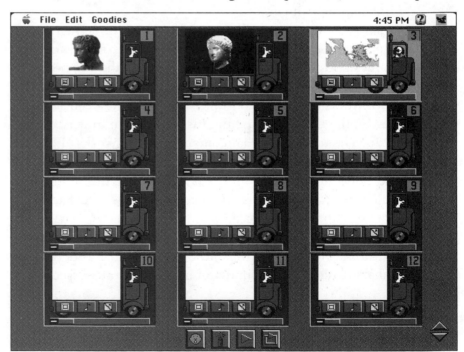

The Moving Vans in the Slide Show feature of Kid Pix help kids quickly organize their pictures, words, and thoughts.

on the Macintosh) in Microsoft Windows. Kid Pix also has strong and easy-to-use drawing and painting features that allow students to author their own illustrations, diagrams, and pictures. The clip art collections available for Kid Pix make this aspect of the program especially useful for student presentations.

- Kid Pix can show a set of slides in a somewhat professional but more lighthearted manner, automatically or with a click of the mouse. The resulting presentation can be compelling and easy to watch. Kid Pix can also add sound and music to the slide show, as we will see in the next two chapters.

To compose and deliver professional presentations, real world grown-up presenters use programs like Persuasion or PowerPoint, which were designed specifically and exclusively for this purpose. Be aware, however, that because these programs are more powerful and versatile than ClarisWorks or Kid Pix, they're also substantially more expensive.

- A program such as Persuasion won't help a child much at the information-gathering stage, but it is especially useful—and structured—for helping organize ideas in the presentation. Persuasion provides a versatile and powerful outlining tool that makes it easy to construct an outline of your ideas and then manipulate its structure. You just click on the part of the outline you want to move and then drag it to its new location.
- You can set jumps on a slide, enabling you to skip to another part of the slide show by clicking a button.
- In the illustration of each slide, the features of Persuasion are hard to match. You can import any kind of picture from a disk file or paste it in from the Scrapbook (on the Macintosh) or Clipboard (both platforms). The Persuasion clip art collection contains hundreds of useful illustrations that pop right in and can be stretched or shrunk to any size without distortion. The program's drawing tools are easy to use and make especially attractive diagrams. There's even a feature

that builds graphs on a slide directly from the numbers you type in.

- In formatting the words on each slide, Persuasion provides utmost flexibility. Words can be of many colors and shades, shadowed, in almost any size, aligned left, right, or center, and even animated so they appear to fly in from space. (Of the kids' programs, Fine Artist comes closest to duplicating this.) In the same way, the background of the slides can be plain, gradient (changing gradually from one color to another), or in a special pattern. A collection of auto *templates* is provided to get you started with some good-looking backgrounds.

*template—pattern for
laying out what each
slide will look like.*

- When it comes time to present, Persuasion provides at least a dozen sophisticated visual effects for the transition from slide to slide. The program also allows automatic operation and the ability to include music, sound, and video on slides.

PowerPoint and ClarisImpact are similar to Persuasion in functionality. No matter what program your child uses, the essential factor in the success of a slide show is the strength of its ideas and the quality of the research. Without good information, well understood by the student, the presentation cannot come off well.

Subjects for Presentation

Just about every school subject assigns oral reports and student presentations in the course of the year. All can benefit from the assistance of the home computer in preparing and presenting the work.

Math

- One of the best ways to understand a problem in mathematics is to illustrate it with diagrams and pictures. Students can use a drawing program such as Kid Pix or ClarisWorks to create a series of diagrams with labels that show how the math problem was figured. These diagrams can then be presented as a slide show, with live oral commentary from the student.

- Word problems are often difficult to figure out unless they are illustrated. Students can draw or copy and paste the characters and elements of the word problem, in stages to match the progression of the words. For instance, "Susie had 6 yards of fabric. To make a tent, she needed $8\frac{1}{4}$ yards. How much more fabric did she need?" might be illustrated with a series of pictures, first one of Susie with 6 yards, next a picture of a tent and 6 yards of fabric, next a picture of the 6 yards and $8\frac{1}{4}$ yards juxtaposed, and so forth. This kind of visual explanation makes for a good oral report, as well as a helpful way to understand and solve the problem.

- Concepts in math often come clear when they are explained with pictures. Even very young children can illustrate ideas such as "greater than," "less than," and "equal to" with pic-

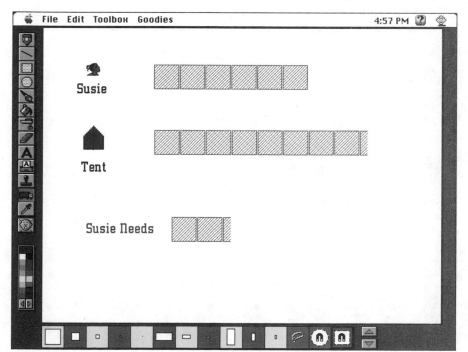

Word problems are often easier to solve when they are illustrated.

tures that they compose with Kid Pix. By stringing together these pictures into a slide show, and talking about what each one means as it comes up, the child can assemble an effective presentation.

- The field of geometry—shapes, sizes, attributes, similarities, and so forth—are best explained with pictures and diagrams. Any of the computer drawing or painting programs can create accurate geometric patterns quickly and color them in for emphasis. By presenting these geometric figures as a series of slides, students can point out the similarities and differences.

- The most mundane of all math skills, the multiplication table can come alive with an "illustrated flash card slide show." Creating the show can help the child understand what multiplication is all about, beyond the facts that must be memorized. Each slide shows one fact in numerals (such as 3 x 4 =) and presents twelve objects arranged in a three-by-

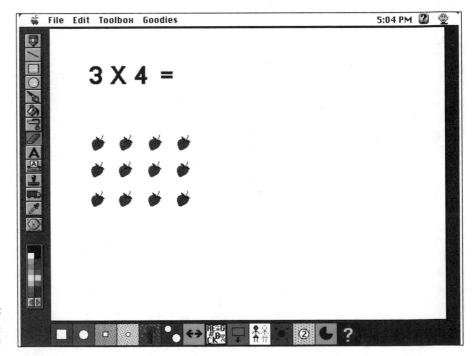

Why not create a set of illustrated electronic flash cards?

four rectangle. As these pictures are shown in a slide show, kids should be prompted to call out the answer.

Social Studies

- In the previous example, Sarah was completing a standard research report for her social studies class. This type of assignment lends itself to a slide show presentation delivery. Just make sure to acquire illustrations and pictures as well as text when researching the report and follow the steps listed earlier in this chapter to assemble the presentation.
- In geography, you can present a series of maps on the screen to show historical trends or compare geographic and political features. Each map becomes one slide in the show. Maps can be copied from the electronic atlas, then modified with a drawing program such as Kid Pix or ClarisWorks to show borders, products, political divisions, and other map features and to add a legend or key; finally, the entire presentation can be titled in the word processor.

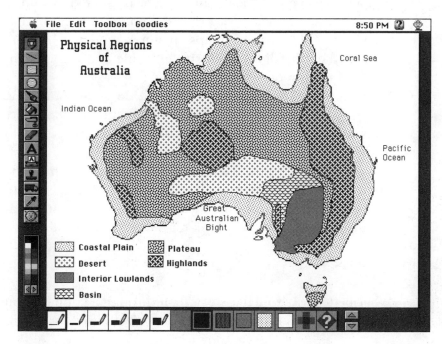

Junior cartographers enjoy using the computer to produce maps.

•the Concord Bridge,

where the British fought the Americans.

Use a regular camera to take your own pictures for a report and put them on a photo CD. Then import them into your computer to use in a slide show or in a word processing document.

- A biography of a historical figure can be presented as a timeline, with each slide representing an important event in that individual's life. Photos, maps, pictures, and text can be combined on the slides to illustrate the life and accomplishments of the famous person.

- Students can illustrate a field trip with a slide show. One easy way is to take along a standard camera and shoot pictures of the salient points. The film can then be sent to Kodak for development into a photo CD and from there pasted into the slide show. Using a digital camera such as the Apple QuickTake, students can wire the pictures directly into the computer and paste them into the slide show. (If that sounds interesting to you, look for more in chapter 8.)

Language Arts

- What better way to tell a story than through a combination of words and pictures? Structure a project based on a children's book, with each slide on the computer containing the pictures and words from a page of the story. Or encourage your child to tell her own stories using this method, each slide showing one event in the story. Children can use programs like Kid Pix, Davidson's KidWorks, ClarisWorks to create such presentations. Storybook creation programs such as Edmark's Imagination Express and MECC's Storybook Weaver work on the same principles and are designed to create slide/story presentations or print out the finished product as a storybook.

- Learning new words can be simple and fun with the use of vocabulary flash cards created on the computer. Construct each screen of the slide show with the word in seventy-two-point type, along with a picture that represents its meaning. As each slide is shown, the child can explain what the word means, in her own words.

- The ubiquitous book report assignment can become an opportunity for a multimedia presentation. Using pictures and text, the student can compose each element of the book report as a slide on the screen: Title; Author; Characters; Plot; Message;

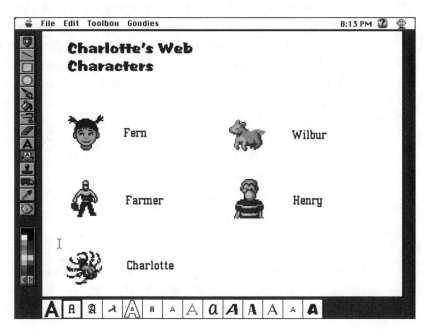

Each element of a story can become part of a multimedia book report.

Illustrations; Commentary; Recommendation. As the slides are shown, the child provides oral commentary on each section of the report. Already done one report as a multimedia presentation? Try constructing an advertisement for a book highlighting the same features.

Science

- To report on a laboratory experiment, construct a slide for each element of the report: the Question; the Equipment; the Method; the Observations; the Result; the Conclusion. On each slide place a graphic that shows a picture and a few words for that part of the lab report.

- The science curriculum, like that of social studies, generally requires students to complete research reports at least twice a year. After doing electronic research, and gathering pictures and text along the way, compose a slide show with pictures and text. Then deliver the report in class, as Sarah did earlier in this chapter, or print out the slides on paper and turn them in to the teacher.

- A good way to explain a scientific process such as electricity or the water cycle or photosynthesis is to construct a series of diagrams on the computer with a painting program such as Kid Pix or ClarisWorks. Each diagram, along with a few explanatory words, becomes one slide in the student's presentation.

- Elementary and middle school science does a lot with classification and grouping of animals, minerals, trees, chemicals, and so forth. An illustrated slide show is a good way to show the attributes of the various groups, which in most cases are based on visual evidence.

Arts

- Visual arts such as painting and sculpture and architecture lend themselves especially well to an illustrated slide show. Students can arrange the history of art on a timeline, make

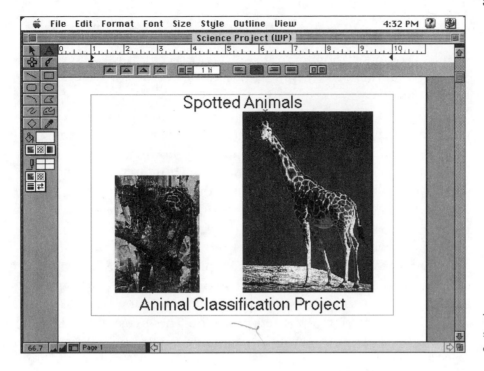

Think about creating a slide show that illustrates the facts of an oral science report.

a portfolio of their own works, or explain a historical period through its works of art. Sources such as the Microsoft *Art Gallery* and Corbis *A Passion for Art* on CD-ROM are very useful for this kind of school assignment.

• In like manner, the history of music can be presented as a series of slides with words, pictures, notes, and even the music itself. (In chapter 9 we will learn how to incorporate music into student reports.)

Getting Ready to Present

Making a slide show is one thing. Standing up and presenting to a group is an altogether different task. It is important to prepare well beforehand and make sure you have the right equipment. No matter how large the group, you will need:

- a personal computer of the same type you have at home
- keyboard and mouse
- computer monitor
- electricity

A group of up to ten people, can be comfortably arranged around the computer screen as you run through your slide show. If you're presenting to a group of ten to thirty, however, use a large TV monitor to show your work. To connect a TV monitor to your computer you will need an adapter that translates the computer's video output to the video input of the television. These adapters cost about $400 and are sold in computer stores. Many schools have a computer outfitted with such a device.

For a group larger than thirty people, you will need a projector that displays the image from the computer monitor onto a movie screen. In many schools you will find a liquid crystal display (LCD) plate that sits atop an overhead projector. These cost about $2,000 but are designed to transfer the computer's image for viewing to a very large group.

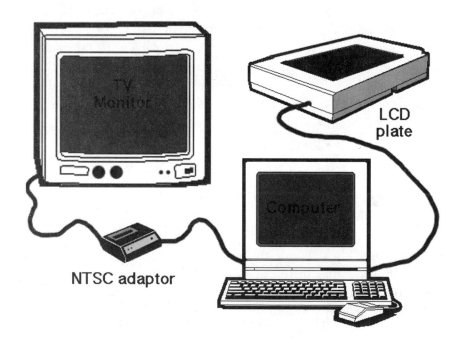

Connecting a computer to a liquid crystal display plate on an overhead projector or a television set allows you to magnify the computer images you want to display to a larger audience.

Recording on Videotape

Most people do not have a large enough screen at home to present their child's computer-enhanced projects to audiences of more than ten people. Neither do most classrooms. But most homes and classrooms do have videocasette recorders (VCRs). Want to record your child's presentation onto video tape? Here's how:

- On some computers, you can record the student's presentation on your VCR at home and simply take the tape to show in other places. The Macintosh AV models include an NTSC video output port that connects directly to the video input on your VCR.

- For other types of computers, you need to use the video adapter described in the section "Getting Ready to Present" to accomplish the same purpose.

No matter which method you use, the process is the same:

1. Connect the computer to the VCR by attaching a standard cable from the video output port on the computer (or NTSC adapter) to the video input port on the VCR. (Use the same cables you would use to connect your videocamera to your television set.)
2. Put a blank videotape into the VCR.
3. Press "record" on the VCR.
4. Run through the slides slowly.
5. Press "stop" on the VCR when you are done.
6. Rewind the tape and watch what you have recorded.

If you want to add your voice to your tape, you will need to attach a microphone to the audio input port on the VCR. Follow the same procedure for putting the slides on the tape, but as each slide comes up, record your speech. The resulting videotape will play on any standard VCR. This option may also be useful if your school does not have a large TV display for its computer or if its of a different type from the one you have at home.

Now you have a portable slide show on videotape!

Applying Some Basic Principles

No matter what method students use to present their slide shows, certain principles always should be followed:

- Engage your viewers. Use images and words and text that will interest them and make them think. Refer to what's on the screen, so your audience will look there as you present the show.
- Design your screens carefully. Make them consistent, elegant, and simple. Use the same typeface and font size throughout. Leave plenty of plain background space around your words and pictures. Don't put more than two pictures on any one slide.
- Advance slowly. Give your audience time to look at the picture, read the words on the screen, and listen to what you say. Count to five (silently) after each sentence. Count to three before going on to the next slide.
- Mix media. In your slide show, use text, diagrams, drawings, and photographs. But don't use more than two of these elements on any one slide. It's okay to have an occasional slide with only words or only pictures, to vary the presentation.

Next Steps

In the next two chapters, we will learn how to add sound and video to students' projects on the computer. Like explorers on an expedition, we will learn how to capture and develop images from a variety of new sources. In this way, we can build on the basic presentation to produce something even more interesting and effective.

chapter 8

Roll the Cameras!
Turn Up the Volume!

When we first discussed writing this book with our editor, she said that we had to remember that today's elementary, middle, and junior high school students are what is known as the "Nickelodeon generation." They expect information and entertainment to move along at a rapid pace, accompanied by lights, images, sound, and action. Our response was that it was high time they realized their computers were fully ready to respond to these needs.

The fact is that most of today's home computers have the built-in capacity to display photographic-quality images and high-fidelity sound. The best-selling software exploits these capabilities, so we have all come to expect pictures and music as a regular part of the software produced for us to view and to use.

But how can students take advantage of these capabilities? How can everyday school assignments be turned into opportunities to incorporate pictures and sound to grab kids' attention and better explain the subject matter?

This chapter provides answers to these and other fascinating questions. In the hands-on introduction that follows, we look at ways to add images, voice, and music to projects assigned for school. We discuss how preteens and teens of the twenty-first century can use their computers to create their own multimedia works, moving beyond the text and numbers that computers are known for and into the modern world of sound and graphics. To do this, we examine some new hardware and software tools necessary for capturing and creating images and sounds: scanners, digitizers, cameras, and microphones. As we introduce each of these, we will explain how they can be used to complete school assignments and how they are best configured for the home computer. Finally, we offer hands-on, step-by-step instructions on how to assemble a student report replete with sounds and images.

But let's start with a typical student delivering his assignment to school. Maestro, a little night music, if you please...

How Did He Do That?

Jimmy produced a multimedia report for his music assignment on Mozart—text, pictures, diagrams, maps, and music all were recorded on the computer. He delivered his report to the class as an oral presentation supported by material in a variety of media. Jimmy, however, is not a computer programmer. Nor does his family own a high-powered, expensive piece of equipment. Jimmy's creation relied on easy-to-use, relatively inexpensive software tools for use on his home computer, which cost less than $2,000.

These kinds of multimedia reports are valuable in many respects. They teach students how to communicate ideas using all forms of information. They increase kids' familiarity with the computer and its capabilities. They offer students the opportunity to produce the kinds of shows they see every day on television and in the movies. And they open up new channels for learning about the content of history, literature, science, and even music.

This year we did something different in music class. Each of us had to choose a famous composer and write a biography. And we had to give it as an oral report. I never liked music very much, especially the old-fashioned stuff. This was not one of my favorite homework assignments.

But the music teacher helped us. So did the librarian. They brought in tapes and CDs full of music from many composers. And they brought in pictures and books and sheet music. And some old instruments as well. We even saw a movie about Mozart. That's what made me choose Mozart. In the movie he was funny and creative.

It was easy to find information on Mozart. He's in all the encyclopedias, and the library has lots of books about him. My father has about a dozen Mozart tapes and CDs. Did you know that Mozart could play the violin when he was four years old? His father was real pushy and made him learn music at an early age. Here in my presentation you can hear a song Mozart composed when he was six. Listen…

I had seen other students do multimedia reports on the computer with sound and music and pictures and all. It seemed too complicated at first, but I learned how to get pictures into the computer and then how to record sound. After that it was easy to put these into my slide show. I even learned how to scan in the sheet music, then enlarge it so I could show the notes on the screen. It took longer than I thought to get this assignment done. In fact, it was a week late. But it was worth waiting for, because it was so interesting. With all the music and the pictures and the funny outfit I wore, you really got the idea of Mozart and his music. Did you know he died more than two hundred years ago, when he was only thirty-five years old?

THE MEDIA GENERATION

Flashing lights. Moving pictures. Loud music. Mindless commercials. That's what's ruining our children. Their minds are fouled by a constant diet of media that keeps them from reading and thinking and reflecting. Rather than promote multimedia in education, shouldn't we fight it? Isn't there enough entertaining MTV-type programming in the environment already? Why should we encourage multimedia reports in school? School should be a special place for dealing with books and ideas and the printed word. Otherwise we put ourselves in danger of producing a generation of media robots who cannot read, write, or think.

This is a legitimate fear. Without reading, writing, and thinking we cannot take advantage of the capacities of our minds, nor can we learn from history, nor can we appreciate literature and the arts. Still, by including multimedia instruction with the computer, we do not deemphasize reading and writing. The first six chapters of this book are in fact devoted to strengthening these basic skills with the computer, and most of a child's hours in school are similarly committed.

But we should remember that not all important ideas come to us through text. The power of Mozart's music, the beauty of Michelangelo's painting, the courage of John F. Kennedy's voice, are best transmitted and understood through image and sound. And many of the basics that we learn in school—the forms of geometry, the structure of the solar system, or the shape of the continents—can be understood only through pictures. Multimedia has been with us for centuries, ever since humans painted on the walls of caves. Today, the personal computer enables our children to combine all forms of human communication in a serious and structured manner, to help them explain their subjects. We need to nurture a generation of children that uses the media not to entertain, but to educate.

Jimmy began work on his report by gathering information. He used all the electronic sources we learned about in chapters 4–6, culling numerous text excerpts and photographs on Mozart. But the bulk of his multimedia examples came from other sources: books, photographs, sheet music, and recorded sound from CDs and tapes. This chapter concentrates on the process Jimmy used to get these kinds of materials—sounds and images—into his computer and later into a polished presentation. We will learn how to capture images and sounds from a variety of sources, then modify them to fit the requirements of a school assignment. We will also learn how to combine these resources into a structured multimedia report. Along the way, we will learn some new software tools, as well as new ways to work with familiar programs.

This chapter also introduces some new hardware: the CD-ROM drive, which we learned a little about in chapter 4; the sound digitizer, the scanner; and the digital camera. It is not necessary to own all these devices to create a report like Jimmy's; but to move into the age of multimedia you will need to have at least one of them. Since many new home computers come already equipped with CD-ROM as well as with sound and video digitizers, you may already have all the tools you need. If not, they can be purchased as peripherals from a computer store. We will introduce each one as it's used in the process of building a multimedia report.

How Digital Images and Sound Work

Most of us use images and sound every day. We peruse them in magazines, we listen to them on the radio, we experience them on television. We shoot photos, we record music on tape, we make our own home videos. Pictures and music are a part of our lives and of the lives of our children. But few of us have worked with all these media, nor have our children used them all in their schoolwork. One problem is that each kind of media needs a different machine and a different kind of material to store it on. We can't very well march off to school with a VCR, camera, slide projector, TV, CD player, and tape recorder just to give an oral report! And there's no way to combine and synchronize all the images and sounds these machines can produce.

But today the home computer can replace all these different machines and enable young media moguls to integrate the various forms of information into a coordinated report. Here's how it works. The computer converts pictures and sounds—which to our eyes and ears appear as *analog information*—into *digital information*. Once in digital form, the sounds and pictures can be stored on the computer's disk, recorded into its memory, and then displayed on its screen or played through its speakers. All forms of information—text, pictures, sounds, even video—are stored in a single digital format on the computer.

analog information—created by manipulating varying physical variables such as the electrical signals that create a television picture or the ink that creates a picture in a newspaper or book.

digital information—information represented by digits or numbers; the computer converts the color and shading of pictures and the various nuances of sounds into numbers it can remember, configure, and display.

Capturing Images for Schoolwork

Students can create or capture images for school projects in a variety of ways. The method depends on where the image comes from and the kind of computer equipment being used. Let's take a look at the most popular methods a typical home computer might have available, from simple imaging drawing to sophisticated digital photography.

183

Drawing and Painting

Just about every home computer comes equipped with a software program for painting and drawing on the screen. For students who want to create an image for a school project, these programs are the easiest place to start. You can create a drawing from scratch, or you can begin with a clip art image or with an image saved in your word processor or Scrapbook (on the Macintosh) from your research. To create a drawing from scratch, use the drawing tools in your program (generally shown as icons along the left side of the screen). Don't be afraid to explore a bit. Most drawing programs come with all kinds of useful tools. (See the appendix for titles of drawing programs.)

To add a piece of clip art, use the Import, Insert, or Open a Picture item from your program's menu; go to a clip art collection (in the same program or elsewhere on your hard drive); then choose the picture you want and bring it into the drawing area. In many cases you will want to modify this picture by using the drawing tools and the eraser. Adding arrows to or circling parts you want to define or emphasize also helps. Just be sure to rename you modified clip art when you save it, so that the original remains intact for the your next use.

A typical approach is to start with a picture from your research. You can either paste it in from your word processor or Scrapbook (on the Macintosh) or, if it was saved as a file on the disk, use the Import, or Insert, or Open a Picture menu item to bring it into the drawing area. Once it's there, you can modify it with the drawing tools. For his music assignment, Jimmy browsed the electronic encyclopedia, clipped a picture of Mozart with his father, pasted it into Brøderbund's Kid Pix, then erased the father and the background, leaving only a portrait of Mozart, which he used on the first slide of his presentation.

Once your drawing looks the way you want it to, you can save it onto the disk as a file that can later be imported into a presentation. (If you have a Macintosh computer, you can copy and paste your drawing into the Scrapbook.)

Drawing and Painting Programs

Most drawing and painting programs have similar features and work very much alike. You choose a painting tool such as a pencil, paintbrush, rectangle maker, or an eraser from the tool palette, then click and drag across the screen to paint with that tool. Earlier in the book we've talked about some of the most common ones, including Brøderbund's Kid Pix, with its myriad tools and rubber stamps that even the youngest users can work with to create masterpieces. The more straightforward art program features are part of adult tool packages such as ClarisWorks or Microsoft Works. Microsoft's Fine Artist is a great program for kids nine and up, who will enjoy its offbeat clip art and the dazzling special effects that can be created by bending and shaping type in all sorts of interesting ways. Davidson's Flying Colors uses a special wavelike effect to create some unique 3-D–style pictures. Art Explorer from Aldus offers incomparable transforming tools and special textures of paint and color. Dabbler from Fractal Design includes many different types and textures but also sports a super learn-to-draw sequence. If a presentation needs some special effects, think about investing in one of these special art packages.

Learning to draw is fun using Dabbler from Fractal Design.

Courtesy of Fractal Design

Scanning

Some of the pictures Jimmy selected to use for his report were available only in books. The best tool for capturing these images is a flatbed scanner. The scanner looks like a miniature duplicating machine. It has a cover with a glass plate on which you place the paper or book you want to scan. Close the cover, open the scanning software, and then press the Scan button on the computer screen. Scanners have no knobs or switches of their own—they are controlled completely by the computer and its scanning software.

The scan proceeds as a light bulb slides across the paper under the glass, along with a sensor that picks up the pattern of the image on the paper. The sensor records the image as a series of very small dots, very much like the pictures you see in the newspaper. (If you look closely at a newspaper picture with a strong magnifying glass, you will see the image is not continuous like a photograph, but appears as a pattern of discrete dots, some darker and some lighter.) The pattern of dots goes from the scanner through the cable, into the computer's digital memory and up onto the screen.

Scanners for home and student use cost between $750 and $1,200, including software. The quality of the software is the key to good scanning, so make sure the program you get can be used easily by your child. One of the easiest software packages to use for this is called Ofoto, which works with many scanners. If you have another software program, chances are it will work like Ofoto.

To start, set the software for the kind of image you need. For most projects you'll need an image that will display on your computer's monitor. Most home computers have a seventy-two-dot-per-inch resolution, in eight-bit color. Many people make the mistake of setting too high a resolution and too deep a color, which creates enormous files that are difficult to work with. So take time to experiment a bit before you launch any serious school project.

At the upper-left of the Ofoto software, set the pop-up selector to match the computer monitor you are using. This will set the resolution automatically for you. Just below, choose the type of image you have in the scanner: color photo, grayscale photo, or line art. Your original should be on the scanner, as straight as you can place it.

If you want to capture the entire document, just press the Autoscan button and the software will go to work, scanning only the "live" area of the image, adjusting brightness and contrast, cropping and straightening it if necessary. Then all you have to do is save the document.

If you want to capture just a part of the document, such as one picture from a page of many items, do not use Autoscan. Instead press the Prescan button. The scanner will make a cursory pass, showing the entire document on the screen. Take the mouse and drag the selection marquee over the exact part you want to scan. Now press the Scan button and let the software do its work.

Help!

Don't have a scanner? If your child wants to use a few scanned images in a report, he or she may be able to arrange to use a compatible scanner at school and save images on a disk to bring home. Larger copy centers in the area might also have scanners and will either rent them for your use or do the work for you. This is definitely one aspect of the project that needs to be planned ahead of time.

Adjusting the Image

Whether you've scanned automatically or manually, you can adjust the image with the scanning software. The menu bar has selections for straightening, sharpening, and cropping the image. You can also use the brightness and contrast controls, located under Tone in the Image menu. Scanning software such as Ofoto often includes many other image enhancement tools, which you may experiment with if you need to.

Saving the Image

In most cases you should save your image as a compressed file. When you choose Save from the File menu, you will see the compression options. Generally, it's best to use the Photo JPEG compression, medium quality. Most half-page color images will compress down to less than fifty kilobytes using this method. Don't forget to save your image in a place where you can find it later. A good method is to set up a new folder on your desktop, into which you save all the items you are capturing—text, images, sounds—for your multimedia project.

Image File Formats

PICT and .PCX format. These are the most common formats for saving image files on the computer. Save your pictures as PICT or .PCX files whenever possible. Often, the software you are using will give you a choice of file formats. PICT or .PCX are the best bets. Just about any Macintosh will read PICT. Windows programs can import or read PICT or .PCX files.

Compression. The QuickTime operating system extension, available for both Macintosh and Windows computers, can automatically compress image files as they are saved, so they take up much less space on the disk. If your software gives you a choice, use JPEG compression, medium quality.

Color depth. The computer can display colors at different levels of quality, ranging from 4-bit (16 colors) to 24-bit (millions of colors). Windows and older Macintosh computers for the home work best with 8-bit (256 colors) images. Newer Macintosh computers work best with 16-bit (thousands of colors) images. If the software gives you a choice, save your images with 16-bit, thousands of colors.

Photo CD

An even more "low-tech" and readily available method for getting images into students' projects, but one that is relatively unknown, is photo CD. Photo CD is a process by which a student can use a standard 35-mm camera to get photos into the computer. For example, to get the picture of the bust of Mozart for his report, Jimmy took his mother's camera to the local library and photographed its Mozart statue. He also went to the music store to photograph some musical instruments, and to a local concert hall to take some pictures of the stage. Altogether he shot one roll of 35-mm film, thirty-six pictures in all. Then he had this film developed into a photo CD right at the local photo store. The photo CD method results in higher-quality images than those from a scanner or video source but takes a little more time because you have to wait for the film to be processed.

To make your own photo CD, use the best 35-mm camera you can find, with high-resolution film and good lenses. Take well-lit photographs of the objects or scenes you need. Bring your exposed roll(s) of film to the camera store and ask them to put the images onto a Kodak PhotoCD. They can put up to 100 color photos or 150 black-and-whites on a single CD. This should cost less than $.75 per picture (cheap when you consider the cost of a reprint) and about $5 for the CD itself (which the store provides), and you'll have your CD in about a week. With kids we sometimes have gotten the pictures processed first, eliminated the ones of feet and the backs of heads and chosen those we really wanted, and then taken in the negatives for CD processing. You have to have at least ten pictures put on at a time, but you can take the photo CD back to the store to have pictures added on until it is full. You can also use older negatives if you want to include pictures from a trip or family pictures you took some years ago.

To read the images from the photo CD into the computer, you must have a CD-ROM drive. You also need some special software as well to get access to the pictures. Make sure you have the Photo Access and QuickTime extensions installed in your System folder on your Macintosh. On newer Macintosh and IBM-compatible computers with CD-ROM drives, this software is often preinstalled. If you have an older computer, you can get the programs you need from your computer dealer. Kodak makes some inexpensive photo access software that will enable you to experiment before graduating to more expensive software that will let you do more things with your pictures. (See the appendix for software titles.)

Once you have settled your software questions, place the photo CD into your CD-ROM drive and wait while the computer creates thumbnails of your images. Click on the Slide Show icon in the photo CD window. You will see a low-resolution QuickTime movie of your pictures. Click the arrows on the controller bar to browse through the images. To view an image in high resolution, select View from the menu bar. A new window will open with your image. To change the size and resolution of the image, use the menu bar. Photo CD stores each picture in five resolutions, ranging from small thumbnail to over 1,000 pixels wide. For most purposes, the 384 x 256 or 768 x 512 pixel sizes are what you want (the first is snapshot size, 3 1/2 x 5 inches; the second is standard size, 8 x 10 inches). You need a lot of RAM to open the larger pictures and print them.

To save an image into your Project folder, use the Save As... item from the File menu. Later, if you need to, you can adjust or edit these images with another set of software tools. Look for a list of some software you might want to try out in the appendix.

Still Images from TV and Video

If your computer has a video digitizer installed in it, you can use a video camera or videocassette recorder to capture images for a school project. This is how Jimmy got pictures from the movie *Amadeus*, which he rented at the local video shop. He brought the tape home and as he watched it captured still shots of Mozart that he used in his report.

A video digitizer takes the analog signal from a videocamera or VCR and translates it into digital information that a computer can understand. The Macintosh AV series of computers have this digitizer built in. On other computers, you can add this capability with an accessory such as the VideoSpigot from Radius (Macintosh) or VideoBlaster from Creative Labs (Windows). These cost less than $300 and can be found at a local computer store or in many of the computer accessory catalogs. (For more detailed software information, see the section in chapter 9.)

Help your kids use pictures
they have taken on vacation
or at local historical sites by
putting them on a photo CD
and importing them into their
writing or slide show project
on the computer.

Once you have settled your software issues, create a still image
with a videocamera by connecting the camera's "video out" jack to the
"video in" jack on the computer, using the same cables you used to
connect your videocamera to your television. Turn on the videocamera and point it at the item you want to capture. You may want to use
the camera's controls to focus and zoom the image at this point.

If your image was captured earlier on videotape, set the camera
to VTR and be ready to press Play after you've set up the software.

Now set up the image-capture software that comes with the
video digitizer you purchased (see chapter 9).

With the Macintosh AV computers, use the Video Monitor program that's in the Apple Extras folder. With VideoSpigot for the
Macintosh, the software is called Screen Play, and with the
VideoBlaster for Windows it's called VidCap. Launch the program,
then set it as follows:

- Window size: Best results happen with the default size, 320 x
  240 pixels, but you can set the capture window to any size

you want by dragging its lower right corner with the mouse or by working from the menu bar.

- Save to: Set the software's Preferences to save the image onto the disk.
- Compression: Use the JPEG or Video compression if your software gives you a choice.

Now set your camera or VCR to play, and you should see the video in the window, just as on TV. It is from this video that you will capture the still images you need for your report.

To snap a picture with the Video Monitor software, choose Copy from the Edit menu (or press Command-C on the keyboard). You'll hear it take the picture, and about two seconds later your picture will appear as a file on the desktop with the name PICT 0. The next snapshot you take will be saved as PICT 1, and so forth.

To snap a picture with Screen Play, simply click on the video in the window and drag it off onto the desktop. Immediately it turns into a new window with a still picture. Use Save from the File menu to record this

Digital Video Formats

There are two different software systems for handling digital video files on a personal computer: QuickTime and Video for Windows. QuickTime is available for both Macintosh and Windows computers; Video for Windows runs only on Windows computers. Both systems allow the computer to store and display moving pictures on the computer screen. QuickTime comes built in to all Apple Macintosh computers. Video for Windows or QuickTime, or both, come built in to most Windows multimedia computers. Both systems consit of special softwware that can compress the video infromation so that it doesn't take enormous amounts of disk space and then decompress that information when it is played back.

Jimmy captured video stills
from the movie Amadeus to
illustrate his report.

picture on the hard disk. When you've got all the pictures you need, drag the files to your Project folder.

To snap a picture with VidCap, choose Save Single Frame from the File menu. You will then be able to choose the drive, directory, and file name under which to save the picture you have just taken from the VCR.

You can use this method to capture images from a VCR or from a videodisk player or from a television with a video output connector. Just connect the video output jack of the device to the video in jack of your computer, press play, and go to work.

Digital Cameras

Probably the fastest, and in the long run, least expensive way to get images into your home computer is with a digital camera. Such devices record images directly into the camera; there is no film, no tape, no floppy disks. From the camera, the images import directly into the computer. The Kodak/Apple QuickTake camera at about $675

is the lest expensive and most appropriate for both the Macintosh and Windows platform home computers.

The QuickTake camera captures what it sees into memory chips that live inside the camera. When you've filled up its memory with images—thirty-two small ones at 320 x 240 pixels ($4\frac{1}{2}$ x 3 inches) or eight big ones at 640 x 480 pixels (8 x 6 inches)—you connect the camera to the computer and transfer the pictures. Software to effect this transfer comes in the package with the camera.

To take pictures, make sure the camera's batteries are well charged, then go to work. Turn on the camera by sliding the lens cover until it clicks. The shutter release is the oblong black button on the top of the camera. Compose the shot so that your subject fills the entire screen, but don't get any closer than 1 meter (3.5 feet). Make sure the subject is well lit.

Back home, connect the camera's cable to the modem port on the computer. Turn on the camera. Launch the QuickTake software previously installed on the computer. Choose View Slides in Camera from the Camera menu. The computer will suck the images from the camera. Soon you will see thumbnail views of each of the pictures in the camera. Double-click on a picture to see it full size. Use the items from the Image menu to adjust the picture as necessary, then save it to your Project folder. It's best to save your pictures in PICT format (.PCX for Windows), thousands of colors, with medium compression.

Capturing What's On the Screen

To copy a picture from the encyclopedia or other source that shows images on the computer monitor but can't copy the image to your word processor, your Scrapbook on the Macintosh, or a disk, try a special screen capture utility program like Flash-It. This kind of software is available as shareware (try now; pay later) and can be obtained from a local computer users group or from the collections of shareware sold by computer stores and catalogs. Many of these programs are also available in the software libraries of the on-line information services. First install the screen capture software into your system, then restart your computer. After the image you want to capture is on the screen, press the appropriate keys to invoke the software. With Flash-It, for instance, you press Command+Shift+5 on your keyboard to change the cursor from an arrow to a cross. Drag the cross over the part of the screen you want to capture. When you let go, the computer will ask you where you want to put the picture. You can save it to the disk as a PICT or .PCX file, place it in the Scrapbook on your Macintosh, or send it to the printer. In most cases, you will save it to the disk. Be sure to credit the picture properly.

Shareware

Can $10 software be any good? You bet it can. Some of the most useful little programs, such as Flash-It for clipping pictures from the screen, are available inexpensively as shareware. This means that the programs are distributed by on-line services and computer clubs at no cost, but the user of the program is expected to send money to the writer of the program. So let's suppose you download Flash-It from America Online and find that it's useful to you. You should then send a check for $15 to Nobu Toge of Menlo Park, California, the author of the program. That's the way shareware works.

Editing and Storing Images

■ ■ ■ ■ ■ ■ ■ ■ ■ ■ ■ ■ ■ ■

You may not need to edit your pictures at all if you are happy with them as you captured them. If you aren't, you will want to edit them. Programs such as Kid Pix, ClarisWorks, and Adobe Photoshop can help you modify images right on the computer screen. We will show you how to use them for this purpose; other image-editing programs will work in similar fashion.

Kid Pix

Bring an image that you have captured into Kid Pix, then use Kid Pix's painting tools to modify it. To get an image into Kid Pix, first copy it from the program you used to create it. Then open Kid Pix and paste the image into the drawing window. Now you can erase parts of it (as Jimmy did when he modified the Mozart family picture), or add to it, or change colors, or make a background for it. When your image looks the way you want, save it to the disk.

ClarisWorks

There are two ways to get a captured image into the ClarisWorks painting program:

- *Copy and Paste from the Clipboard.* To do this, first open your image in the program you used to create it. Then copy it, using the Copy item under the Edit menu. Now open a new ClarisWorks painting window and use Paste under the Edit menu to place your image in the window. Using the ClairsWorks painting tools, you can modify the image extensively, adding items, erasing, changing colors, lightening, darkening, rotating, flipping, adding text, stretching, shrinking, and distorting. You have at your command the entire array of painting tools, plus the options under the Transform menu. When your picture looks right, save it as a PICT or .PCX file, using the Save As... command under the File menu.

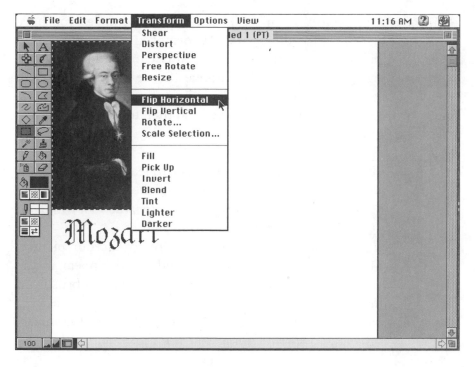

There are lots of options for modifying images in the Transform menu of the painting program of ClarisWorks.

- *Import from a disk file.* If you have saved a picture to your disk from one of the sources listed above, you can import it directly into ClarisWorks. Make sure that it was saved in the form of a PICT or a .PCX file, or else ClarisWorks will have trouble importing it. Go to the page in ClarisWorks where you want the picture to appear. With the arrow tool selected, go to Insert under the File menu. Use the dialogue box to find your way to the place where you had previously saved the file, and select it. You will see the picture appear on the page. Now you can use the arrow tool to move it around, stretch it, or shrink it as necessary.

PhotoShop

The most powerful (and substantially more expensive) tool for editing photographic-style pictures is Adobe Photoshop. Launch Photoshop, then open your picture from the File menu. The images you have saved in your Project folder are in PICT format (.PCX on Windows), which Photoshop and most other programs can read. Photoshop offers many tools to modify your image. Some affect the overall nature of the image, such as the image adjustment tools, brightness, and contrast. Others allow you to select and then touch up small sections of the picture. Features that are fun to play with:

- *Eraser*: clears out whatever is under it, leaving a white spot.
- *Pencil* or *Paintbrush*: select one and then choose a color, using the big squares in the color selector; the tool will paint this color over whatever is on your picture.
- *Eyedropper*: use to match a color already in your picture; "pick up" a color with this tool, and it will appear in the color selector square. Now the pencil or the paint brush will paint in that color.
- *Lasso*: Use to copy a piece of the background of the image, then paste it over something you want to hide.

Photoshop has tools for doing almost anything you want to your image. When you are done, save your edited image—in compressed form—to your Project folder as a PICT file (.PCX on Windows).

Capturing Sound

Sound and music were essential to Jimmy's school project on Mozart. Almost a dozen different samples of the composer's music highlighted points in his report; to get this sound into his computer, he used several different techniques, all available on a properly equipped home computer.

Your computer needs sound digitizing hardware and software to record sound and music. On an Apple Macintosh computer, this capability is built in and you need no further equipment. On a Windows computer, however, you need to add a sound board such as

SoundBlaster from Creative Labs, unless you have recently bought a multimedia system. You may also need some additional software, depending upon the kind of sound you want to record.

Sound Digitizer

In the real world, in the air around us, sound occurs in analog form. It comes in waves of air molecules that move back and forth in a continuous flow. The computer cannot deal with this kind of continuous analog information. So in order for us to use sound with the computer, we must digitize it, change it from the analog to digital form. If an analog sound looks like a wave, a digital sound looks like a series of dots that outline the pattern of the wave. With enough dots, you'd begin to think it was really a continuous wave. A sound digitizer changes sound back and forth between its digital (computer) and analog (natural) forms. All Apple Macintosh computers have the sound digitizer built in, as do most Windows multimedia computers. You can add a sound digitizer to your regular Windows computer for about $150 with a product such as SoundBlaster from Creative Labs, Inc.

If you have an Apple Macintosh computer, all the tools you need for a short and simple sound capture are built in to the operating system. If you want to capture sound with more flexibility, you can use the SoundEdit software from Macromedia or the AudioShop software from Opcode. The instructions that follow show you how to capture sound with both methods and to edit sounds with SoundEdit.

Silence Is Golden

When you work with sound at home or in a school classroom, it may be appropriate to use headphones so as not to disturb others. Common Walkman-type headphones work well. Plug in the headphones at the back of your computer under the Speaker icon. Plug in your microphone under the Microphone icon, or refer to your owner's manual.

Short and Simple Sound Capture (Macintosh Only)

For a quick capture of live sound, place the Macintosh microphone near the source and shut off all extraneous noises. Open up the Sound icon in Control Panel, located under the Apple menu. Click on the Add button. Click on the Record button in Control Panel, make your sound, and then click Stop. Give your sound a name and save it. The name will show up in the list of Alert Sounds. Click on it to hear it.

Your sound is saved as a resource in the System file on your hard drive. To see it, double-click on the System icon in the System folder. Double-click on your sound to hear it. From here you can drag your sound file to your Project folder. (Dragging items from the System suitcase can be accomplished only when no programs are running on the computer.) Once in your Project folder, you can import this sound into your presentation.

Recording with SoundEdit (Macintosh and Windows)

Using SoundEdit or AudioShop to capture sound involves a similar process, except that the control panels in these sophisticated programs offer additional features that allow you to exert more control over your sound. We'll use SoundEdit for this example; other sound programs work in like fashion.

Open SoundEdit and make sure the Recording Options are set to take sound from the built-in microphone. Check the sound level by clicking on the Meter icon and making some sound—you will see a moving green bar representing the amplitude of your sound in the SoundEdit window. (Keep the microphone away from the speaker at this point or you will get audio feedback.)

When you are ready to record, click the red Record button. Make the sound. The sound will *not* show up in the window as it is being recorded. When you're done, click the Stop button and the recording will stop. Now an image of your sound will show up in the SoundEdit window. You can edit the sound by selecting parts of its image with the mouse. You can cut, copy, and paste your selection, just as you would with words in a word processor. SoundEdit is to sound what a

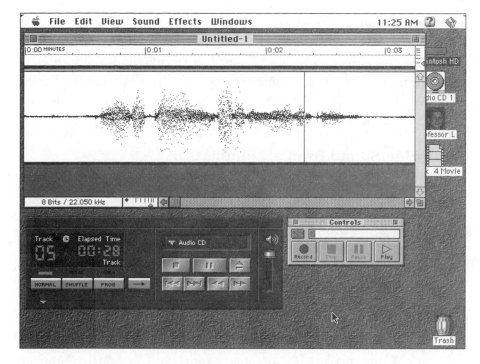

 File Edit View Sound Effects Windows .... 11:25 AM

Jimmy used SoundEdit to create just the right moods with the music he chose for his report.

word processor is to words. Jimmy edited the music for his project with SoundEdit. For one special segment of his report he made it fade up from nothing to a crescendo.

You can select a portion of your sound and apply sound effects to it. Just select the part of the sound you want to modify, then choose a treatment from the Effects menu. You can insert another sound into what you have by placing the cursor at the desired spot and recording from there. You may also open a new window in SoundEdit from the File menu, record a new sound there, then copy and paste it into another SoundEdit window.

To blend several sounds, choose Add Track from the Sound menu. Then record or paste a sound into this new track. Make a third or a fourth track if you need to. Then choose Mix from the Sound menu, and the computer will combine all your tracks into one.

When you have the sound the way you want it, save it to your disk as an Audio IFF file or as a QuickTime movie. These two formats are the most useful.

Recording from External Sources

To record sound from a tape recorder, connect the audio output jack from the tape recorder to the microphone jack on the computer. Then, to capture the sound, use the Sound icon from the Control Panel or SoundEdit as described above.

Capturing Sound from a Compact Disc

Sound on a CD is already in digital form. Jimmy gathered many of the Mozartean musical excerpts for his report from his father's collection of audio CDs and from some that he borrowed from the library. This is a very easy way to capture music into a computer.

On a Macintosh computer, you can use MoviePlayer software to convert sounds from a CD directly into sound-only QuickTime movies. MoviePlayer comes built-in with many Macintosh computers, and with many multimedia software programs. It is also available from computer stores and catalogs and on-line services.

To use this method of capturing sound, put your music compact disc into the CD-ROM drive on your computer. Launch MoviePlayer. Use Open from the File menu to open one of the tracks on the CD. Select the track you want to use, then click on the Options button. From this control panel, you will be able to preview the track you want to record and choose the exact piece of the music you want to capture. You can also set the quality (sampling rate) of the sound from this control panel. The sound will be saved to your disk as a sound-only QuickTime movie, from where it can be imported into almost any other program.

MoviePlayer can turn any sound file into a sound-only QuickTime movie, which is important especially if you plan later to import it into ClarisWorks or Aldus Persuasion. To do this, launch the MoviePlayer program. Use the File menu to open the sound file of your choice. MoviePlayer will ask you to choose a name for your sound movie. Save this QuickTime movie into your Project folder.

Sound File Formats

Sounds can be saved on disk in several file formats—SND, WAV, and AIFF—and as sound-only QuickTime movies. When you save a sound, your software often gives you choices as to the file format:

- SND files are used mostly on Macintosh computers. A short and simple sound recorded with the sound control panel is saved as an SND file. But not all programs can import SND files, so it's not the best choice.
- WAV files are used on Windows computers. Like the SND format, WAV files are not universally accepted so are not the best kind to use.
- AIFF (audio interchange file format) sounds are more universally readable so are a better choice than WAV or SND format.
- QuickTime sound-only movie files are the newest and probably most flexible format for saving your sound files. QuickTime files can play on both Macintosh and Windows computers. QuickTime files can be imported into ClarisWorks, Persuasion, Aldus Premiere, and most of the other programs we will use to assemble our multimedia presentation. And it's easy to edit QuickTime sounds with the MoviePlayer software.

Incorporating Sound and Images into Student Projects

Now that you have captured and edited your sounds and images, it's time to assemble them into a presentation. There are many tools to choose from for this purpose. We will start with the simplest, ClarisWorks, and work up to the more complex Persuasion.

Making a Slide Show with ClarisWorks

Open a new ClarisWorks word-processing document. Open up the tools palette. Use the Page Setup menu item to effect a horizontal format. Each page of this document will become one slide in your multimedia slide show.

To put a title on a slide, simply type into the word processor. Select and center your title. Set the font size to a larger number (seventy-two or more). Access the Style menu to choose a nice color for the title.

To bring a sound or image onto a slide, follow these steps:

1. Make sure the arrow tool is selected from the ClarisWorks tools palette.
2. Use Insert from the File menu to bring in sounds or images from your Project folder. (Sounds must be saved as QuickTime movies for ClarisWorks.)
3. The items you insert will appear on the page; drag them wherever you want. (If they won't drag, that means you did not have the arrow tool selected before you inserted.)

To get a new page (and thus a new slide), select Insert Break from the Format menu. Type another title. Insert some more items. Use the ClarisWorks draw and paint tools to embellish your slides. Continue this process until you have finished.

To play your slide show, select Slide Show under the View menu. Use the Slide Show dialogue box to format your presentation. Check off the box for fade to make the show fade to black between slides; select a background color (pastels work best); and set the movies to "auto play." Now start the slide show. Click the mouse or use the arrow keys to move from slide to slide. To stop the slide show, press Command+period from the keyboard.

To reorder the slides, drag them to different places in the list of slides on the upper left of the Slide Show dialogue box.

Slide Shows with Persuasion

Persuasion helps you construct slide shows that include text, pictures, sound, and video on a graphic background. Persuasion is used by many businesses to prepare slides. To make a simple slide show, follow these steps:

1. Gather your resources. Choose the items you want to include in your presentation and gather them onto a folder on the

computer's hard disk. These might include text, pictures, graphs, sounds, or QuickTime movies created earlier.

2. Give Persuasion some room. Find the Persuasion Program icon on your hard disk. Select it (but don't launch it) by clicking once on it. Under the File menu on the Macintosh, select Get Info. Set the Memory Requirement Preferred Size to as much memory as you have available in your computer. To do this on your Windows machine, refer to your Persuasion manual. Persuasion should have as much memory as it can to handle the information you will be putting into it.

3. Choose an auto template. For your first presentation, choose one of several predesigned backgrounds for your slides. Launch Persuasion. From the title screen choose Open Presentation. From the folder Auto Templates in the Persuasion folder, choose one of the On-screen/video templates. These can be previewed in the little window to determine the style that's most appropriate to your presentation. Open the template of your choice.

4. Build the text of your presentation. You will see the first (and only) slide of your slide show on the screen, along with some of the tools for working with it. To add text to a slide, just click into the title and body text place holders that you see on the slide, then type in what you want. (If you leave these place holders alone, they will remain empty when you view the slide show.) Add a second slide with the New Slide button on the bottom left of the screen (in the gray area). Add slides and enter text as necessary until you have a rough draft of your presentation. Use the arrows down in the gray area to move back and forth among your slides.

5. Add graphics, sounds, and movies. Go back through your slides and add multimedia elements where you want them. Use the Import command under the File menu. You can import pictures (graphics) from the PICT files (.PCX on Windows), sounds from QuickTime files, and movies from QuickTime files. With the full installation of Persuasion 3.0, you ill get a folder of clip art specially designed for Persuasion. You may also draw items on the slides, using Persuasion's

built-in drawing tools. The items you import or draw will appear on the slide, from where you can move or resize them as necessary.

6. Rearrange your slides. Use the slide sorter, available under the View menu, to see thumbnail images of all your slides on a "light table," where you can rearrange them as necessary by dragging them with the mouse.

7. Show your slides. Under the View menu, select Show All Slides. Check the buttons in the resulting dialogue box to alter the form of your slide show. When you press OK the slide show will play on the computer screen.

Multimedia: Next Steps

In this chapter we have learned to capture and employ images and sounds in our schoolwork. With this capability we can construct interesting and provocative reports and presentations. In the next chapter we will add to our repertoire by learning how to make digital video movies and simple animations and incorporate them into our work. A video is really just a combination of images and sounds displayed over time, so a lot of what we mastered in this chapter will apply in the next.

chapter 9

Action! Ideas in Motion

In the real world, things are always in motion. The earth revolves around the sun, rivers flow, children scamper, and cars speed. You can't understand the world without observing the way it moves. Albert Einstein developed his theory of relativity by imagining the movement of one object relative to another. Shakespeare's plays rely on the movement of actors across the stage to convey their meaning. Motion is key to making sense of science, history, the arts, and literature.

Motion is also endemic to our current forms of mass communication. The movies, television, video games, sports, and MTV all rely on moving images to pass on their messages and keep our attention. It's part of our culture.

So far, the things we have built together with the computer in this book have been static. They don't move. Our students have handed in homework printed on a fixed page, presented as a still image in a slide show, or embedded in an inanimate map. In this chapter we will learn how to animate schoolwork, using movement and video to capture and explain subjects in which motion is key to understanding. We will learn how to create simple animations with programs like Kid Pix, produce our own video clips on the computer, and use some kids' animation programs, which can become part of a homework report.

Just about any Windows or Macintosh computer can create simple animations. All you need is enough memory to fit the needs of the software. For creating your own digital video, your computer will need a video digitizer. The Apple Macintosh A-V series of computers comes with this capability built in: you can plug your videocamera right in and see the movies on the screen. If you use a different computer, you can add this capability with a video digitizing card, which we will explain in this chapter.

How Did She Do That?

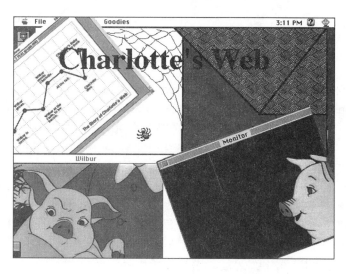

I had already read *Charlotte's Web* by E. B. White at home. Twice—once when my mother read it to me as a bedtime story and then again last summer. So it was pretty boring when Mrs. Young assigned us to do a book report on it.

I had always had this picture in my mind of Charlotte crawling around in mid air spinning her web, sort of like one of those nature shows about an insect ballet. So I asked the teacher if I could work on something like that instead of this book report. She said I had to turn in a book report covering all the usual items, but she wouldn't mind if the spider dance was a part of it.

So I went to work. I got my friend Janet to show me how to do animation with Kid Pix. It was a lot of work, but when it was done I had exactly what I wanted, a movie of Charlotte spinning her web.

Then I used the same method to show the plot, you know, the ups and downs of the story. I made a sort of graph with the drawing program on the computer, showing how the story was going. I drew a circle to represent each big event. Then I could play this back as a slide show that explained the story.

My dad went to the video store and rented the cartoon movie of *Charlotte's Web*. It was fun to watch the things I had been reading about. My mom showed me how to hook up the VCR to the computer so I could make little movie clips of my favorite parts of the story. I made one little computer movie for each of the circles on my plot graph. It was easy to make movies: just press the Record and Stop buttons on the computer.

All the kids read *Charlotte's Web*. And they all have an opinion about it. I decided to make little movies of what some of the kids thought about the book. I hooked our home videocamera to the computer, sat my friends in front of it, and recorded little movies of them explaining what they thought of the book. Some of my friends were shy in front of the camera, others tried to talk like Dan Rather, but at least two of the movies turned out okay.

So now I had the spiderweb animation, the plot graph, the video clips, and the students all in my computer. When I showed them to my teacher, she asked me to make a report to the class. It was fun to show the book in this way. It made everybody think a little differently about *Charlotte's Web*.

Ellen used her computer to make *Charlotte's Web* come to life. Animation helped her and her classmates visualize the life of a spider spinning her web. A moving graph outlined the ups and downs of the plot, and accompanying video clips illustrated the story in yet another way. Ellen also captured the opinions of fellow readers in a lively manner. Finally, she used the computer to present all of these as an integrated report. She put her ideas in motion with the computer.

How did she start? With a good idea. She did not start her work by sitting at the computer and calling up data. Good reports start with good ideas—in Ellen's case, an image in her mind of an animated spider spinning the web. Her next step was to seek a way to express this idea with her computer. She called on a friend to teach her some new tricks: specifically, how to animate a drawing.

Simple Animation

Ellen used Kid Pix* to create her animated spiderweb. Janet showed her first how to draw a web that would always be in the background. Ellen made this look more realistic by drawing in the wall of Farmer Zuckerman's barn as part of the background. Ellen saved this "background" picture on the disk twice, just in case she lost or saved over it accidentally. Next she found a Kid Pix rubber stamp that looked

* You need a version of Kid Pix that includes the Slide Show feature, such as Kid Pix Companion, Kid Pix 2, or Kid Pix Studio.

frame—in animation,
a single picture or
single page, like a
single picture in a
flipbook.

like a spider but had only six legs. She edited the rubber stamp using the Edit feature in the Toolbox to add two more legs so she had a good-looking spider to represent Charlotte.

Into her background drawing, near the corner of the screen, Ellen placed the spider. Then she carefully saved this picture on the disk as "Spider 1." She closed this picture and opened the background picture again. Onto this picture, a little farther away from the corner, she stamped the spider again. She saved this picture as "Spider 2." Repeating this process, she saved twenty pictures on her disk, each with the spider a little farther along the wall. Each of these pictures became a *frame* or cell of her animation.

Next she brought up the Kid Pix Slide Show tools. Into each blank square on the slide show (each square was actually a little truck that "carried" the slide through the show) she imported one of her twenty pictures. Then she told the computer to play these back as an animation. Sure enough, the spider seemed to walk along the wall. But it went much too slowly! It looked like the spider was hiccuping along the wall while half asleep.

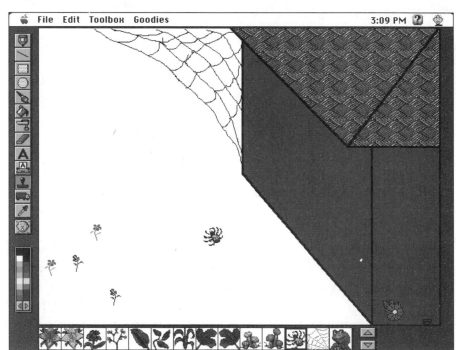

In Ellen's animation, Charlotte, the spider, slowly made her way up the wall to the web.

210

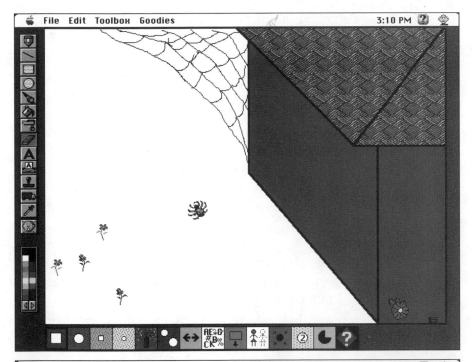

In each frame, Charlotte moved a little closer to the web.

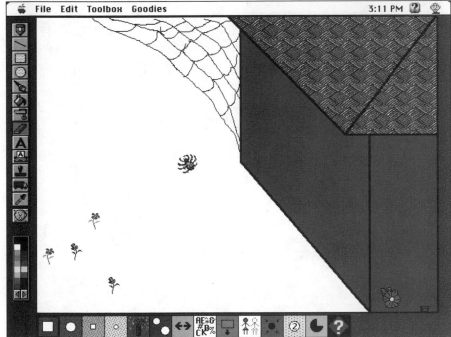

After Ellen adjusted the timing, Charlotte crawled smoothly up the wall towards the web.

Ellen found the Kid Pix manual and looked up information on animation. It suggested that she make the timing of each slide in the slide show as short as possible, so that the animation would run quickly. She went back and adjusted the slider on each truck all the way to the left. Now when she ran the slide show, the spider naturally crawled across the wall.

Ellen's last step was to save the animation. Here she had two choices: she could save it as a Kid Pix slide show, as a QuickTime movie, or as a Stand Alone. If she saved it as a Kid Pix slide show, she could show it on any computer, even those without the Kid Pix program (in some versions this mode is called Stand Alone). But she would not be able to import it into any other programs. If she saved it as QuickTime movie, it would play on other computers, and it could be imported into most other programs, such as word processors and presentation tools. The QuickTime movie format would also be smaller in size. Ellen chose to save her animation as a QuickTime movie so she could use it anywhere in her project and play it on the computer at school.

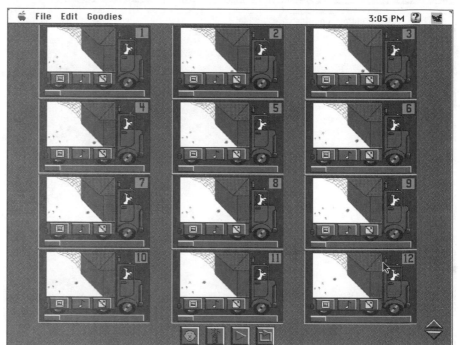

Ellen imported each one of her pictures into a Moving Van of the Slide Show feature of Kid Pix.

Steps for Making Animations with Kid Pix

1. Draw a background picture, containing only those elements that will be included with every frame of the animation.

2. Save this background to the disk, twice, as a backup to be sure you don't erase it accidentally when you are creating your animation.

3. Open the background and add the animated element(s) in the place where you want it to start.

4. Use Save As… to save this picture to the disk as "Picture 1."

5. Open the background picture again.

6. Add the animated element(s) in a location just a little ahead of where it was in the last picture. About one centimeter (three-eighths of an inch) away is just about right. (To make this easier, place a piece of clear plastic wrap over the computer screen and mark the locations of your animated characters with Magic Marker.)

7. Use Save As… to save this picture to the disk as "Picture 2."

8. Repeat steps five through seven to create Pictures 3, 4, 5, 6, and however many are necessary to complete the animation.

9. Open the Kid Pix Slide Show program.

10. Click the square on the first truck (upper left) to get a choice of pictures to import.

11. Import Picture 1 into truck 1.

12. Do the same to import Pictures 2, 3, 4, 5, and so forth into their respective trucks. Remember that the trucks read across.

13. Set the timing of each truck to zero by sliding the timing bar all the way to the left.

14. Name and save the slide show.

15. Use the arrow at the bottom of the screen to run the slide show to see if it forms a natural-looking animation.

16. Revise the timing, or insert new pictures, as necessary to make the animation smooth and natural.

17. When you are happy with the animation, and depending on the version of Kid Pix you have, save it as a Kid Pix slide show, self-running Stand Alone, or as a QuickTime movie.

Graphing the Plot

Children have for decades drawn diagrams to show the plot of a book: rising lines to show growing action, circles to denote key events and crises, down-slanting lines to show sadness or despair. Ellen created nothing new with her particular plan for *Charlotte's Web*. But by building it with the computer, she could embellish and enhance it. By using simple animation, she could make it come alive for her audience. To do this, Ellen used the drawing capability of ClarisWorks to build her plot graph.

Setting up the Pages

First she used the Page Setup function under the File menu to make the pages of the drawing sideways (the landscape view), just like the computer screen. Then she used the Document function under the Format menu to set the piece to six pages, which was the number of key events she had planned. Using the Edit Master Page function under the Options menu, Ellen put "The Story of *Charlotte's Web*" as a title at the bottom of every page. Under the View menu she chose Page View so she could see each page as it would look on the screen. At last she was ready to build her plot graph.

Building the Graph

By constructing simple lines, circles, and text, Ellen showed the ups and downs of the story. On the first page she drew a line with the line tool, then set it to 4 pixels wide using the thickness tool. She drew a circle, again as thick, to represent the first key event in the story, the saving of the runt piglet, Wilbur. Then she used the text tool in the drawing program to label this event. That was Ellen's first page. To construct the second page, Ellen selected all the elements on the first page by dragging the mouse over them, then used Copy from the Edit menu. She moved the cursor to the second page, clicked once, then pasted in the items from page one. To these she added another thick

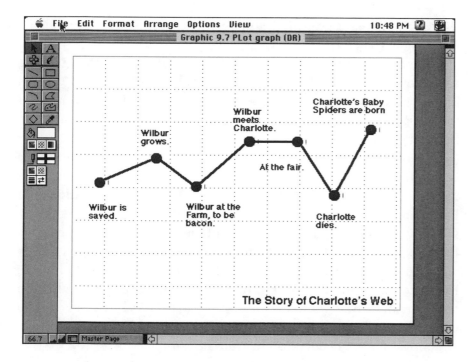

 File   Edit   Format   Arrange   Options   View   10:48 PM

Graphic 9.7 PLot graph (DR)

Charlotte's Baby
Spiders are born

Wilbur
meets
Charlotte.

Wilbur
grows.

At the fair.

Wilbur is
saved.

Wilbur at the
Farm, to be
bacon.

Charlotte
dies.

The Story of Charlotte's Web

66.7   Master Page

Ellen graphed the plot of
Charlotte's Web in the
drawing program of
ClarisWorks.

line and another circle. This she labeled to correspond with the next
event in the story. She repeated this process for each of the six events.

Making an Animated Slide Show

When all six pages were complete, Ellen chose Slide Show from the
View menu. In the dialog boxes she was presented, she chose a background color, and set the slides to advance automatically every four
seconds. After she pressed OK, she watched her plot graph animate
the story of *Charlotte's Web*. She saved the show on the disk. At this
point she was ready to embellish this piece of work with video.

Making Digital Video Clips

. . . .

From the video cartoon movie of *Charlotte's Web* (Paramount, 1972),
Ellen captured six short video clips, one for each of the key events in

the story. She also captured still pictures of the main characters. Here's how she did it.

First she connected the family VCR to the computer (use the same cables you would to connect your videocamera to the TV set). This involved connecting cables from the audio and video output of the VCR to the audio and video inputs of the computer. Then she pressed play on the VCR to start the tape rolling.

Second, Ellen launched her video recording software, which was called FusionRecorder and came built in on her family's Macintosh A-V. (Look at the tip box to see what kind of digitizing hardware fits the needs of your computer type.) This showed her a window, about one-quarter the size of the screen, where the video from the movie showed on the monitor.

Third, Ellen fast-forwarded to the piece she wanted to record, then clicked on the Record button on the video capture window on the computer. She watched until she had what she wanted, then pressed the Stop button. Each clip was only a few seconds long, which was all she needed to illustrate her story.

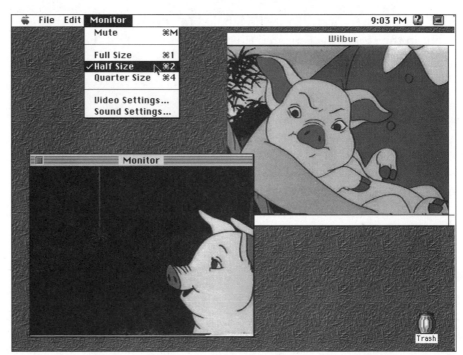

Ellen connected her computer to her family VCR to capture video clips to use in her report.

The computer took a few minutes to compress her work into digital video movies. When this was done, Ellen saved the movies as a file on the hard disk inside her computer. Later she imported these movies into her presentation to the class.

Compression

Video takes up a lot of room on a computer's disk drive. Each frame of even a small video (240 x 180 pixels) contains 43,200 bits of information! Multiply that by fifteen frames per second, and you will find that one minute of digital video can take up 38,880,000 bits of space on the disk. That's too much. So scientists have invented schemes to compress this video information so that it takes up less space. There are several different ways to compress the video, but they all do the same thing: save to the disk only those pixels that are absolutely necessary to make the video appear.

Here's how it works. Suppose you have a 30-second digital video of a baseball game. The first frame shows the field of green grass and brown dirt and players in white uniforms. Most of the pixels in this frame are either green (grass) or brown (dirt) Now let's look at the second frame of the video. Most of the green and brown pixels have not changed at all from the first frame. The only thing that's different is the pitcher, whose arm has moved three pixels to the right. The only pixels that change between frame one and frame two are those of the pitcher's arm, perhaps 35 pixels (560 bits). All else remains the same. So the computer does not need to save the unchanging parts of the picture; it only needs to record the changes from one frame to another. Instead of saving 43,200 bits for every frame, it can get away with saving one complete frame (frame #1) but from then on it needs to save the changes, about 560 bits per frame. By this method the 38 megabits of information can be compressed to about 5.

To get the still pictures of the main characters, Ellen used similar software, called Video Monitor on the Macintosh A-V. (See the tip box for software to fit your needs.) With this software, she simply watched the movie play and when she saw the character she wanted, she clicked on the Copy button to take a snapshot of a single frame of video. The program automatically saved these snapshots as image files on the hard disk.

Capturing Video on a Computer

Preparing a digital video clip involves two steps:

1. capturing video from tape, videodisc, and live sources
2. editing and mixing this video with other information into a short movie

Before you can capture video, your computer needs a digitizing card, which costs about $300. This circuitry coverts analog video (the kind we use on videotape and in television) to digital video (the kind we use in the computer). Look at the list to see what fits your needs.

The Apple Macintosh A-V comes already loaded with

- FusionRecorder for capturing and digitizing video into the computer
- MoviePlayer for viewing movies

To an Apple Macintosh, add a VideoSpigot card from Radius to have

- ScreenPlay for capturing and digitizing video and stills into the computer
- MoviePlayer for viewing movies

To a Windows machine, add a VideoBlaster card from Creative Labs to have

- VideoCap for capturing and digitizing video and stills into the computer

- MediaPlayer for viewing movies

If you recently bought a multimedia machine, check your owner's manual to see if you already have this capability. Optional for any of these machines is an additional program such as Adobe Premiere for editing and mixing the video on the computer.

Capturing Video

You have read about how Ellen captured video, but what about doing the same on your computer? After you have settled the hardware and software needs for your computer, try digitizing some video from tape or a videocamera into a file on your computer.

Connect the Videocamera or VCR to the Computer

Connect the VCR or videocamera's "video out" connector to the "video in" connector on the computer (using the same cables you would to connect your videocamera to the TV set). Connect the "audio out" connector on the VCR or videocamera to the microphone jack on the computer. Turn on the videocamera and point it at the item you want to capture. You may want to use the camera's controls to focus and zoom the image at this point. If your image was earlier captured on videotape, set the VCR to play, or the camera to VCR and play.

Set up Your Digitizing Software

Make sure that no programs are running on your computer. Capturing video requires all the memory you can spare! Open the FusionRecorder, Screenplay, or Video Cap software. It will bring up a video window on the screen, about 3.0 inches wide and 2.5 inches high. You should see the image from the videocamera or VCR in this window.

If you don't see the video, check the Video Settings item under the Record menu. Set these as follows:

- Compression: Compressor
  - Video
  - Depth
  - Color
  - Quality: 50
  - Frames: 15
  - Key Frame: 15
- Image: All settings to 50, unless they need changing by the looks of the video
- Source: Digitizer
  - Built-in video
  - Input: Composite
  - Format: NTSC
  - Filter: VCR

(You shouldn't have to change these settings once they are set correctly.)

Set the Record Window Size to 240 x 180. This is three-eighths of the computer screen, a good size to work with for your project at this point. Larger sizes will take up more space and be slower to work with.

Set the Sound settings if necessary, to the following:

- Compression: None
- Sampling: 22.050 MHz, 8 bits, mono
  - Source: Device
- Built-in
  - Input: Microphone
- Speaker: On

You should hear the sound from the video source and see it flashing in the indicator.

Set the Record Preferences under the Record menu as follows:

- Record Directly to Disk
- Post Compress
- Show Available Space

These settings will grab frames of video as they are played and save them to the disk. When you stop recording, the program will go back and compress the movie from the frames on the disk.

Record Some Video onto the Computer

On the recording window, click on the record button, and the computer will capture whatever is coming in from the video source. Click on the Stop button when you are done. (At first, record just a brief selection of video to make sure everything is working correctly.) At this point the software will *postcompress* your movie, which will take some time. When it's finished, the movie opens in a new window.

postcompress—compression that takes place once you are done working on your movie.

Inspect the movie you have made. If something seems wrong, recheck the video and sound settings to make sure they match the values described above. Make another recording. When you are happy with your movie, save it into your Project folder.

Keep your movies short. Digital video takes up lots of memory and lots of space on your hard disk. If you have trouble recording, you may need to clear off some space on your disk to fit all the new information.

Disk Space

Making movies and animations requires considerable free space on the hard disk of your computer. The programs actually save, albeit temporarily, every frame of the video to your hard disk. This means they will not work well, or at all, unless you give them room to save this information. It's best not to attempt digitizing your own videos unless your hard drive has 50 megabytes of free space.

You can use this same method to capture movies from a VCR or from a videodisc player. Just connect the audio and video out jacks of the device to the microphone and video in jacks of your computer, click on the play button, and go to work.

Editing Video

■ ■ ■ ■ ■ ■ ■ ■ ■ ■ ■ ■ ■

Just as you can cut, copy, and paste the words you have written with your word processor, you can do the same with the video that you captured. Take a short piece of a movie to help illustrate an idea in a school report. Or link together two or three movies to tell a longer story. The possibilities are endless.

Simple cut, copy, and paste editing can be accomplished with the MoviePlayer (Macintosh) or MediaPlayer (Windows) program. Launch the software. Open a digital movie that you have previously saved on your disk. To select part of the movie, hold down the shift key as you play it. The part you have selected will turn black in the controller bar. You can cut or copy this selection, using the standard commands under the Edit menu.

Whatever you cut or copy goes into the Clipboard, from where it can be pasted into another program, put into the Scrapbook (on the Apple Macintosh), or used to create a new movie. You can assemble a new movie from bits of several movies by opening them all with MoviePlayer, selecting New movie from the File menu, then copying pieces and pasting them one after another into the new movie.

Whenever you save an edited movie from MoviePlayer, you have two choices: you can save an alias of the movie, which is simply a pointer to the original movie file; or you can save the movie as a self-contained movie. In most cases, you should save your movie as a self-contained file. Also, it's best to save movies onto the hard disk in your computer; only very short movies will fit onto a floppy disk. Do not work to and from a file server, because sending movies back and forth across the network will bog it down.

Presenting Video and Animation

■ ■ ■ ■ ■ ■ ■ ■ ■ ■ ■ ■ ■

The types of videos and animations that Ellen created can be presented alone, simply by double-clicking on the files. But best results are often obtained by integrating these moving works into reports and presentations. That's what Ellen did to present her book report to the class. Today's computer software makes this easy to do.

Animations and Videos in ClarisWorks

In earlier chapters we learned how to create and present a simple slide show with ClarisWorks. It's easy to add video clips to such a show. First, create a slide show with titles, images, drawings, and photos as described in chapter 7. Next, go to the page of the slide show where you want the video clip to appear. From the File menu choose Insert and find a digital movie file that you had previously saved on the hard disk. (In the dialogue box, you may need to set the Show button to "QuickTime Movie" or ".AVI file" in order to see your videos.) When you choose the movie, it will appear as a window on the page, with one frame of the movie showing. Drag the movie to the location desired. Then go on to insert other movies on other pages in your slide show. Ellen put each of the six "key event" video clips into the proper pages of her Plot Graph slide show in just this manner. When you go to Slide Show under the View menu, don't forget to check the box titled Auto Play under QuickTime options. When the slide show plays, the movies will appear and play through on each slide.

In a similar manner, you can import animations into ClarisWorks. Simply save the animation as a QuickTime movie and follow the previous instructions. You can also import these same digital movies and animations into Persuasion, PowerPoint, or Digital Chisel presentation programs, using the Import function under the File menu.

Animation in a Can

. . . .

Does all of this sound really interesting but a bit technical, to you? Besides Kid Pix, there are some other user-friendly software programs on the market that help kids take their first crack at computer animation without much instruction. They come with backgrounds, props, characters, sound clips, and other special effects to create fun animated movies quickly and easily. They also contain tools so that young animators can do some simple editing of their creations.

Most kids use animations first to tell stories. The graphics and sound assist in conveying the meaning and add to the mood and the feeling of the tale. Programs such as Amazing Animation from Claris and Magic Theatre from Knowledge Adventure are so easy to use that even preschool age kids can put together dynamic clips with minimal help from adults. Older kids will enjoy Nickelodeon Director's Lab from Viacom New Media, an electronic production studio for the design of minimovies and animated cartoons.

All of these programs contain backgrounds that kids can use as backdrops for their presentations if they don't want to draw in their own. The backgrounds range from under the sea to on the moon, with a variety of landscapes in between. Once the scene is set, kids can then bring in characters and props. Click on any one and drag it across the screen, and it displays a set motion when the animation is run. In Amazing Animation, for example, a beaver can juggle, fish shimmy through blue waves, hot-air balloons float through the sky, and monkeys can swing through the trees.

Sounds can also be added. Each program contains a collection of realistic sounds and whimsical sound effects. Dogs bark, crickets chirp on a summer's night, or a raucous calliope tune can change the mood of a scene. You can also record your own sounds or voices. Transitions, to blend one scene into another, can be added between scenes.

Amazing Animation and Nickelodeon Director's Lab (as well as Kid Pix Studio—the CD-ROM version of Kid Pix) allow the animator to save a finished presentation to a disk and run it on another computer of the same type even if the program itself isn't on that computer. This is a great feature for taking an animation clip to school for a quick assignment. You can also be up and running on any of these programs in less than an hour. They are simple to learn and easy to use. Neither you nor your kids have to be artists or programmers to create engaging multimedia presentations.

Amazing Animation lets kids quickly choose or create a background and add animated stickers to produce an animated movie.

Courtesy of Claris

Programs, such as Magic Theatre, are so easy to use that anyone can create an animated movie within minutes.

Courtesy of Knowledge Adventure

225

Camera! Action! Homework!

Animation and video can enhance schoolwork in just about every subject area. Here are a few ideas that might help liven up some typical assignments.

Reading, English, and Language Arts

- The standard book report is an ideal forum to set forth plot diagrams, video clips, and interviews that help clarify the main points and interpretations of a book or selection of literature. As Ellen showed in her assignment, even the simplest and most traditional of stories can profit from the addition of movement.
- Animated ads make a great way to introduce a book for an oral report.
- Short stories, folk tales, jokes, riddles, limericks, and poems can be brainstormed, enhanced, and just plain fun to write when using one of the "canned" animation programs.
- Students can stage the production of a play as a series of pictures that change as the characters enter and exit; their lines can be delivered with sound files and their personages visualized with digital video clips, then the entire play can be presented as a slide show with ClarisWorks or Persuasion or with one of the "canned" animation programs.
- When you think about it, a sentence is an idea in motion: it moves from beginning to end, from noun to verb to adverb to prepositional phrase. A student can create an animated diagram of a sentence, in much the same way that Ellen animated the plot plan of *Charlotte's Web*. This is a great way to help understand the grammatical structure of a sentence.
- Some words, especially verbs, are best illustrated with motion. A student can analyze a passage from literature by illustrating each verb, and many adjectives, nouns and adverbs, with animated diagrams or short video clips. When

Words come alive when illustrated by short video clips or animations.

presented in a series of slides, these become a multimedia analysis and explication of the story.

Social Studies

- Next time your student has to report on a memorable battle, the voyage of an explorer, or an important event in history, let him do it with an animated map that shows the chain of events in concrete moving detail on the computer screen. Starting with a map clipped from an electronic atlas as a background, use the animation technique described previously with Kid Pix to produce the final result.

- Many of the most studied historical events and figures from the twentieth century are featured in various movies or documentaries on video. Clips from these movies can be used to embellish otherwise static reports for social studies. Your child can find these clips in the electronic encyclopedias or at the video store in the documentary or historical films section. From there they can be captured into the computer and then imported into ClarisWorks, Persuasion, or Digital Chisel slide shows. Make sure you credit your sources.

- Most of the geographical locations that students study in school can be found on videos from the video store. Look in the travel or nature section. The series from National Geographic is especially useful. Follow the directions offered previously to capture short clips from these films to use in your student's next geography report.

- Next time she goes on a school field trip, let your child take along the family videocamera. She need not record the entire event, just a few short clips of the most interesting sights and sounds and events. Her report of the field trip can come to life as these scenes are digitized and displayed on the computer screen as part of her interpretation of the field trip.

- Just about every student writes a report of the westward movement of population across the United States. What better way to illustrate this than with an animated map of the United States on which the density of population is plotted? Use the census data and show every ten years as one map. Make each map a page in a ClarisWorks slide show or a frame in a Kid Pix animation. You will be surprised at the power of this moving image to capture the true meaning of the shift.

Science

- A science laboratory is a hotbed of motion and animation. Using a videocamera, still camera, or QuickTake digital camera, take still pictures of your experiment over time. Arrange these into an animation with Kid Pix, and play it back. This is similar to time-lapse photography and helps show the process of the experiment in a dramatic way.

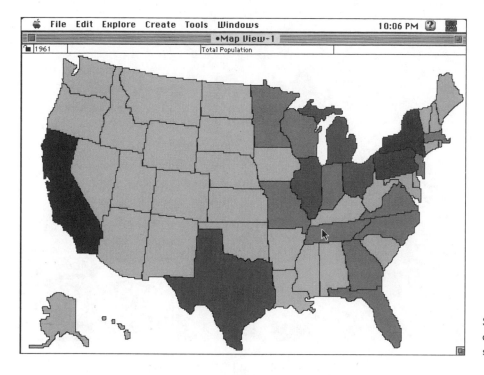

Shifts in population can be dramatically portrayed in slide shows and animations.

- Many middle schools have a video microscope, which is simply a videocamera mounted on top of a standard microscope. Connect the output of the video to the input of the computer and record whatever is happening in the microscopic world. These short film clips can make this part of science much more understandable.

- The processes of biology—hearts pumping, flowers growing, cells dividing—can all be illustrated with simple animations. As Ellen did, use Kid Pix to create a background (for example, heart, arteries, veins), then animate the moving items (such as oxygenated and depleted blood) over several frames and play it back rapidly, in a loop. This can show how the process works where words and still pictures cannot.

- What better way to show the growth and flow of a volcano than with a combination of computer animation and video? Scan in a photo, or draw your own volcano to use as a background, then animate the lava flow by drawing it frame by frame with Kid Pix. Couple this with a video clip drawn from

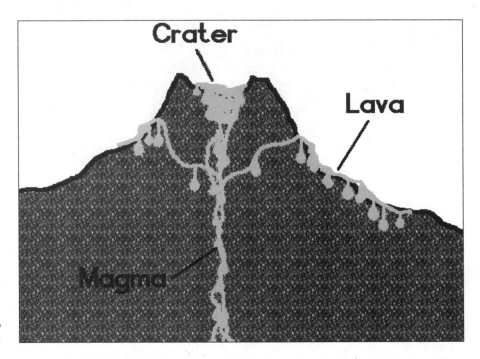

Create an erupting volcano
for a science report!

the electronic encyclopedia or from a videotape, and you have
an impressive student science report.

Flipbooks

Remember those old-fashioned flipbooks you had as a kid? Well, if you
make an animation such as Charlotte spinning her web, a flower growing,
a heart beating, the route of an explorer, or a volcano erupting, your child
can also make a fast flipbook out of it with a piece of utility software called
Flipbook from S. H. Pierce. Just save your animation as a QuickTime movie
and open it in Flipbook. Flipbook will print it out complete with dotted lines
so you can cut it out quickly. I use these when I am teaching kids about
animation. These flipbooks are also a great way to remind teachers of
what was done in a presentation that included computer animation.

Math

- Much of math in the middle school hovers around measurement: how many, how much, area, perimeter, volume, and so forth. A great way to visualize the measurements, and how they change under different circumstances, is to animate them with Kid Pix. To illustrate area, for instance: In frame one, show a blue square with a 1 cm side and the numeral 1 to represent its area. In frame two, make a 2 cm square with area 4. In frame three it's a 3 cm square with area 9, and so on. The rapid increase in volume as the sides lengthen will show up dramatically when the animation is played back.

- A good way to set up a word problem is to make a video clip of it. Use the camera to capture Susan with four candy bars and Jason with two, then show them eating one each. Make a ClarisWorks slide show that plays this as a digital video clip, then asks, "How many candy bars are left?"

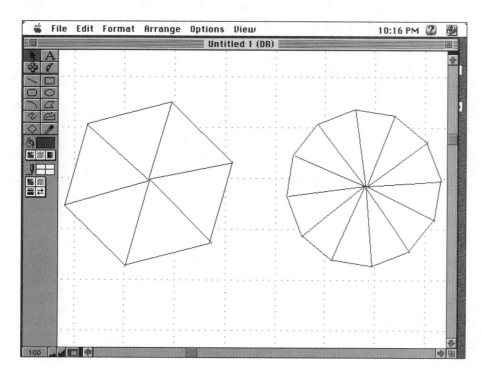

Math concepts can be examined and understood by constructing animations on the computer.

- Advanced mathematical concepts can be worked out by taking measurements, on the computer screen, of events that you have recorded with digital video. Make a video of a child swinging, taken from the side so it looks like a pendulum going back and forth. Digitize it on the computer by following the directions in this chapter. Look at the video one frame at a time. On each frame, measure the distance of the child from the center of the swing set. Enter these measurements into a spreadsheet. When you plot these measurements (by making a graph with the spreadsheet program), they will produce an interesting geometric curve. (A software program called Measurement in Motion from Learning in Motion can be purchased to make this measuring and plotting much easier.)
- The ancient Greeks figured out the formula for the area of a circle by dividing the circle into an ever-narrowing series of triangles, until the short side of the triangle was almost nothing; then they added up the combined area of the triangles to get the area of the circle. A child can clarify this difficult concept in a similar fashion with a series of ClarisWorks slides or frames of Kid Pix animations.

Arts

- Animation is in and of itself a form of art. Let students work with animation as part of their art curriculum—encourage them to use the computer at home to do this work.
- By cutting and pasting video clips, students can produce works of art on the computer that cannot be duplicated in any other medium. Encourage them to express their ideas in this manner.

Next Steps

. . . .

The next chapter goes beyond the use of simple motion in school work to the use of complex simulations that combine motion with logic, graphics, sound, and even video. You'll be surprised how the computer can enhance a child's understanding and help build homework tasks that go far beyond the simple reports we started with in chapter 1.

part

4

· · · · · · · · · · · · ·

You Won't Know
Unless You Experiment

chapter 10

Simulating the Real World

The most successful series of lessons I ever devised when I was teaching high school social studies centered around the concept of revolution. My job was to make the history of Western Europe come alive and be relevant for three classes of urban kids who felt very little connection to Europe, history, or school in general. I was young, but I learned early on that all the conventional approaches I had experienced or been taught to use had little effect on most of these kids.

By the time we had reached our study of the French Revolution I was up for trying something different: I gave the kids a scenario that resembled their school situation. The king (who coincidentally had the same name as the principal) was the First Estate. The Second Estate comprised those in control, a ruling class whose members sounded a lot like the teaching staff and the deans. The Third Estate, made up of the lowly drudges, might easily have been the students, toiling away endlessly and turning in homework as "taxes."

I suggested that students devise a plan for changing the situation. In each class, meeting in small groups, they all neatly obliged me by plotting a revolution—complete with overthrow of the king and those in power. Their plots made a great platform for teaching about the stages of revolution and making comparisons to the French and

Russian Revolutions. The kids were also interested in how their simulation of a revolution matched up with what really happened so long ago. As one student, who had cared little about history before this point, remarked, "Those French people were very smart."

The point of this story is that simulations—of historical events, the building of towns and cities, running businesses, science experiments, aquariums, and other generic models—are a great way to grab kids' attention when you want them to learn. They also enable kids to use in a practical way some of the principles they have learned. And guess what? Simulations are also something the computer does well.

In this chapter we are going to look at a variety of popular computer simulations and discuss how they can contribute to schoolwork and help kids develop a more positive attitude toward learning. Simulations are another way for students to "mess around" with learning and information, much as they did with the on-line and CD-ROM resources we told you about in the last section of the book. We are going to suggest how these simulations can help create parts of projects for homework assignments, but we are also interested in how these programs can help kids to feel connected with the subjects they are studying. Simulations can add a depth to certain subject areas that can't be delivered by lectures, reading materials, or videos.

How Did He Do That?

■ ■ ■ ■ ■ ■ ■ ■ ■ ■ ■ ■

Lincoln, a seventh-grader, turned a simple health fair project into an experiment that everybody in his school could try out on the spot. He started by building his own stethoscope out of a balloon, some rubber tubing, two small funnels, and a rubber band. This worked really well. He could hear the sound of his heart valves closing and opening. Watching the animation of the human heart that was part of his electronic encyclopedia, he learned that the longer sound he heard is made when blood flows out of the heart and the two heart valves shut. The shorter dub sound is made when two other heart valves

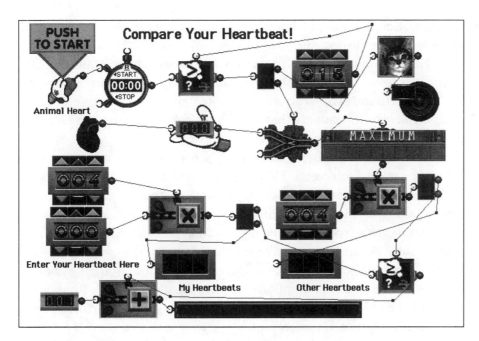

It was time for the annual seventh-grade spring health fair. I had seen a plan for building your own stethoscope in a science fair book. It looked pretty easy, so I chose to do a display on the heart. Mrs. Bode, my science teacher, mentioned that someone else had done that last year. The way she said it made me think that I needed to add something to get a good grade. Then I remembered that I had seen some hearts in the Widget Workshop program from Maxis on my computer that I could use to compare the heartbeats of people to cats, dogs, elephants, tortoises, and even gerbils. It was easy to put together, complete with sound, and it was really cool to watch in action. The first time I compared my heartbeat with that of the tortoise though, I thought something was wrong with the computer. A tortoise's heart beats so slowly compared with ours. But I went and looked it up and that really is how their hearts work.

I borrowed one of the computers at school and set it up at my booth. I let people come by and use my handmade stethoscope to count their heartbeat rate in fifteen seconds while an animal's heart ran the same amount of time. When they finished counting (a cat meowed on the widget to let them know that fifteen seconds was up), they input their heart rate and the widget displayed a message saying "Your heartbeat is slower" or "Your heartbeat is faster" depending on the animal they chose. Kids were really surprised at how fast the gerbil's heartbeat went, and some couldn't believe a tortoise's heart really goes that slow. The line in the gym got pretty long coming to my booth. A lot of teachers came by, too. I talked to the kids about life expectancy, weight, and all sorts of factors that were related to my display about the heart. At the end Mrs. Bode came by with a big smile and commented on how I had helped to make this one of the most interesting health fairs ever.

open and blood flows into the heart. Lincoln probably would have been satisfied just to demonstrate his stethoscope at the fair if Mrs.

Bode, his science teacher, hadn't mentioned that another student had done the same project the year before.

Her comment made him think about what else he could do. His mom had given him the software Widget Workshop from Maxis for his last birthday. The software consisted of a bunch of somewhat realistic tools and gadgets that can be dragged onto the screen from a tool bar and connected to create various kinds of devices. The devices can then be turned on and off with the stop and go buttons that appear on the screen. He loved messing around with the Rube Goldberg–style puzzles that came as part of the program. He also liked making up machines of his own out of the timers, switches, keypads, converters, speakers, displays, transformers, tuning forks, and other tools. When he remembered that you could experiment with hearts that could be set to beat at different rates, he thought of building a widget that could compare the heartbeat rate of a human with those of the animals included in the database (gerbils, tortoises, rabbits, and elephants, for example).

But where to start? Lincoln brainstormed a list of steps into his word processor that looked something like this:

1. Get your own heartbeat using the stethoscope.
2. Input that rate into the machine.
3. Use a heart from the Parts Bin set to an animal's heart rate.
4. Start and record a rate for that.
5. Compare the two rates.

It looked like a simple enough process, but Lincoln took a few minutes to look over the tools in the various Parts Bins to give him some ideas on how to proceed. Suddenly he remembered that when you go to the doctor, the nurse usually takes your pulse for a minute, so he started out by finding a tool that would time your heartbeat for a minute. He used a timer that looked like a stopwatch and a digit displayer to show the heart rate at the end of sixty seconds. He got the whole thing started by hooking up a mouse that had to be clicked to start the timer. When he tried it out, he found that it was hard to listen to your own heartbeat through the homemade stethoscope, count the beats, and can keep an eye on the clock. To remind himself when a minute was up he added a cat that was preset to meow at the end of sixty seconds.

So much for human heartbeats. Next Lincoln chose a heart out of the Parts Bin and connected it up with a counter. That worked well when he started the simulator. The counter clicked off the heartbeat precisely. Just for fun he tried it out by switching the data for the rate first to a gerbil's and then to that of an elephant. He was amazed to watch the clicker and hear how fast the little gerbil's heart went. The elephant's heartbeat seemed much like his own.

Now to compare the two heartbeats. Lincoln chose a switcher to connect both sets of information. He ran the simulator again and recorded what heart rate he got for himself when he used his stethoscope and counted out loud for a minute. He recorded that information in a display. Then he connected up a comparer—a nifty little device that will compare two numbers and indicate which is greater than, equal to, or less than. He set the widget to register the heartbeat of the animal after a minute as recorded on the clicker and then compare the result with the information he collected about himself after a minute on a digital display. But what to do with that information? Lincoln decided to hook up an adder that would indicate whether the human heartbeat was faster or slower than the animal sample, and a message light to the comparer. If the message light got an input of "1," it displayed the message "Your heartbeat is slower." If it got a "2," the message was "Your heartbeat is faster."

Lincoln tried out the widget with his little sister. She had a lot of trouble sitting still for a minute while he got her heart rate, but she loved watching the little heart on the screen beat rapidly when it was a gerbil's and slowly as a tortoise's. He mentioned the fidgeting problem when he tried the simulation out with his dad that night. His dad had played with the software a bit too, and suggested that if he used a multiplier, he could take a fifteen-second heartbeat reading, multiply it by four, and get a reading for a minute. That worked out well. (Lincoln was very glad that he had done that on the day of the health fair when everybody at school was lined up to try out his simulation!)

Lincoln did some more research on the relationship among size, heart rate, and longevity and recorded the information on some posters, which he put up behind his table at the health fair. He also prepared a little talk about how his homemade stethoscope worked.

Next he got the computer part of his display ready. Widget Workshop lets you save your simulations as "Stand Alone Widgets." This meant that all Lincoln had to do was borrow a machine at school that was the same type as his machine at home and he could run the widget without even having the full software program with him. That was helpful because the school didn't own Widget Workshop.

Displaying Projects at School

PLAN AHEAd!

My father had a sign like that in his basement workshop when I was growing up. It's a key maxim to remember if your child is planning to use a school computer to display any part of a project. First, make sure that whoever is responsible for the computers at school is alerted to what plans are in the works. A compatible computer with enough hard drive space, RAM, and a sound card (if you are using a DOS/Windows machine) must be available on the day and at the hour it will be needed. Second, settle any software issues. If the school doesn't own the same piece of software, you will have to get permission to put that software on the hard drive. That permission might take some time to get, so check on it early in the planning stages. Technically that software should be on only one computer at a time, so make sure it gets deleted after the project has been shown. Also make sure there are three prong outlets and adequate electricity wherever the projects are being set up. Some older buildings are not wired the same everywhere, so do a little snooping beforehand. If possible, visit the school a few days early to try out the project on the computer that will be used for the display. That way, if there are any problems, you'll have time to talk to the computer resource person at school for help or to consult with the technical support staff at the software company.

When Lincoln got to school the morning of the health fair, he set up his display with his homemade stethoscope. Previously, he had arranged to borrow one of the school's mobile "computers on a cart," so he was able to get his program up and running without a hitch. And printing some copies of the widget with additional labels on it helped him later on to explain how the whole thing worked.

His working display was the most popular stop at the health fair. Kids standing in line tried to relax enough to slow their heartbeat to that of a tortoise. Others ran in place before taking their rate to see if it could match a gerbil's. Everyone went home knowing that different animals have different heartbeats and some even had some notions about why after talking to Lincoln and looking at his posters.

Open-Ended Software

Simulation software such as Widget Workshop represents a growing segment of the children's software market. The package offers

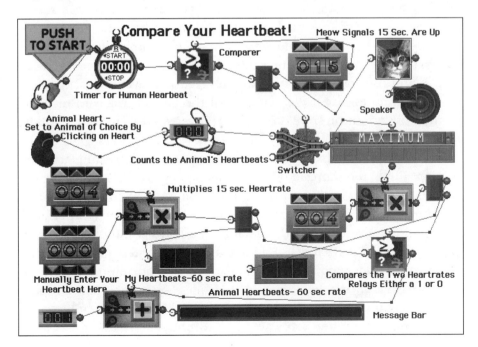

For his final display, Lincoln labeled all the parts of his widget.

Manuals

When my oldest child was very young I quickly learned that I had to watch the videotapes she was watching if I wanted to understand some of the analogies she drew between things she had seen on television and tape and things she encountered in the real world. The same goes for software. The pieces of software that come with step-by-step tutorials in the manual are probably the ones you want to start with. Play with them by yourself for a while, then work along with your children. Kids tend to be intuitive when it comes to the computer and are often disdainful of manuals. As programs become more open-ended, though, it's almost impossible to make full use of them without consulting the manual. A glimpse through the manual will show you the parts of the program you might have otherwise missed.

games and puzzles to solve, but is also open-ended. Kids can create their own puzzles and machines as well as playing the games provided for them. They can mess around and experiment with all kinds of devices from timers and switches to mathematical devices to hearts and tuning forks. Unfortunately, like any workshop, this one has its limitations. But the contents of the Parts Bin gave Lincoln a chance to try out or simulate a few things, such as animals hearts, that were not otherwise available to him.

Along the way, he also did some logical thinking and problem solving. First he organized what he was trying to create, isolating the various steps involved in constructing a machine to compare animal and human heart rates. Then he drew on his personal experience (having his pulse taken at the doctor's office, for example) to design each aspect of his widget. Lincoln also confronted problems that cropped up after he finished his basic design (shortening the time it took to get a heart rate sample to fifteen seconds, for example). Finally, he polished his presentation by trying it out on various members of his family and truly went "multimedia" by adding posters about heart rate and longevity and the creation of a homemade stethoscope. All in all, it turned into a first-rate project.

Linking Up with the World of Computer Simulations

There is good news and bad news about the world of affordable computer simulations for kids. At this writing, the good news is that there are some excellent simulations in a variety of subject areas. The bad news is that simulation programs are still emerging as a genre, so there isn't one to fit every purpose. Here we include information about those that are available to help you locate them, use them in an imaginative way with schoolwork projects, and to remain interested enough to stay on the lookout for others as they are released. The appendix in the back contains more information about suggested titles.

Applicable to almost every school subject, simulations can be a useful tool for the student seeking help with a project. They are also a great way to use skills from other subjects to solve a problem or create a model. Let's take a look at how all this works.

Science Simulations

Physical Science

A computer simulation may be used in science class to create a model to try out a hypothesis or demonstrate a phenomenon that might otherwise be difficult, messy, or dangerous. Software such as Widget Workshop lets kids try experiments like finding out what will fall faster off the Empire State Building—an elephant, a baseball, or a feather. (Remember Galileo?) The great thing about Widget

Workshop is that you can easily change the relevant height: drop an object from six feet up or from the top of Mt. Everest. You can also customize the height. Or change the object. Or change the gravity to that of the earth, the moon, the sun, or *Apollo* to see what effect that will have on the drop rate.

Even games such as Sierra's The Even More Incredible Machine have a "create your own" or free-form segment that allows you to create machines using inventive parts. To familiarize yourself with the devices in the game, you can do the tutorials section and solve some of the Rube Goldberg–style puzzles. Then you can play with balls of every description, nails, bellows, trampolines, balloons, generators, pipe, pulleys and eye hooks, gears, light bulbs, candles, and even cannons to create various kinds of gadgets and realistic or fanciful machines. You can also change the gravity and air pressure factor. While many of the devices in this particular game are rather imaginative, the scientific principles behind them are real and can be used to create and tinker with machines that can illustrate various scientific principles or theories.

Rolling balls, falling objects, and swinging weights can all be simulated by children using Fun Physics from Knowledge Revolutions.

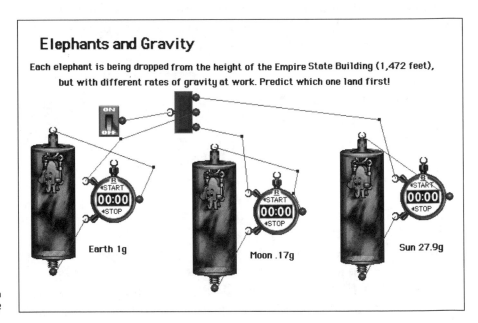

Elephants and Gravity

Each elephant is being dropped from the height of the Empire State Building (1,472 feet), but with different rates of gravity at work. Predict which one land first!

Earth 1g

Moon .17g

Sun 27.9g

Can you predict which elephant will land first?

Incline- Objects go up or down on this. It's used to direct floating balloons too. Dynamite can't blow inclines up.

Belt- Refer to the Belts section on page 13 for more info.

Gear- Use a belt to connect to a power supply part. Mesh gears together to change direction of power supply.

Conveyor- Belt this up with a power supply part. It carries objects short and long distances.

Jack-in-the-box- Belt this up to a power part. Jack pops up and flings objects up in the air.

Windmill- Blow on it to make it spin. Use with a belt to power another object.

Magnifying glass- Use with any light source to ignite any objects which have a fuse.

This manual page from The Even More Incredible Machine displays only a few of the many devices available in the program.

Courtesy of Sierra

Children draw objects on the screen, which act as they would in the real world: they have mass and velocity and subject themselves to the law of gravity. Fun Physics can be used to create on-screen experiments or animations of real-life events. The results of what children build can be saved as QuickTime movies and from there included in slide shows and presentations.

To simulate the world of lines, circles, triangles, and squares, Geometer's Sketchpad from Key Curriculum Press provides an electronic chalkboard onto which students draw their shapes. Then they can take measurements, which change as they move and resize the objects. This program's results can be saved as pictures, or printed on paper, and used to support assignments in math and science.

Using these simulations kids can create working models to supplement science presentations, or puzzle through single homework questions about forces and motion or even math. They can also take a crack at creating futuristic machines to substantiate projects; such assignments often crop up in both science and social studies classes dealing with the environment. In some cases the programs can also be used to brainstorm science projects or to present diagrams that illustrate the functions of machines past, present, or future. Given the limitations of the various Parts Bins, the programs will not work for every problem or question. For the mechanically minded, they are a great place to putter; for the not so mechanically minded, they offer an opportunity to discover how things work.

Biology

Perhaps you have a child who gets a bit queasy at the thought of dissecting a frog, or maybe your children want to know more about what each structure they encounter. In either case Operation Frog from Scholastic allows kids to snip away and view frog body parts and systems, but then allows them to put everything back together again so the frog can come back to life and jump off the screen.

Thanks to detailed color illustrations in *A.D.A.M.: The Inside Story* from A.D.A.M. (Animated Dissection of Anatomy for Medicine), the user can peel away one layer of the body at a time and take a look

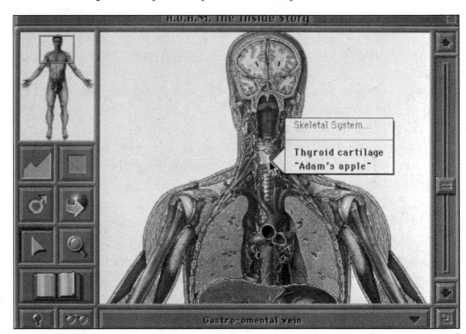

In A.D.A.M.: The Inside Story, users can quickly peel away layers and look at the systems and structures of the human body they are interested in.

Courtesy of ADAM

at various bodily functions. Interactive puzzles allow the user to piece together systems. Animations illustrate more fully how the human body works. This CD-ROM is a cross between a reference disk and a simulation. It probably is the closest thing to working with a cadaver as a young student is going to get. The animations are very clear and simple and if Lincoln, our seventh grade student, had been able to borrow a second computer, he could have run the sequence on the chambers of the heart so that his audience could have seen what was going on internally when they were listening to their heartbeat with his homemade stethoscope.

Beyond dissections, there are simulations that let kids become members of the animal world to test their survival skills. Odell Down Under from MECC simulates the life of a fish in a tropical reef. You have to learn to find food, avoid electric eels, identify predators and prey, avoid poisonous snacks, and use your body energy wisely. The program can be played on different levels, from surviving as a small fish to reigning as a great white shark. It is a stimulating way to learn about food chains, food webs, and natural communities while creating and testing hypotheses and doing a bit of problem solving.

In Wolf from Sanctuary Woods kids become either a timber, arctic, or plains wolf and learn to survive in the wilderness. They can

Try roaming the ocean as a great white shark!

Odell Down Under™ copyright and trademark owned by MECC. Used with permission. All rights reserved.

249

live in the world of the wolf using one of forty different scenarios or an open ended free-form mode. Many different factors are at work, from weather to predators to food supply. Only the smart, strong, and swift survive, so kids must quickly learn the lessons of the wolf.

There is also a mini-interactive documentary of the skills and habits of the wolf, along with a brief overview of wolves and their history (including many people's misconceptions about them). The forty mission scenarios include such missions as "Kill a Hare," "Find a Partner," and "Win a Fight." Within each scenario players can learn more about their wolf (including age, sex, endurance, health and hunting record) and check out the weather, the amount of potential prey, and the size of their territory. They can also find out how many humans are around and if there is a bounty set on wolves. As wolves, players can see, eat, bark, hear, howl, drink, sleep, dig, scent mark, and much more. Health is a major concern—each wolf must eat, drink, and sleep enough and learn to evade approaching humans. Through repeated use of the program students find out how the family hierarchy and survival techniques of the wolves really work.

Wolf would make a great addition to any social studies or science presentation about current issues involving wolves—for example, whether to readmit wolves into Yellowstone National Park and other locations in the West. A project could incorporate a simulation to study wolves and their habits, testing theories about what will bring them into conflict with humans in their natural habitat and making comparisons with news reports about their progress in the western national parks. Wolf could even be used as a courtroom scenario for a mock debate on the place of wolves in the United States.

Maxis also offers three sophisticated simulations of interest in this area. SimAnt is an up-close look at the inner workings of an ant colony. Here kids can learn about and manipulate an ant colony as it searches for food, reproduces itself, and fights off enemies, including spiders, ant lions, floods, pesticides, and human feet. SimEarth looks at the world as an interrelated living organism, enabling users to design and nurture planets from their creation to the evolution of their life forms. In SimLife, users build their own ecosystem from the ground up, playing geneticist and designing unique animals and plants. All the programs are quite complicated; if your child's inter-

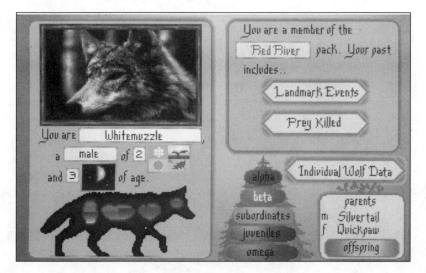

Run with the wolf pack in Wolf!

Courtesy of Sanctuary Woods

ests run in this direction, the Maxis trio can be very stimulating—but be prepared to have to read and use the manual in great detail.

All these simulations offer kids the chance to experiment in environments they would not normally have access to. They can manipulate the lives of creatures ruled by instinct, survival of the fittest, and pure chance. Other programs such as El-Fish from Maxis and Aquazone from Desktop Life allow kids to do much the same with fish in aquarium environments that can be constructed and adjusted at will. You can raise or lower the temperature, add or subtract plant life, add chemicals, add various species of fish to see how they mix, mate fish, raise newborns, withhold or add extra food, and lots more.

A Word of Caution

Simulations are fun, but some of them require a bit of study to master. Don't buy any of the simulations mentioned in this chapter thinking that you will be able instantly to help your children with a school project. All require serious playing time and a bit of reading to learn how to use them to the fullest degree.

Having an aquarium in
your computer allows you
to isolate the factors for
survival.

Courtesy of Maxis

Programs such as these make excellent science projects themselves or can be used as supplements to science project presentations. For example, a student could have a tank of real fish that displays the best factors for survival and health, such as light, food, companionship, chemical balance, and temperature control (perhaps discovered by experimenting with the aquarium programs to begin with). The student could then demonstrate the effect of a particular factor on an aquarium by simulating its deprivation or addition. Exploring via simulation could save fish and plants that might otherwise die in the name of science!

Social Studies Simulations

The first computer simulation we ever saw for kids in upper elementary and middle school was a program called Geography Search (now marketed by its creator, Tom Snyder Productions). We saw it at a social studies teachers convention, and it took the audience by storm—not because of its graphics or sound qualities (this was actually back in the early 1980s), but because built into it was a catch that made kids in the classroom cooperate with each other. The premise of the program was that students took on the roles of early navigators, teaming up on different ships crossing a large ocean in search of the City of Gold. The computer gave them information about wind direction, wind speed, water depth, the location of the North Star above the horizon (to determine their latitude), a chance to watch the mast's shadow grow and shrink (to help determine their longitude), temperature, and food stores. The catch was that kids had to act together to get the information because it appeared on the computer screen for only thirty seconds. That meant each member of the team had to watch out for one piece of assigned information. To determine where they were and what they should do next, teams had to gather the information from their individual members. Every member of the team had to cooperate or all were hopelessly lost.

The thirty-second time limit caught many kids and adults off guard. Most of them had never had to cooperate quite like that before, and the first few turns at the computer left them grumbling. Then, once they'd gotten the hang of it, all were addicted. Interesting things happened, too; for example, quiet kids who never contributed much before took center stage when reporting they must be near land because the water depth was falling.

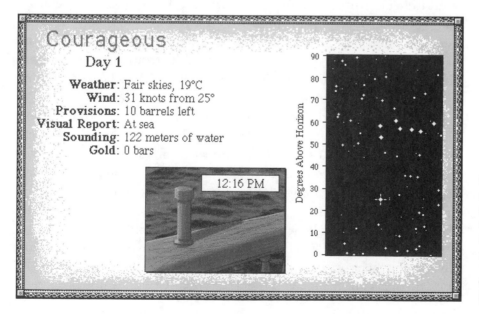

In Geography Search, kids are asked to find their position, as the early navigators did, by observing the North Star and the shadow of their mast at mid-day.

Courtesy of Tom Snyder Productions

Tom Snyder and his team have built a number of other simulations like Geography Search. Check at your child's school to see if they are using some of these cooperative simulations or might be interested in doing so. They are an exciting way to capture kids' imaginations and draw them into the subject they are studying.

Perhaps the most famous social studies simulation available for the home market is the Carmen Sandiego series from Brøderbund. There are many titles in the series including Where in the World is Carmen Sandiego? and Where in the USA is Carmen Sandiego? These and other programs in the series are designed to help kids use primary sources such as atlases and almanacs to find information that will help them catch the notorious Carmen Sandiego, who roams the globe stealing famous landmarks. Kids in upper elementary school and middle school seem to enjoy these programs and learn a bit about geography, landmarks, and culture along the way. These are great additions to a home software library even for general use and fun. The second most famous social studies simulation is The Oregon Trail from MECC, now available in an enhanced CD-ROM version. In this adventure simulation, kids pick a route (Oregon, California, or Mormon Trails) to travel as pioneers across the American continent between 1840 and 1860. Video footage, sound effects, three-dimensional graphics, and digitized speech all add to the perilous journey across the unpredictable American frontier. Kids get to ride the rapids; hunt for their next meal; suffer at the mercy of the weather; grieve for those who die from disease, bad sanitary conditions, and snakebites; and deal with other day-to-day problems that crop up as they move west.

MECC has added The Yukon Trail and The Amazon Trail to their line of historical simulations. In Yukon Trail players become prospectors during the Gold Rush of 1897. Again kids can ride the rapids, wager money on a game or cards or dog sled race (and risk losing everything), grab a shovel and dig for gold, buy supplies, and talk to historical figures such as Jack London, Nellie Cashman, and Mountie Sam Steele. Their decisions along the way have life-or-death implications.

In The Amazon Trail, the mission is to travel up the Amazon River—and back in time—to search for a tropical cure to save the ancient Incas from malaria. Dangers such as wild animals, greedy

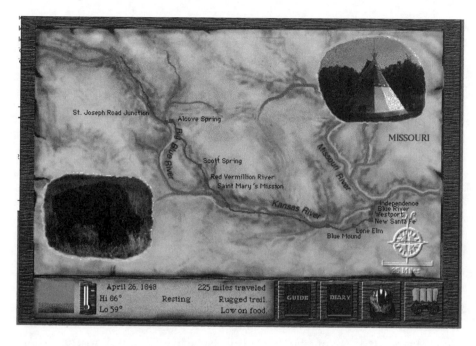

In the Oregon Trail, kids experience all the perils of being early pioneers.

Conquistadors, and hungry piranha add to the excitement of the simulation. Naturalists, scientists, indigenous peoples, and other explorers are on hand to offer advice and encouragement.

Lawrence Productions offers similar simulations. Discovering America lets kids accompany a group of early Spanish explorers on a quest in the Americas. The Tribe has a prehistoric theme, in which the player becomes leader of a tribe of prehistoric people who have lost their village in a volcanic eruption. The tribe seeks a homeland known only from ancient legend. There is a bit more whimsy to The Tribe than to some of the others, but kids still need to make hard decisions and become involved in some conflicts between tribe members.

These simulations are valuable interactive research tools for the periods of time they cover. They are a great way to begin a student's research on a particular time period or even to supplement an ongoing unit in social studies class. Students are often asked to imagine themselves as pioneers in the American West and to write a journal about their experiences; a simulation like Oregon Trail can give them lots of material. (The program even has a built-in feature that enables kids to keep a journal of their adventure.) Simulations such as these can also serve as starting points for different kinds of writing and research projects as kids encounter people, places, or interesting ideas to pursue.

Other social studies–oriented simulations take a different tack. DinoPark Tycoon from MECC lets kids run their own dinosaur park à la *Jurassic Park*. Young entrepreneurs have to make decisions about how to spend their limited budget for land, fencing, employees, dinosaurs, and food. They have to set admissions prices and expand the business. All the basic economic decisions of running a business are covered. This quick and easy way to use or acquire knowledge about running a business offers kids the opportunity to work with some of the basic economics they are learning in class. They might even be able to incorporate their experience into a homework assignment about starting a small business.

Some simulations explore how government works. For example, Capitol Hill from Mindscape simulates what it's like to be a freshman member of the House of Representatives. Players navigate their way through the process of passing a bill. SimCity (Maxis), on the other hand, offers kids the chance to plan and manage cities from the past, present, and future. In the role of mayor they are responsible for

- planning and zoning the city;
- the infrastructure—water, power, and transportation

Young entrepreneurs run their own dinosaur park in DinoPark Tycoon™.

- government services—fire, police, hospitals, and prisons
- education—schools, colleges, libraries, and museums
- recreation and open spaces—parks, zoos, stadiums, and marinas
- city budgets and taxes
- The health, wealth, and happiness of the "Sims" who live in the city

Players can try out scenarios built into SimCity such as coping with a problem or a disaster; they can also start their own city. Scenarios have "win" conditions. If you meet the condition within a specific time, you receive the key to the city and are allowed to keep your job as mayor. If not, you get run out of town. When you start your own city, there are no time limits or conditions to meet.

Maxis has come out with a less complicated version of the SimCity programs for kids 8–12 called SimTown. The program puts you in control of building a small town. You can take charge of adding various kinds of terrain and vegetation, houses that open up for inspection (including one that's haunted!), places to work, community buildings, movie theaters, pizza parlors, and fast-food restaurants. If you like, you can design your own "Sims" (people who live in the town). Each Sim in the town has an individual profile, generated either by the user or by the computer, complete with likes and dislikes and a diary.

The local newspaper keeps you up-to-date on how things are going in town. Like the various versions of SimCity, SimTown allows to try out scenarios of towns with problems such as a lack of water, crops, trees, or clean air. Such issues arise even when kids build their own town but in that case, advisers are available to help them maintain ecological equilibrium. Options enable users to add random EcoVillains such as the Litterbug, Water Hog, or Food Pig or to face disasters such as drought, earthquakes, or fire. To gain points quickly to use to keep up the town's natural resources, kids have to balance the number of houses and number and types of businesses so the town can grow steadily

Both the more sophisticated SimCity and the slightly fanciful SimTown, allow kids to explore and create new worlds. To substanti-

A visit to SimTown can give young students a whole new perspective on the problems of running a city.

Courtesy of Maxis

ate a science project on pollution or a lack of resources, they can use these programs to experiment with potential solutions. If they're interested in these cities from a more social angle, they can creatively look at issues such as zoning, providing government services, and maintaining the economics of a town or city. They can also look at cities from a historical angle: where have our cities' problems come from? What are their historical and socioeconomic roots? These kinds of simulations offer endless possibilities for a personal study of cities and their problems. They can even generate fun creative writing projects. Kids can create their own town or city, invent some inhabitants, follow their progress, and then write about their creations. What would it be like to be part of a simulated town or city?

Spreadsheets

. . . .

Spreadsheet programs or spreadsheet portions of integrated tool programs like ClarisWorks and Microsoft Works can be used by kids to simulate models of everything from the quantity and cost of the food and drink for a party with an ever-growing or -shrinking invitation list to more complicated science projects, where keeping track of variables such as temperature, weight, pressure, and other physical factors is important. Spreadsheets can also be used to keep track of statistics in a social studies survey or a comparison of countries' vital statistics.

The Cruncher from Davidson teaches kids how to use a spreadsheet. The program begins with tutorials that explain everything from the basics to some of the more powerful features of a spread sheet. Once those have been mastered, kids can try some of the projects that are set up within the program. There are examples of how to conduct a survey and graph the results, plan the cost of a trip, plan a party, and convert recipes. Kids can also track what it costs to own a pet or create a budget so they can save up to buy something they want that seems out of reach.

From playing with these programs, kids can create their own projects to keep track of and manipulate test results in science experiments, do opinion surveys, and experiment with equations in math.

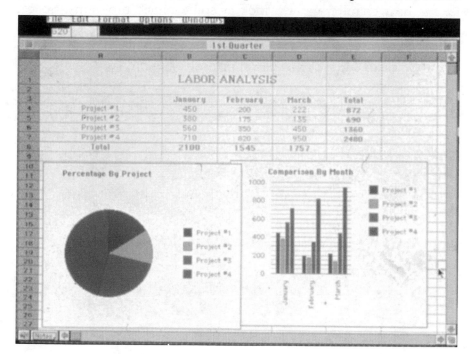

The cruncher includes tutorials for kids on how to use a spreadsheet.

Courtesy of Davidson and Associates

Lincoln, our fictitious student in the beginning example, could have made a spreadsheet to keep track of the heartbeat rates of the students at the health fair where he introduced his heartbeat rate machine. At the end of the day he could have displayed the figures he'd accumulated and done correlations with weight, height, temperament, sex, or other factors. He also could have done a survey on what people knew about the human heart and entered that information into a spreadsheet. He could have looked up what parts of the world are home to most of the medical problems related to heart attacks and then correlated other data such as the number of beef cattle in those regions, in a spreadsheet. Any project that deals with numbers and formulas can be projected on a spreadsheet. Graphs and charts can also be generated easily and make powerful additions to any school project.

Next Steps

In the next chapter, we will look at some music programs. So get ready to boogie, swing, jive, and rock to sounds that you can create on your own computer for your listening pleasure, for an assignment, or as an add-on to a special project.

chapter 11

Soothe the Savage Breast— Music and Schoolwork

Music has been a part of the school curriculum for hundreds of years. The ancient Greeks studied music as a branch of mathematics. Today it plays an ever-increasing role in the lives of young people. Music is all around them, at home, at school, in the car, in the streets, at the shopping mall, and in the concert hall. It is in their ears, and is constantly rattling around in their heads. Whether they are tethered to their Walk Mans or struggling with music lessons, most of our children are listeners and performers of music. As poet William Congreve noted:

> Music hath charms to soothe a savage breast,
> To soften rocks, or bend a knotted oak.
> I've read that things inanimate have moved,
> And with living souls have been inform'd
> By magic numbers and persuasive sound.

Congreve might be surprised at the charms of some of the music our children listen to these days. But he would not deny the power and fascination of music for our minds. Long before Mozart performed as a child prodigy or Shirley Temple sang in the movies, young people have been drawn to music. It moves them. It teases their minds. It gives them a powerful avenue to perform and to express themselves. And as Professor Harold Hill reminded the citizens of River City, involvement in a musical enterprise can keep kids out of trouble.

The computer offers some new and interesting ways for a student to work with music, to use it for homework projects, and to express ideas with "magic numbers and persuasive sound." This chapter provides an overview of computers and music, with a close look at some of the tools that can help your children bring rhythm and melody into their assignments. We cover many things, from MIDI keyboards to printing sheet music, from recording digital music to performing original works. Some sections will appeal more to the child who already has some musical training while others can be enjoyed by all.

We also take a different approach in this chapter by starting with an interview with Lee McCanne. Lee, a music educator at Boston University, helps teachers and students understand the links among computers, music, and schoolwork. Our questions and Lee's answers provide a quick overview of a vast topic.

Where to Start? An Interview with Lee McCanne

I knew I should have joined the band! Instead I took "Introduction to Music." Now Mrs. Babar, my teacher, wants us to do a final project. It can be a report on a famous piece of classical music, or we can write an original score, or we can do a music video by making up a tape of song clips that fit the mood of the pictures. I hope when I get home my mom has one of her good ideas about this project. Maybe the computer can help.

Q. What do computers have to do with music?

A. A computer's forte is its ability to manipulate complex structures—and since music is one such structure, the computer is a great match for music. By using a computer to help students uncover and create complex musical structures, teachers and parents can excite their learning. Research has shown that students learn more when they use a computer in their work.

Q. Is a computer enough?

A. No. Computers can't teach, only teachers can. A computer is a tool, and like all other tools it has its place in the curriculum and at home. Students get very excited about using computers and synthesizers, and you can use this excitement to your advantage. And it can be just as much fun for the teacher and the parent to use these tools as it is for the student.

Q. Isn't all this technology too new to have proven itself?

A. Music technology is not an emerging field anymore, but rather a mature voice that has greatly impacted the music industry. Recording studios, film and TV production houses, and the compact disc business all depend on computers. And the same technology is entering the schools, emerging as wonderful tools for manipulating music. Just as word processor software edits text, sequencer software edits music. It allows the user to arrange the parts of the music played simultaneously by various instruments. It can then be quickly played back and rearranged.

Q. Do you really need a computer just to play a melody?

A. The real power of the computer is to help you organize the complex structure of music. A computer enables people with little musical training or skill to compose, arrange, and perform their own music in ways that were never before possible.

Q. What kinds of software are available?

A. There are many kinds for different purposes:

- Music *tutor* software teaches a child how to play an instrument.

- Music *history* software helps students learn about instruments, compositions, and composers, in interactive multimedia CD-ROM format.
- *Notation* software helps students transpose or write music that can be printed as sheet music or scores.
- Music *sequencers* enable children to build musical arrangements by letting them set the melody lines or parts for various instruments that play together to form everything from songs to symphonies.
- Music *recording* tools let students capture live music or clips from CDs to use in their multimedia works.

Q. How should we get started at home?
A. First get a good computer that can handle the kinds of programs listed above. A CD-ROM is essential. Second, add a MIDI keyboard, preferably one compatible with the general MIDI standard. The keyboard should also be polyphonic, or capable of playing more than one melodic part at a time, and multitimbral, meaning that it can play multiple tones of different timbres or tones simultaneously. This means that the piano, bass, and drum can sound their notes at the same time in the song. You'll also need a MIDI interface and cables to connect the computer to the keyboard. Finally, you'll need software for what you plan to do: teach music, write music, print scores, and so forth. A good set of software to get started with is the EZ Music Starter Kit from Opcode, which includes Music Shop, Band-in-a-box, and a MIDI interface all in one box.

Tools for Music on the Computer

You don't need to be a musician and you don't need a synthesizing keyboard to employ music in school projects. On even the simplest computers, you can record music and play it back as part of a presentation. On computers with CD-ROM drives, you can capture music directly from a regular music CD; you can also purchase interactive CD-ROMs that teach about the music as you listen to it.

MIDI

A student at the U.S. Naval Academy? No, MIDI stands for musical instrument digital interface. It is an international standard for sending signals from a computer to a music synthesizer. MIDI represents each sound as a series of numbers: one number tells the pitch, another the type of instrument, another the length of the sound, and so forth. Each note in the song is represented by a set of numbers; these are strung together in a file and saved on the computer's disk. When the computer sends these numbers through a wire to a MIDI instrument, the instrument plays the appropriate notes. And when you play notes on the MIDI instrument, it can send them to the computer, where they can be remembered on the computer's disk. MIDI files are very compact and efficient—an entire movement of Mozart's *Divertimento*, for instance, will fit into a 39-kilobyte MIDI file. Saving a non-MIDI recording of the dame piece would require 3.9 megabytes—a thousand times more space!

Recording Music

In chapter 8 we describe how to record sound into your computer. You can use the methods described there to record short pieces of music. Set up your computer and software as described in the "Capturing Sound" section of chapter 8. Next set up the source of your music, such as a musical instrument, church choir, CD player, tape recorder, or radio. Set the software to record, and play your music. The music will be digitized into a file on your computer's hard disk. From there it can be imported into a slide show as described in chapter 9.

Capturing Music Directly from CDs

It's easy to convert the digital music on music compact discs to files on your computer if your computer has QuickTime capabilities (most Macintosh computers come with this as part of the system). Follow the directions in the "Capturing Sound from a Compact Disc" section of chapter 8. Choose a track that has the music you want, and it will be saved on the computer's hard disk as a QuickTime movie file. From there it can be imported into a slide show as described in chapter 9.

Interactive Music Compact Discs

To learn about Mozart as you listen to his music, purchase a copy of the composer's String Quartet in C Major as published by the Voyager Company. Place the CD into your computer, click on its icon, and you will read and see Mozart and his notes on the screen as you listen to the music. This interactive program includes musical analysis, narration, notes in the score, and even a Quartet Game that tests whether you've learned anything. Similar CD-ROMs are available for Beethoven's Ninth Symphony and Stravinsky's Rite of Spring. To learn more about the instruments of the orchestra, kids might also be interested in Microsoft's *Musical Instruments* and Opcode's *Musical World of Professor Piccolo*. (See the appendix for more titles.)

Young music students can gain new insight into classical music by using interactive CD-ROMs.

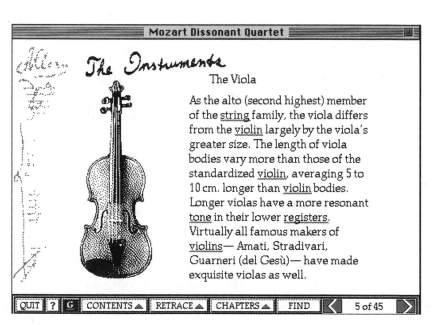

Playing Spin Doctor

Everyone likes to play around with music. CD-ROMs such as *Rock 'n' Roll Your Own* from Compton's New Media and *Rock Rap 'n' Roll* from Viacom/Paramount Interactive gives you the chance, whether or not you know a b flat from a half step. With these software programs you construct a song form pieces of music on the disk. You drag rhythm lines in to their places, start them up, then use the keyboard and mouse to provide melodies, accents, riffs, and vocals. it sounds like the real thing. There are sections for blues, reggae, rap, jazz, and other forms.

Learning to Play an Instrument

There are even tutorial programs for learning to play a musical instrument from your computer. The *Miracle Piano Teaching System* from Mindscape is an electronic keyboard that you connect to the computer, along with software that puts interactive piano lessons on the screen. It shows you what notes to play, you play them on the piano, and the computer analyzes your accuracy. With a carefully structured series of lessons and exercises, *Miracle* takes you through a beginner's course.

Synthesizer Keyboards

Here is where we start to need some musical knowledge and sill to take advantage of the computer's capability. A MIDI keyboard is an instrument that can be attached by wire to the computer and exchange information with it. You can run software on the computer that causes it to play a song on the keyboard, just like the player-piano of old. Conversely, you can play a song on the keyboard and let the computer record your music as a MIDI file. The possibilities of such a system are almost endless. Most of the keyboards can play several parts at once, so you can imitate a small ensemble even when you're the only person playing.

Sequencer Software

To work with a MIDI keyboard, you use software that sequences the notes on your computer. The sequencer software, such as Cubase from Steinberg, Master Tracks from Passport Designs, Vision from Opcode Systems, ConvertWare Music Studio from Jump Software, or Music Shop, allows you to enter the notes for each instrument on the computer screen, usually in a spreadsheetlike format. Then you can adjust the timing, pitch, and other factors. When the song is complete, you click on the Play button and your composition issues forth from the keyboard.

Notation Software

Programs such as Finale from Coda, Encore from Passport Designs, Music Time from Opcode, and Songworks from Ars Nova Software allow you to build notes on a musical staff that appears on the computer screen, using the notes and rests of standard musical notation.

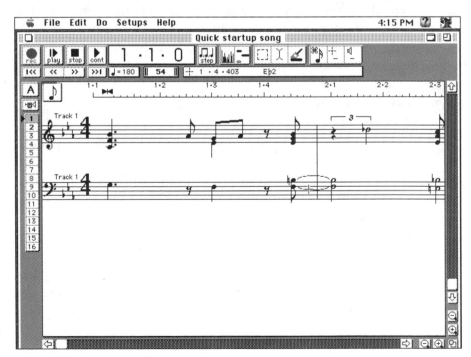

Kids enjoy creating their own musical compositions using sequencer software like Music Shop.

These passages can then be adjusted, transposed to a different key, copied, and pasted by the computer. From there they can be sent for playing to a keyboard, or for printing to a printer, or for saving on the disk as a MIDI file.

Many of the software programs in the sequencer and notation genres are fast converging to cover some of the same capabilities. While a number of them continue to have a forte in one area, as noted here, it is far more fun to use either kind with a keyboard. If you are planning to purchase either genre, make sure to add the cost of a keyboard into the price.

MIDI QuickTime Movies

Today, on Apple Macintosh computers, and on PCs with the newest versions of Windows, you can turn a MIDI file into a QuickTime movie, since version 2.0 of the QuickTime software allows for a MIDI track in addition to the QuickTIme sound, text, and video tracks. QuickTime is described more fully in chapter 9. To make a QuickTime movie file from a MIDI file, use the MoviePlayer software from Apple, also described in chapter 9 to open a MIDI file that you made with your music sequencer program. movie Player will convert the MIDI file to a QuickTime movie with a MIDI track. This movie can be imported into a slide show or other work to add music as necessary. QuickTime MIDI movies are very small in size compared with digitized music, so they take up much less disk space and need much less memory to play. you may also find QuickTime MIDI movies for downloading from most of the commercial on-line services.

So What Did Our Student Decide to Do?

When our unhappy music student from our opening assignment got home and had a chat with her parents, she found that her computer offered many solutions to her problem. She decided to do her own music video, much like the slide show we describe in chapter 9. She chose and labeled ten pictures and recorded a song, picking from the various styles of music they had discussed in class—everything from classical to rock, folk, and country and western songs, with a little blues, bluegrass and jazz thrown in along with a traditional Japanese piece. For her last slide she wrote her own song, using Music Shop, which her mom had bought her older sister for her music theory classes. It was very effective, and the teacher asked for a copy to show to her classes the next year as an introduction to the kinds of music the class would be studying.

Next Steps

Most homework assignments are pretty mundane stuff. Memorizing spelling and vocabulary words, states and capitals, and math facts, as well as writing short paragraphs are often part of the nightly homework ritual. The final chapter looks at various genres of software that can help chase away the everyday homework blues.

part

5

Relief for Everyday
Homework Headaches

chapter 12

Everyday Homework Helpers

If you have gotten this far in the book, you've learned to use the computer to research, analyze, write, and present the larger school-work projects that are assigned on a regular basis. These truly are the skills children are going to need for school and work in the twenty first century. But what about the more mundane, everyday home-work assignments such as spelling, memorizing map facts, math, and all the rest? What can the computer do to help with those?

One of the computer's best skills is patience. It can be an untir-ing tutor, assisting kids with skills that need to be practiced over and over again, such as learning math facts and reviewing weekly spelling lists. The trick is to buy the right software, the kind that is flexible and will grow with your child's skills. Some software will be used only a few times, such as the geography program that helps your child mem-orize the fifty states and their capitals, or a drill to help master the multiplication tables. But even that software must be able to capture your child's imagination with detailed graphics, lively sounds, rewards for gaining new levels, a high degree of interactivity, and a sound educational approach to the content and skills to be practiced.

It would not be wise to inundate your hard drive with these kinds of programs or to buy every new math drill CD-ROM that hits the market. Kids should use the computer to explore and be creative. They should have access to software that fosters an open and playful attitude toward learning. But the reality is that, to do well in school, kids still need to learn how to spell and master the facts of addition and subtraction, memorize the multiplication tables and fill in the map of Europe with country names. So there is a need for some of this "drill" software and for the computer's skills as a patient tutor.

This chapter looks at how to use software designed to help chase away the everyday homework blues. In addition, we have offered suggestions about similarly using some of the more open-ended software discussed in other parts of the book. Finally, we've also thrown in a bit of information about software tools for creating posters, signs, banners, and models. This is not meant to be an exhaustive look at the subject; it's just an overview of what's available, what you should look for in a product, and how you can use what's out there.

Taming the Homework Blues

This has been *some* week at school. They weren't kidding when they said that we would have more homework in middle school. Vocabulary words—spelled properly, of course—with all kinds of new meanings; sheets of math problems; countries for Asia to be memorized for a current events quiz; and a book report and an upcoming research paper. I even had to create a drawing of a typical frontier cabin complete with something called a dogtrot.

Homework is often a problem for both parents and kids. And problems with homework have no simple solutions. What works in one household may not work in another. The homework issue can easily become a battleground with parents and kids on opposing sides. Want to avoid the conflict? Start by helping your kids develop effective and responsible home study habits:

- Help kids establish good study habits early in their school career. Even if your kids don't have a homework assignment, talk with them about what they learned in school that day. Encourage them to bring home books that you can read with them. Enjoy together some of the resource CD-ROMs now available on a variety of topics of interest to you both. Set aside time for reading and special projects.

- Get kids involved in projects such as telecommunicating with other kids throughout the world, creating newspapers for classes or clubs, making databases of their collections, and creating graphics on the computer. Tap into the other creative computer resources discussed in this book. These will help motivate students to grow in their academic subjects and in their use of technology.

- Insist that your children write down and bring home information about when tests are scheduled, when short- and long-term assignments are due, and what outside reading assignments exist. If a problem develops with this, call your child's teachers and set up a joint plan of action. Some teachers check home assignment notebooks and initial the pages to indicate that the assignments have been copied correctly. It is then your job to follow up by asking your child to show you the initialed page each day.

- Maintain a regular time for your children to study and read, along with a set time for you to look at their homework. Create a study area with a minimum of distraction. Make sure that you check in with them periodically. Kids are capable of looking like as if are studying when they are really daydreaming. Be sure to review their progress and praise their efforts.

- Encourage your children, as they move up in school, to use the computer to recopy class notes, make outlines, write essays, create reports, write plays, practice spelling and vocabulary, learn math facts, look up information in encyclopedias, and use online resources.

- Insist that homework be done neatly and accurately. Don't accept the excuse "My teacher never collects it." Doing homework on the computer helps students with neatness, organization, and editing.

- Work with your children to help them get directly into their homework without wasting time. Help them set priorities so they start with what needs to be done first.

- Help your children develop effective review techniques for tests. If they have been doing their homework and using the computer for organization and help with learning, preparing for tests should be easy. If they seem to be doing their homework well but are having trouble on tests, talk to their teacher about the kinds of test being given and how to help your children prepare.

- Be enthusiastic about your children's nightly homework assignments and projects.

- Never do homework for your children. Encourage, cajole, correct, and assist them, but do not do their work.

- Unplug the television set and replace it with a computer and some good books. And do the same for yourself—this will help both of you spend time with the tools that will expand rather than pacify your minds.

How Else Can the Computer Help?

Earlier in this book we looked in great detail at how to create reports and projects using the wordprocessing, desktop publishing, and multimedia capabilities of the computer. That was the "razzle dazzle" part, and also the part that most parents know the least about. This chapter is a bit of a reality check, aiming at homework assignments that still deal with drill and memorization. This chapter may seem rather old hat to you if your home is full of drill and tutorial programs for your children. Even so, you might pick up some tips as we look at the genres of software that might be useful on an everyday basis.

Spelling Programs

The most important feature of a spelling program is its ability to enter a customized weekly spelling list. If it can't do that, don't buy it unless your child is trying out for the local spelling bee and needs practice with random words. Early readers might enjoy a program that throws random words at them, but most kids just want to get the weekly spelling list out of the way and move on to other things on the computer and in their lives.

Two programs that give you the flexibility of customization are Super Solvers Spellbound from The Learning Company and Spell Dodger from Arcadia/Davidson. In Super Solvers Spellbound, kids are challenged to take on Morty Maxwell, the Master of Mischief, and his robot pals at the National Spelling Bee. Before competing against Marty, kids hone their spelling skills by playing three interactive games: "Word Search," "Flash Cards," and "Criss Cross." In Word Search they hunt for words that are hidden in blocks of letters—a format based on the traditional word search games. Flash Cards are just that, but with a high-tech, imaginative twist: kids have to spell words properly after viewing the cards. Criss Cross is a crossword puzzle that helps the student get through a weekly spelling list. The goal orientation and element of excitement in SuperSolvers Spellbound are enough to keep this game going for many weeks.

In Spell Dodger, the game plan is a set of five hundred ladder-and-platform mazes in which kids must dodge bad guys and collect points by spelling words accurately. It looks a lot like the Mario Brothers games on Nintendo, which is part of the appeal. There are five different types of spelling questions: multiple choice, where you pick out the correctly spelled word from a list of similar or misspelled versions of the word; complete-the-sentence, with the spelling words in context; scrambled words, where you must unscramble a word from your spelling list; sound-to-spell, where you record your own voice pronouncing the word; and definition questions. You also have the option of picking the kinds of questions you are asked. This game is a fast-paced way to practice a weekly spelling list.

Another variation on the traditional method of practicing spelling with your children is to read off words and ask your children to type each one into a wordprocessing program rather than writing them all down. When you've finished the list, ask them to run the spell check and see what it comes up with.

These games will help kids do the rote practicing needed to spell words accurately and swiftly in a testing situation, but they cannot substitute for your help in other areas: it's still important for you to go over the weekly spelling lists with your children to point out quick or funny ways to remember how to spell various words, find small words within words, recall definitions, or help your children construct fast sentences that can be scribbled down to show they know the meaning of a word in context.

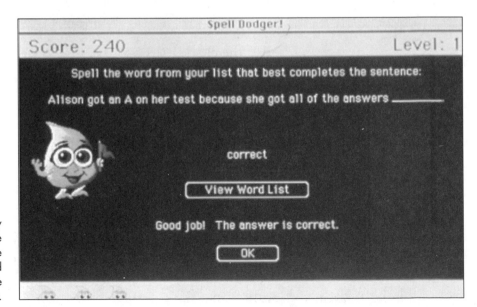

Polishing off the weekly spelling list will never be the same after your kids have had a chance to play and learn with a program like Spell Dodger.

Vocabulary Builders

▪ ▪ ▪ ▪ ▪ ▪ ▪ ▪ ▪ ▪ ▪

As kids move up the academic ladder they often work with vocabulary lists, where more emphasis is placed on the meanings of the words they must learn to spell. Programs such as Word Attack 3 from Davidson allow kids to enter their own vocabulary list into the computer and then provide a set of games that test their definition recall, spelling and using the word in a sentence. In one game, the main character—who looks like one of those dots on the 7UP commercials—eats his way through a maze as the player matches the meaning to the word to be gobbled. There are also crossword puzzles to do and a mah-jongg-like game to unstack. The sound component of the program allows your child to hear the words as well as see them—a definite plus in working with unfamiliar words. The game may move a little slowly for arcade addicts, but it advances at the user's pace, which is helpful for those who find timed games hard to conquer. Word Attack 3 also contains lists of words at various levels for kids who need to work on their word power.

If your child needs some remediation in this area, and you are willing to work with lists already in the computer's memory, try Word City from Sanctuary Woods. This arcade like game can help kids work on skills from speed reading to vocabulary to alphabetization. It does emphasize a race against the clock, however, so it may not be appropriate for every child.

Writing and Grammar

▪ ▪ ▪ ▪ ▪ ▪ ▪ ▪ ▪ ▪

A word processor is the basic tool your child needs for creating and presenting most everyday homework assignments. In chapter 2, we reviewed all the common features of a word processor and how to put them to use in a variety of subject areas. One of the bonuses of buying a word processor developed especially for kids are the special student features. A program such as the Student Writing Center from The Learning Company includes

- templates for creating reports, newsletters, journals, letters, and signs
- automatic text wrap around graphics
- a clip art library of pictures relevant to regularly assigned homework assignments
- a bibliography maker, in which kids are prompted to fill in boxes with the entries they need to complete a proper citation for the variety of resources
- a title page maker, with boxes for the title of the project, the student's name, subject, date, and the teacher's name
- grammar tips on punctuation, capitalization, plurals, abbreviations, and numbers, plus definitions of commonly confused words such as "than" and "then"
- a journal with a password feature and a calendar
- letterheads and sign borders

With tools and templates like these, kids can quickly compose, edit, and print everything from a short paragraph to full-fledged and formal presentations. They can author lab and book reports, and compose research papers. With the clip art library that is included and the ability to import pictures from art programs and photo CDs, they can quickly jazz up a Renaissance menu, social studies report, science fiction story, and much more. Student Writing Center is a full-featured word processor, but the buttons, rulers, bells, and whistles are oriented to the homework needs of the young student.

Other children's word processors such as Creative Writer from Microsoft and the Amazing Writing Machine from Brøderbund are great for students in grades three, four, and five, who may need more help with creative writing assignments. These programs contain story starters and clip art, to give kids ideas for stories and other creative writing pursuits. Storybook creation programs such as Storybook Weaver Deluxe from MECC and Imagination Express from Edmark also make great additions to a home software library for inspiring young writers. However, kids over twelve who are in a hurry to format a standard assignment may be frustrated by all the fluff.

Find out from your child's teachers what writing assignments are acceptable if they are accomplished on the computer. If they give

Did You Know...

If you want your kids to use the computer as an everyday tool, they need to see you using it for everyday tasks. Kids follow the models they see and live with. If you're anxious about using the computer, ask a friend to help you to learn to do a little word processing or to use a program to help you balance your checkbook. Try your hand at playing some of the games the kids are so wild about. Find out how to get online and make use of the myriad services available there. Try taking an introductory computer course at a local computer store or community college.

you carte blanche, encourage kids to do all their brainstorming and prewriting tasks on the computer as well as their rough drafts and final products. Use the computer for even the simplest assignments, such as the creation of a paragraph about "my summer vacation." If your child's teachers restrict what can be done on the computer, help your child live within those guidelines. Find out if there are any schoolwide guidelines for completing assignments on the computer. This is an issue most schools have not yet faced, so don't be surprised if you cannot get a universal answer to your questions.

▶ TO COMPUTER OR NOT TO COMPUTER? ◀

Some tasks are done better on the computer and some aren't. For example, if keyboarding is a problem, your child should probably write class notes with a pencil rather than laboriously type them into the computer. On the other hand, if children compile a research report using the computer, they shouldn't copy out by hand summary notecards for an oral report. Remind them to use the copy and paste features of their wordprocessor to create the notes they need. This question—when is it most efficient, and therefore appropriate, to use the computer—is going to pop up now and then. Be sure to weigh the advantages and disadvantages of doing things by hand versus using the computer.

Students who need some drill and practice help with grammar skills may benefit from Grammar Games by Davidson. Four activities, centered on a rain forest theme, help kids with editing for proper punctuation, plurals and possessives, subject and verb agreement, identification of sentence fragments, and verb and word usage problems.

Unfortunately, this kind of exercise can get pretty boring fairly quickly. The best way to learn grammar is to do lots of writing and get other people to read it. With help from you, siblings, the computer, and other family members critiquing and correcting their work, students will soon begin to find and correct their own grammar errors. Encourage kids to use the grammar tools on whatever word processor they are using. We all need all the help we can get!

Many kids find it fun to keep a private journal on the computer. Programs such as Student Writing Center, the Amazing Writing

How to Find Good Homework Software for Kids

1. Find out what programs your child is using at school. Ask the teachers what their favorite programs are and ask for suggestions on using them. Your child's teachers can also be asked if they can send home an update on what programs are being used throughout the school year. Urge your PTA to bring in speakers or to sponsor a technology fair at your school.

2. Talk to other parents about what software their children enjoy and why. Also ask about how the kids have used the program. Is it drill and practice, a game, or a creativity tool?

3. Keep your eyes open for reviews in the newspaper and free family resource magazines.

4. Subscribe to a newsletter such as *Children's Software* and/or a family computer magazine such as *Family PC* that includes software reviews as well as articles on technology of wider interest to families. (Look for a list of other titles in the appendix.)

5. As you begin to buy software or hear about it, make note of some of the brand names that seem consistently to put out high quality software. The brand name is no guarantee, but it is a good indicator of what your money will buy.

6. Don't feel you have to buy every piece of kids' software on the market. There are lots of duplications out there—for example, there are now more than 10 kids' art programs on the market each of which has its merits—so don't buy a new program unless it offers lots of features you want and don't already have. Keep your child's interests in mind when you're looking for an addition to you collection.

7. Make sure you have a balanced collection of software. You don't need a lot of programs, but you need a variety. You should have software to help create art and documents as well as tutorials in math and reading and keyboarding. A simple spreadsheet program is useful to older children. Games are also important—from serious ones that simulate life to the fanciful and even the arcade variety.

Keroppi Day Hopper is a fun way for kids to keep track of their calendar, address book, and write a daily journal on the computer.

Machine, and Keroppi Day Hopper from Big Top Productions can make keeping a computer journal more fun. This is a great way to encourage kids to write at the keyboard a little bit every day even if it's only a couple of sentences.

Math

In every kid's home software library there should be a least a couple of different kinds of math software. First and foremost, there should be drill and practice software to help your child practice computational skills; this should be flexible enough to work with them at their own pace on the skills they already have and to help them with the skills they have yet to acquire. Some math software can be customized to correspond one on one with the problems your child brings home every day. This kind is best for getting kids up to speed on numbers facts and for reviewing for tests.

Other types of math software should probably be more exploratory, helping kids acquire mathematical concepts and explore the world of numbers and patterns. They should be full of fun and different ways to use math (such as solving mysteries) or filled with puzzles that challenge and intrigue a young problem solver. Some kinds of software contain both drill and practice and a broader look at math concepts, and it's fun to have a couple of pieces of math software with completely different but equally valid approaches to math.

The best known math software on the market is the Math Blaster series from Davidson. At the beginning level, Math Blaster: Episode 1—In Search of Spot teaches the most basic math skills. As you progress through the series, though, kids encounter increasingly sophisticated topics. In Math Blaster: Episode 2—Secret of the Lost City, problems involve decimals, fractions, equations and percentages. Math Blaster Mystery: The Great Train Robbery involves strategies for solving word problems. Alge-Blaster 3 (Alge-Blaster Plus for the Macintosh) teaches algebra.

All of these drill programs combine game play with math practice. There's a video game quality to them, including some old fashioned shoot-'em-up games as part of the bonus rounds. These programs are customizable: problems can be set up to suit your children's individual needs so they can work at home on whatever they're studying at school.

Another classic piece of math software is Super Solvers Outnumbered from The Learning Company. In this program, the Master of Mischief is trying to take over the Shady Glen TV station. In order to stop him before midnight (at which time he will change all the station's programming to boring stuff), kids have to visit various rooms in the station and solve word problems by using charts, graphs, and maps. This allows them to discover the code that will lead them to the Master of Mischief's secret hideout, where they can put an end to his dirty deeds. This is a great program for those who need practice with word problems. Kids seem to enjoy solving the mystery aspect of this (mostly) drill program. But if yours find this aspect too frustrating, the program can be customized to offer straight computational problems.

Programs like Math Blaster can help make learning math facts fun.

Two math software programs that start with basic number recognition and run through decimals and fractions are Number Maze and Decimal and Fraction Maze from Great Wave Software. Both are calm but colorful math games where children navigate through a series of mazes in order to reach a castle or house. Along the way kids encounter gates, hedges, walls, and other obstacles that they open or breach by answering math problems. As they progress through the mazes, they are rewarded further by seeing their treasures pile up in the castle or house and by receiving award certificates that can be printed out.

This program is customizable so that kids can work on the same kinds of problems that they've had at school that day, advance to new challenges, or go back to review concepts from earlier lessons. These programs seem to have a magical appeal for some children, perhaps because kids actually see themselves advancing on their goal or because the problems are not timed. Drills are done at a child's own pace, and kids are sometimes able to teach themselves higher math concepts using them because of the software's patient approach to all levels of math. If your kids don't respond well to time pressure, these games are a good bet for drill and practice software.

Kids who do like to race the clock will appreciate Math Ace from Sanctuary Woods, a program that covers everything from basic math skills to pre-algebra concepts. The basic premise of the game is that a virus has invaded the Global Math Archives and the player must help Bit-Bot, the Keeper of the Archives, protect the repository. The only way to trap the virus is to answer math problems correctly. This game is fun, but the problems become complicated quickly, so players must be careful not to choose a level too far above their ability. The action moves right along, and if players dawdle too long over a question the virus starts munching away. In another part of the program, called the Smart Lab, players can practice the same problems that appear during the game but without pressure: they can take time to think through solutions and get on-screen help if they need to. Math Ace is definitely an intense game; it's lots of fun, but not for those who don't like to be rushed.

Another speed demon favorite is Mental Math from Word-Perfect. This is a very basic, straightforward program with arcadelike games for practicing addition, subtraction, multiplication, division, fractions, percents, and decimals. As their skills improve, kids advance to higher stages. As of this writing, Mental Math is the fastest paced entry of the lot.

WordPerfect also publishes Memphis Math: Treasure of the Tombs for older students—particularly budding archaeologists and Egyptologists—who want to practice their fractions, decimals, and percents. This program is a mystery game with clues and rewards handed out as kids solve the problems that are displayed. The program can be customized to offer specific brain teasers with imposed time limits.

Another classic, but more exploratory, math game is Number Munchers from MECC. General math operations such as addition, multiplication, and division are not the focus here: instead, the program teaches some of the basic, underlying concepts upon which all mathematics is based, such as prime numbers, factors, and multiples.

Number Munchers looks and plays a lot like the old arcade game Pac Man. Kids help their Munchers roam around the game board, gobbling up numbers depending on the math topic they have chosen to study. At the same time, they have to watch out for the

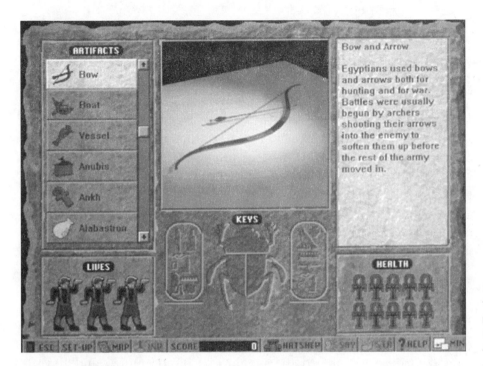

Exploring the mysteries of the tombs provides many problems for young mathematicians in Memphis Math.

Troggles, which love to swallow Munchers whole. Numbers Muchers is not a fancy game, but it has the kind of staying power that kids enjoy and parents appreciate. And it's great for practicing multiplication tables as well as experimenting with number concepts.

Another less conventional math program is Math Workshop from Brøderbund. Along with the traditional drill and practice section for computation (addition to division) and estimation (if you can call bowling with a gorilla traditional), there are a whole host of activities to help kids grasp larger math concepts. The activity for working with fractions links their manipulation to musical beats and rhythms demonstrated by a relative of Woody Woodpecker. Puzzles that become animated upon completion help kids practice problem-solving skills and assist their comprehension of geometry and spatial relations. Other puzzles ask kids to form pictures cards that complete certain patterns. (That one is *hard*!) A third set of puzzles works on proportion, scale, and symmetry; logic in a game with rockets that take off with a roar; even a little geometric art. Brøderbund also includes a parent guide right on the CD-ROM that supplies additional ideas for math activities, a list of readings and national math and computer organizations, and an overview of current math strategies.

Another math program that can be used for supplemental purposes is Counting on Frank from Electronic Arts. Frank actually is a dog, and the games on the disk involve the adventures of Frank and his master, Henry and their friends. The main part of the program deals with solving problems that require multiple steps and includes a jelly bean counting contest. There are also four math activity games with different levels that involve matching numbers and equations in a concentration-style game, forming magic number squares, Geometron (an updated electronic version of completing shapes by connecting the dots), and a math machine to challenge kids' operational and problem solving skills.

A second innovative supplement for kids who love math and different kinds of math challenges is Real Word Math: Adventures in Flight from Sanctuary Woods. This game doesn't really go along with homework but is great for children who need to see some of the real world aspects of the subjects they are studying. Kids are transported to an airport (thanks to the magic of the computer) and have a chance to explore and try their hand at some of the day-to-day calculations undertaken by airport and airline workers. For example, kids see how pilots use air speed and distance to calculate estimated time of arrival; help flight attendants use graphing skills to seat passengers on a plane; or learn longitude skills to find out what time it is in another part of the world. A trip to the control tower gives them a peek at how air traffic controllers make use of place value when reading a radar screen and then gives them a chance to try it themselves. Each kind of math calculation is first demonstrated and then kids have a chance to take a quiz and try their hand at it in order to win "air time" points. These points earn them certification as pilots of various kinds of airplanes, starting small and working up to the space shuttle. They don't actually get to fly the planes but instead receive certificates or paper plane patterns or models they can assemble to represent their progress. This is a great way to practice measurement, estimation, geometry, map skills, calculation, and graphing! Real World Math is a very innovative approach to math, but unless kids are interested in aviation or mechanical things, they

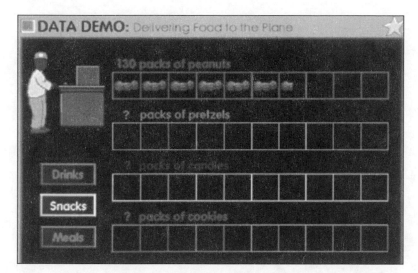

Do your kids ever ask you why they have to learn math? Real World Math: Adventures in Flight demonstrates how workers in the airline industry use math everyday in their jobs.

might not take the time to get into it. Nevertheless it really does a great job of showing the place of math in our daily lives.

Social Studies

All through this book we have given suggestions for using the computer to do research, design maps, and produce projects, reports, and papers for social studies classes. The computer is a useful research and creation tool for any modern student of the social studies. But students are still asked to memorize the fifty U.S. states and capitals or countries of Africa. And lots of kids love to know a bit of trivia about maps and geography.

Here again, the computer can be a patient tutor. National Geographic has three programs in their ZipZapMap series—World! USA! and Canada!— that can help kids learn the names and locations of cities, states, provinces, countries, and major geographic landmarks. Regions of the world or the states and provinces of the United States and Canada are divided up in a game format, (at different levels of difficulty and speeds of play) where countries, states, or geographic names float down the screen until "captured" with a click

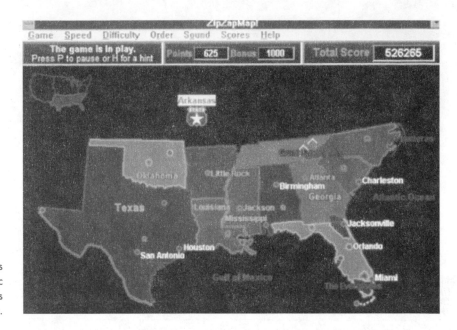

The ZipZapMap Series from National Geographic is a great way to help kids memorize map facts.

and placed correctly on the map to gain points.

Another program called Cross Country USA from Didatech lets the player "drive" an eighteen-wheel truck across the United States, picking up and dropping off freight and learning about the country at the same time. Kids love all the detail that programmers have put into letting them operate the truck, which makes this a good "learn-by-doing" program for absorbing information about states, capitals, and the natural resources of the United States. Programs such as the ever popular Where in the USA is Carmen Sandiego? and Where in the World is Carmen Sandiego? from Brøderbund also can help kids learn about the landmarks and geography of the United States and the world.

Software for Creating Print Products

Print Artist from Maxis and Print Shop (in any of its many versions) from Brøderbund are two great pieces of software to have on hand for creating signs, posters, postcards, and all the other incidentals that can be helpful for school projects. Both are jam-packed with graphics, clip art, and design templates for creating a variety of print products that can jazz up simple assignments. Other fun projects your child might want to try include

- creating a business card or decorated stationery for the detective or main character in a story or for a small business project they are running at school
- designing postcards as part of a project on a country or landmark
- writing a persuasive letter using some inventive letterhead (such as a letter to Santa from the Easter Bunny) or creating stationery for a fictitious society to protest or support a facetious stand on a topic
- producing an ad for a book they have reviewed and enjoyed, to use as a title page or part of the report
- procuring a menu for a particular period in time, a particular historical or fictious event, or a special occasion

Ace Kendall
Pet Detective
10 Alley Cat Way
Purrville, TX 77777

Dear Mrs. Jones,
    A ransom note for your dog Prince has arrived. The kidnapper wants 2000 cans of tuna delivered to a litter box at Acme Pet Food by 5 p.m. today.
    The whole thing smells. I think your neighbor's cat, Fang, may be involved.
    At this point, we have no choice but to start buying the ransom. But have no fear, Ace Kendall is on the case!

Fanciful stationery devised in a print program such as Print Shop or Print Artist can inspire the work of young authors.

These are only a few ways such programs can "spice up" a writing or social studies assignment. And remember, if you don't have a color printer, you can still have fun designing in these kinds of programs and printing out your final project on paper with a pre-printed border or background.

Models, Maps, and Diagrams

Kids are often asked to do some research and draw a diagram or map of the inside of a traditional home or castle, or to draw a map of their room or a part of their neighborhood. My daughter has had assignments to draw everything from her room to a castle to a traditional Korean home. Drawing programs such as Kid Pix are fabulous for making maps and diagrams. The stamp feature is a great way to add details to a map or label a diagram. The drawing and painting portions of integrated tools programs such as ClarisWorks and Microsoft Works can also be used for this purpose.

If the enterprising young architect or engineer at your house would like to try building a 3-D model, consider buying a program called Kid Cad from Davidson. Kid Cad is a bit like an electronic set of Lego blocks. You can choose single, multiple, angled, or arched blocks to build with, or you can use a sample building to start with, such as a house, a castle, or an apartment building and then add on. Menus are available for adding furniture, people, and even animals. Building tools let the user move, copy, rotate, link, unlink, and hide objects in the design. You can get either a top-down or side view of your project. Other features like the Zoom and Pan Camera buttons enable you to look at your design close up or pan around to see the parts not currently in view. Paint tools let you paint, wallpaper, or use building materials such as tile, marble, wood, terra cotta to decorate your handiwork. Older children who really get into designing structures may want to research more professional CAD (computer-aided design) programs but Kid Cad is a fun and useful piece of software to start with, especially for quick school projects.

Young architects will enjoy constructing everything from castles to their dream house of the future in Kid Cad.

Homework and the Online Services

. . . .

In chapter 5 we discussed how to help your child use online resources for projects and reports. Don't forget that those same online services are also helpful on an everyday basis. Whether your child needs a newspaper article for help with a social studies assignment, a magazine article on a topic currently being studied in health class, or a sample book or movie review for a language arts class—all are easy to find and print out using online services.

Any current events or "hot" topic in the news or the arts that might be assigned is sure to be covered or discussed somewhere online. So the next time your child comes to you at 9 P.M. and says he has to have something on the impending solar eclipse in Siberia—by tomorrow morning—don't panic. Go online!

Homework and the Computer

■ ■ ■ ■ ■ ■ ■ ■ ■ ■ ■ ■ ■ ■

The computer cannot do kids' homework for them, but it can coax kids through some of the rough spots in their school careers. Certain things still (and may always) have to learned by going over and over them, and the computer can take the drudgery out of some of that with its colorful and amusing graphics and encouraging rewards. The computer can also be a useful tool for keeping kids organized and focused on the task at hand, whether it's this week's spelling or writing the most in-depth research report of their elementary or middle school career.

appendix A

Kids, Homework, and the Internet

The American Dream

The concept of an information highway is the latest manifestation of the American dream. Americans have always been dreamers, explorers, and builders. Each generation reinvents the dream, in its own realm of activity. Back when our generation was growing up, Americans built free-flowing highways of concrete and steel as part of the dream that would link us and our goods and services without delay, across state boundaries.

Today, in our middle age, America still dreams about free-flowing channels, but they are not made of concrete and steel anymore. They are made of wire, fiber-optic cable, and microwaves. Just as the America of our parents' generation dreamed that the interstate highways would bring us increased travel, commerce, and communication, so we dream that the Internet computer networks will bring us and our children data, information, and ideas.

In time we all became drivers on the concrete highway. Every one of us has gone for a spin on the interstate highway. Many of us use it every day. We depend on it to get to work, to do our shopping, and to visit our friends and relatives. But few of us are regular commuters on the information highway. At least not yet.

Our children may in fact learn to drive on the digital networks before we do (perhaps even long before they are old enough to travel the concrete byways alone). They will use the Internet to research their school assignments. To them, the Internet is not a dream, it's an everyday reality.

What is the Internet?

Once upon a time (actually about thirty years ago), a scientist working on a government project at University A needed to use a computer at Institute B in another city far away. In those days, computers were expensive, and only Institute B had the right kind for our scientist to use. Rather than travel to the institute to use the computer, the scientist convinced the university, and the government agency sponsoring the research, to pay for a cable connecting the computer at his university with the computer at the institute. This worked well and saved money, and soon everyone in that business began connecting their computers. After a few years, most of the universities and institutes and government agencies had established connections between their computers: there was a cable connecting the computers at Boston University to those across the river at MIT; from MIT another cable ran to Dartmouth College in New Hampshire; from there, cables led to McGill University in Canada and to the State University of or in New York at Albany. And so it went, this mammoth "Web" of connections.

It also came to pass that a scientist at Boston University wanting to send a computer file to a colleague at Stanford University way out in California would put an address on it, such as "scientist#5@stanford.edu," then send it along the cable to MIT; MIT's computer would see that it was addressed to Stanford and automatically send it along the cable to Dartmouth: Dartmouth would route the file to Albany ... and eventually it would arrive at the Stanford computer, which would place it in the designated colleague's electronic mailbox.

In this system there is no central post office, no hub through which all messages pass, no brain controlling the whole enterprise. This decentralized design was created on purpose, so that no enemy could destroy our electronic communications capability simply by blowing up the nerve center.

As this web of connections grew, it came to be known as the Internet. The web grows bigger very day and now extends all over the world, even to Russia, China and India. You or I or a scientist or your child can address a message to anyone else on the Internet, and it will find its way there, no matter where they are.

The World Wide Web

As the Internet grew, so did its uses. A few years ago a group of scientists in Switzerland wanted to develop a system so that they could share their scientific papers with each other over a computer network. Their papers were in word-processing files already, and each of their universities or institutes had a computer network that linked them together. So each scientist set up one computer as a public information server by putting all of his or her articles onto its hard drive, along with an annotated directory of what each article was about. Then they connected the computer to the Internet. Now the other scientists could "log on" to that server and browse through the articles, thus keeping up with the growth of scientific knowledge. This idea expanded around the world, so that most scientific groups—and many other kinds of folks—set up a public computer "site" on the Internet. A group at the University of Illinois then created a new software program that would allow people to more easily connect to and browse the information on these servers. As more sites began using the same software to organize and search their works, this cyberspace forum collectively became known as the World Wide Web. Today, the Web is the fastest-growing part of the Internet and the easiest to use. To tap into the resources of the World Wide Web, you need a full connection to the Internet, as well as a Web browser software program on your computer. Mosaic and Netscape are two popular (and inexpensive) Web browsers.

Connecting to the Internet

Family-oriented information services are easy to use for schoolwork. But "intermediate"-level users might further benefit from a connection to the Internet. Here are some ways to make this connection:

- If you are in some way affiliated with a college as staff, faculty, or student you may already have an Internet account. The college computing staff can help you connect to it. Visit the personal computer support center or the information technology office at your college and ask for the software you need to hook up. You'll still need a computer, modem, and phone line to make the connection from home to college. The software you get will depend on how your college's Internet servers work but in most cases includes two kinds of programs: one to establish a connection between your computer and the college net-

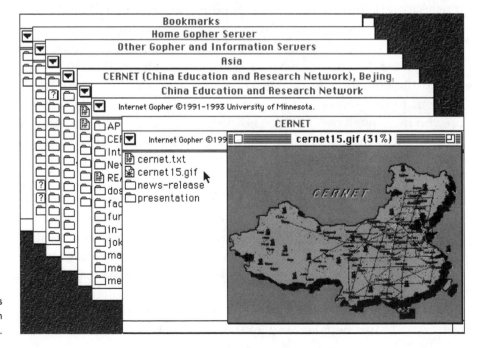

You can retrieve graphics from this server in Cern, Switzerland.

A welcome screen at a
university site.

work; and one to "browse" the various Internet servers. The college
will also assign you an account name and a password and a phone
number, which you must use to make the connection. Once you're connected, there is usually no monthly charge.

- If you have no university affiliations, you can purchase a connection
to the Internet from an Internet service provider such as PSINet or
NetComm. For a monthly fee ranging from $20 to $200, depending
on where you live these companies provide a dial-up connection to
their Internet server. Like the college, they will provide you with connection software and browsing software, as well as a phone number
(usually a toll-free 800 number), password, and account number.
Using the software they provide, you establish a connection to their
server and from there are allowed to browse other servers on the
Internet.

Some of the on-line information services offer a Web browser as part of their package of services. These are not full Internet connections, such as we describe later, but they will allow you to get to just about all the Web sites we list in this appendix. Getting onto the Internet first through the on-line services, though, is a great introduction to this monumental resource.

Hypertext Searching

The World Wide Web uses a system of hypertext links between its documents and sites. The authors of the documents embed (implant) the links in their works. Click on a highlighted phrase in one document, and it takes you to another document at another site, and so forth, so everything is linked to everything else. All documents are created (written) using a common system called the hypertext markup language, or HTML. The Web browser software on your computer can interpret and automatically interlink any HTML document on any other computer in the Web. Hypertext cross-referencing, searching, and back-tracking are new skills that students must learn to navigate successfully in today's interlinked webs of electronic information.

Connecting to the Internet

The first step in using the World Wide Web is to purchase an Internet connection from an Internet service provider. (Remember that you can do some preliminary research on the Internet through the commercial on-line services.) The kind of connection you want at this stage is a dial-up PPP (point-to-point protocol) connection or SLIP (serial line interface protocol), available for about $50 per month. This type of connection lets your home computer become a full-fledged, two-way "node" on the Internet, but you'll need a good machine (about $2,000) and a fast modem (about $200). You'll also need some "Web browser" software, such as Mosaic or Netscape.

Internet Service Providers

If you are in some way connected with a college or university as staff, faculty, or student, you may well have an Internet account. The college computing staff can help you connect to it. Visit the personal computer support center or the information technology office at your college, and ask for the software you need to connect up. You'll still need a computer, modem, and phone line to make the connection from home to the college. The software you get will depend on how your college's Internet servers work but in most cases includes two kinds of programs: programs to establish a connection between your computer and the college network; and programs to "browse" the various Internet servers. You will be assigned an account name, a password, and a phone number, which you must use to make the connection. Once you are connected, there is usually no monthly charge.

If you have no university connection, you can purchase a connection to the Internet from one of the Internet service providers such as PSINet or NetComm. (See the list of publishers and service providers on page 345.) For a monthly fee ranging from $20 to $200, depending on where you live, these companies provide a dial-up connection to their Internet server. As with the college, they will provide you with connection software and browsing software, as well as a phone number (usually a toll-free 800 number), password, and account number. Make sure you ask for a PPP or SLIP connection. Using the software they provide, you establish a connection to their server and from there are allowed to browse other servers on the Internet.

Finding Your Way

Once connected to the Internet, you will find there is no "Town Center" or "main menu" as there is with the family-oriented information services such as America Online, Prodigy, or eWorld. Instead, you are on your own to connect to one of the thousands of Internet servers and see what's there. To connect to these servers, you use a program called an Internet browser such as Gopher, Mosaic, or Netscape. These programs put onto your screen a list of the information items that exist on the server you are connected to. With Gopher, these items show up as little file folders: You click on the folders to see what's inside.

With *Netscape*, the items show up as highlighted words in a paragraph of standard text, or in a list, or as icons. You click on the word or icon you want to see the information.

Many of the Gopher and World Wide Web servers that you find will have folders or highlighted words that point to yet another Internet server. In this way, you can "cruise" the Internet by connecting from server to server, looking for the information you want. But remember, there is no official index to what's out there on the Internet, so for most students the on-line service will get them more information, faster.

Knowing Where to Look

For the Internet to be useful to a young student, it must first be set up and organized so he or she can use it. The information must be arranged so that the student can get what he wants and make good use of it. Most children will need some kind of index, directory or starting points—such as the list in this chapter—in order to make sensible use of the Internet.

The second key is the quality of the information available. This too demands intelligence in gathering, summarizing, and organizing the sources so they are meaningful and reliable. Not all of the information on Internet servers is useful, relevant, or appropriate to a young student's schoolwork. In fact, most of it isn't. Your child needs pointers to the most useful and relevant sources among the vast array of Internet sites.

Safety Tips for the Information Highway

Your child may also need supervision as he or she surfs the Internet. No one censors the Internet, so a crafty browser can find dirty pictures and obscene stories, just as you can at the local library—if you know where to look. By sticking to the sites listed here, your child will remain in safe territory. The best way to make sure your children are not drifting off into things that are not appropriate for them is to stay in touch with what they are doing. Ask them to teach you how to access the services. While kids need a certain amount of privacy, they also need parental involvement and supervision in their lives. Some good rules of thumb:

1. Think very carefully before giving out any personal information—this includes age, address, phone number, school name, marital status, and financial information.
2. Get to know the services your child uses. If you don't get on-line yourself, have your child show you. Do some exploring.
3. Remember that people on-line may not be who they seem. You can't see them or hear them, so a message from a ten-year-old girl could actually be from a forty-year-old man.
4. Set reasonable rules and guidelines for computer use at your house, and stick to them.

An excellent free brochure entitled *Child Safety on the Information Highway* is available from the National Center for Missing and Exploited Children at 800-843-5678.

Internet Sites for Schoolwork

Here is a small but carefully selected collection of computers on the Internet that contain information useful and relevant to homework projects. All of these are open for public access without fees or subscriptions. Most are maintained by respected and reputable institutions or organizations. Each site is described briefly so you know what's there. Internet addresses are also included.

To get to one of these sites, make your Internet connection using Netscape or Mosaic or other Web browser, then select Open Location from the menu bar. Type in the URL (universal resource location) exactly as it is listed below. In a few seconds, your computer will connect to the "host" computer, and the information will appear on your screen. From there, just point and click to the items you want.

Here's how to interpret the URL we list for each site. Think of it as the electronic address of the computer:

$$\underset{1}{\underline{\text{http:}}}//\underset{2}{\underline{\text{www.bu.edu}}}/\underset{3}{\underline{\text{COM/netcom.html}}}$$

1. *http:* hypertext transport protocol, the format of the signals that this computer sends. Computers on the World Wide Web all use http.
2. *www.bu.edu* is the electronic identifier of the university that sponsors this site. *www* stands for Word Wide Web; *bu* for Boston University; and *edu* for educational organization. Other designations you might see are *com* for a commercial organization or *gov* for a government site.
3. *COM/netcom.html* is the name of the file that you are reading. Here you are reading the *netcom.html*, which resides on the disk drive called *COM*.

All addresses on the World Wide Web follow this form.

Directories and Indexes

Even though the Internet has no official central directory, some people have attempted to make a list of what's out there. Others have developed tools that search out things on all those interconnected computers. By learning to use these directories and indexes, your child will be able to find the needle of an idea in the haystacks of data.

Yahoo Directory

The staff at Stanford University have organized many of the Internet's servers in a subject-area directory, sort of like the Yellow Pages. From art to zoology, you click on the subject, getting more detailed at each step until you find what you want. This may be the best place to start if you don't know exactly what you are looking for but want to learn what's there.
http://akebono.stanford.edu/users/www_server

Lycos

The experts at Carnegie Mellon University in Pittsburgh set their up their computer to search out all the new information that is posted on the Internet, like a spider crawling continuosly along the Web. Then they put the information into a big index, which you can search by typing in key words. This comprehensive, popular search engine is often busy.
http://agent4.lycos.cs.cmu.edu/lycos-form.html

Web Crawler

The computer scientists at Washington State have programmed their computers to search the Internet for information and save it in a big index. By typing in key words, you can send the Web crawler out along the Internet to find what you are looking for. Type in a word or two, and the Web crawler finds you a site that refers to it.
http://webcrawler.cs.washington.edu/WebCrawler/WebQuery.html

Commercial Sites

Many companies, corporations, and services ply their wares on the Internet. This site has a search engine that can help you find the company or business you want, with a key word search engine.
http://www.directory.net

Reference Works

Dictionary

This point-and-click hypertext *Webster* interface to the dictionary provides definitions, pronunciation, and cross references for almost every word you can think of. Its search engine even helps you find words you can't spell.
http://c.gp.cs.cmu.edu:5103/prog/Webster

French-English Dictionary

For those foreign-language assignments, this interactive bilingual dictionary can be quite useful. It includes key word searches, clickable cross references, and help for bad spellers.
http://mlab-power3.uiah.fi/EnglishFrench/ef.html

Roget's Thesaurus

Can't think of exactly the right word? Get ideas from the thesaurus. Synonyms and antonyms and other connected words all arrive at the click of a mouse, with key word searching.
http://tuna.uchicago.edu/forms_unrest/ROGET.html

Bartlett's Familiar Quotations

Dredge up a pithy quote for a term paper, or find out who authored that witty remark. This key word–searchable version of the famous 1911 edition is great for English assignments.
http://www.columbia.edu/~svl2/bartlett

Arts

. . . .

The Smithsonian Institution

This site provides a directory of the many museums that make up the Smithsonian, everything from air and space, art, and history, with information and electronic exhibits for many school subjects.
http://www.si.edu

ArtsEdge

This site is a large collection of student art galleries, school art projects, and ideas from the National Arts and Education Information Network.
http://k12.cnidr.org/janice_k12/artsedge/artsedge.html

Allen Memorial Art Museum—Oberlin College

Students will find here large, high-quality images of ancient, European, American, Asian, and African art from the collection at Oberlin College.
http://www.oberlin.edu/wwwmap/allen_art.html

Dallas Museum of Art

You can view or download more than 200 images of artwork from the Dallas Museum of Art, including African, Asian, American, European, and contemporary painting and sculpture.
http://www.unt.edu/dfw/dma/www/dma.html

The Louvre

Browse the collection, or take a guided tour of the famous paintings, sculpture, and even music at this great museum. Many pictures are available to download and use in student reports. Extensive commentary and explanation are also included.
http://www.cnam.fr/louvre

Science

Periodic Table

The Periodic Table of the Elements, live on your computer! This interactive chemistry resource allows you to click on an element to find its atomic weight, valence shells, bonds, properties, and much more.
http://www.cchem.berkeley.edu/Table/index.html

Center for Earth and Planetary Studies

At the National Air and Space Museum of the Smithsonian Institution, this site contains a collection of research and images of earth and the planets, with an especially useful collection of photos taken from the space shuttle.
http://ceps.nasm.edu:2020/rpif.html

The Weather Processor

See an up-to-the-minute weather map of the US in full color. This site helps students visualize the weather with maps, satellite photos, temperature and radar readings.
http://thunder.atms.purdue.edu

Science Fair

At the Cyberfair Virtual Science Fair, students in grades 3–6 can see student projects, look for science ideas, and share their results with other students. From Mankato, Minnesota.
http://www.isd77.k12.mn.us/resources/cf/welcome.html

Global SchoolHouse

This site is a directory with pointers to science projects, curriculum ideas, software tools, and contacts with schools all over the U.S. It's sponsored by the National Science Foundation.
http://k12.cnidr.org/gsh/gshwelcome.html

Reading and Language Arts

Written Works

This site contains a collection of classic literature for reading or searching. Several books and stories by Edgar Allan Poe, Mark Twain, Charles Dickens, and others are included. You can read them on the screen, or download them onto your computer and read them later. Some provide information on the author.
http://www.wonderland.org/Works

Book Reviews

Many people contribute book reviews to this site. You will find brief, pithy opinionated reviews of recent works, mostly of the best-seller variety.
http://sunsite.unc.edu/ibic/IBIC-Journal.html

Alice in Wonderland

Lewis Carrol's classic work is available in its full unabridged text. From the rabbit hole to the tea party to the Queen of Hearts, your child can read to enjoy, or quote a passage in her next research report.
http://www.cs.indiana.edu/metastuff/wonder/wonderdir.html

Social Studies

The Declaration of Independence

Thomas Jefferson would have loved the Internet. The Declaration that he helped to author can be quite useful for history and social studies. It can be read from the screen or copied to your own computer.
http://www.house.gov/Declaration.html

The U.S. Constitution

The full text of this law of laws includes the Bill of Rights and all the subsequent amendments. The clickable index makes it very easy to find the part you want for law or history.
http://www.lm.com/~damon/Constitution.html

The Emancipation Proclamation

During the Civil War, Lincoln freed the slaves. Or did he? Let your child figure it out by reading the original document on the Internet. This copy includes commentary and a bibliography useful for history students.
http://www.cs.indiana.edu/statecraft/emancipation.html

The Gettysburg Address

Practice your speaking ability with this most famous of American locations. The Gettysburg Address is useful in understanding history and the art of speaking.
http://www.cs.indiana.edu/statecraft/gettysburg.html

Bureau of the Census

Here you will find complete census tables for anywhere in the country, as well as maps, statistical briefs, and economic indicators for social studies. There's even a gallery of population art.
http://www.census.gov

Central Intelligence Agency

The CIA's *World Factbook* has information on every country in the world, with maps, demographics, government, and economy. It's updated regularly and is great for research reports.
http://www.ic.gov

U.S. Geological Survey

This site provides maps, water resources information, surveys, and reports full of ideas and facts for earth science and geography projects.
http://www.usgs.gov

Navy Online

A collection of information and resources from the U.S. Navy, searchable by key word. Photos of ships, text about navy missions and weapons.
http://www.navy.mil

The White House

Learn about the executive branch of the federal government, and about the president and his family. You can download pictures and voice clips from the people and even their pets.
http://www.whitehouse.gov

The Supreme Court

You can search and read the Court's decisions in hypertext with this well-indexed collection, searchable by key word. This site will help with assignments in history, government, and law studies.
http://www.law.cornell.edu/supct

House of Representatives

Find information here about members of Congress, bills in progress, new laws, and schedules. Along with information on how a bill becomes a law, this site also includes links to individual members' home pages.
http://www.house.gov

Senate

Senators, bills, and government information, mostly in text form.
gopher://gopher.senate.gov

States

. . . .

Arizona

Download pictures, sounds, and documents from the Grand Canyon State. This site can be useful in social studies and geography assignments.
http://www.state.az.us

Delaware

Your child can learn quite a bit about Delaware's elected officials and agencies on this computer. Even their e-mail addresses are included. This site can provide facts and history for reports.
http://www.state.de.us

Florida

The Florida Communities Network provides information on business, government, tourism, and information for the Sunshine State. A key word search engine will help you find pictures and text at this easy-to-use site.
http://fcn.state.fl.us

Hawaii

Take a trip far to the west to this island state. Read the governor's speeches and learn exactly what each branch and agency of the state's government does.
http://hinc.hinc.hawaii.gov/soh_home.html

Indiana

Click on a map to be a "virtual tourist" on the Indiana network. Read the new laws being proposed by the state legislature. You can even search for job openings.
http://www.state.in.us

Kentucky

Your child will find maps, weather reports, and a message from the governor at this site, along with information on tourism, government agencies, and historic sites, all with a key word–searchable index.
http://www.state.ky.us

Louisiana

This site can provide information for a students report, such as facts on the people, history, and culture of Louisiana. Excellent photos and maps, as well as census data and weather, are included.
http://www.state.la.us

Maine

This site contains the most colorful state seal, as well as weather for any part of the state. Like Indiana, it includes a clickable tourist map, along with factual information about the state and its government.
http://www.state.me.us

Missouri

From historical manuscripts to community profiles with photos and facts, this site can help your child learn about the Show-Me State. You'll find government data, city home pages, and other Missouri information.
http://www.ecodev.state.mo.us

List of State Sites

For a complete list of all the states that publish information on the Internet, connect to this site.
http://www.yahoo.com/Government/States

Foreign Countries

. . . .

Hungary

The prime minister's office publishes pictures, speeches, and interviews with government officials. Some are in English, while others are published in Hungarian.
http://www.meh.hu

Mauritius

You probably don't even know where this country is. Find out by connecting to the pictures, maps, and interactive questions and answers about this island country. You'll find high-quality pictures, along with text about Mauritius' history, economy, and geography.
http://www.herts.ac.uk/~cs4bw/index.html

Belgium

Agatha Christie's famous sleuth Hercule Poirot was from Belgium. At this Internet site you will find (in English, French, or Dutch) information about the king and queen, the different language groups, and the agencies of the Belgian government.
http://www.innet.net/belgium

Code Civil du Québec

A great way to practice reading French, for students and teachers. This full text of Quebec law outlines the rights and responsibilities of citizens in this Canadian province.
http://www.droit.umontreal.ca/cgi-bin/ccfTDM

Japan Window

This site on the World Wide Web lets you read about the structure and function of Japan's government, business, and kids' lives, through diagrams, text, and maps. Information here is published in English.
http://jw.stanford.edu

New Zealand

You'll find New Zealand's Constitution, maps, pictures, geography, history, and economy, as well as a collection of text that can help with student reports. Read what the government is up to down under.
http://www.govt.nz

United Kingdom

Britannia rules the waves, but can she surf the Internet? Find out at this site, where you'll find government information from England, Scotland, and Wales. Many items are included, from the history of Hyde Park to the Queen's annual awards. This site can help students come up with an interesting comparison to the United States.
http://www.open.gov.uk

Peru

Because this site is bilingual—you can select to read it in either Spanish or English—it is good for working with Spanish in a practical situation. Your child will find text and pictures about education, government, business, and organizations in Peru.
http://www.rcp.net.pe

Canada SchoolNet

Bilingual (French and English) information on Canada's schools and Canada, with many links to ongoing projects and schools.
http://schoolnet.carleton.ca/schoolnet

Maps

▪ ▪ ▪ ▪ ▪ ▪ ▪ ▪ ▪ ▪ ▪ ▪

The Virtual Tourist

This site organizes all the public World Wide Web computers onto a series of maps that you can click on, to establish a connection to that server. Click on a country and get a list of the World Wide Web servers in that place.
http://wings.buffalo.edu/world

Xerox PARC Map viewer

From the world map that this site draws on your computer screen, you can click on a spot, and it will draw a detailed outline map for you, instantly. It can draw a map at any longitude and latitude: tell it the coordinates, and it draws a map for you. The making of maps can be an interesting interactive experience.
http://pubweb.parc.xerox.com/map

The Perry-Castañeda Library Map Collection

This site at the University of Texas contains a great collection of beautiful color maps that you can download and see on your screen. It has maps of just about any place on this earth, great for student presentations and reports. The maps are organized by continent and country.
http://www.lib.utexas.edu/Libs/PCL/Map_collection/Map_collection.html

U.S. News

▪ ▪ ▪ ▪ ▪ ▪ ▪ ▪ ▪ ▪ ▪ ▪

Time Daily

Time magazine provides short summaries of each day's news, both national and global. Organized by subject, *Time* provides hypertext links among articles to make browsing interesting. A key word–

searchable index lets you find related stories from past issues of the magazine.
http://www.timeinc.com/time/daily/time/1995/latest.html

Tacoma News/Tribune

This newspaper provides you with access to its files of daily stories on world and national events. There are no pictures here, only text, but it's a great resource for current events.
http://www.tribnet.com

San Francisco Chronicle and Examiner

These two newspapers provide in one place an extensive collection of lengthy world and national news articles, on-line. They also provide stories on weather, along with feature stories with pictures.
http://sfgate.com

InternetMCI/Reuters New Media

These very brief summaries of today's news are drawn from both national and global sources from Reuters news agency. This site is good for current events assignments.
http://www.FYIonline.com/infoMCI/update/NEWS-MCI.html

International News

The Electronic *Telegraph*

The *London Daily Telegraph* newspaper puts its stories, in their entirety, on-line each day. They include British and world news, as well as interesting perspectives on the American scene.
http://www.telegraph.co.uk

Kyodo Cyber Express

Japan's largest international news agency provides photos, text, maps, and features, in both Japanese and English. This site is useful for social studies projects.
http://www.toppan.co.jp/kyodo

Welcome to Iceland!

Find out how volcanoes thaw Iceland and many other interesting facts about this advanced yet isolated nation. Daily news and cultural information is sent out in English. This site provides a good comparative perspective on the day's events.
http://www.centrum.is/icerev

China News Digest

A billion people make a lot of news. This site publishes daily news from China, along with a collection of pictures, articles, and classic literature. Most articles are in English, and some material is published in Chinese.
http://www.cnd.org

St. Petersburg Press

A few years ago it was Leningrad, and it was definitely not in the Internet. Things are still changing in Russia; this site can help you understand them. Find news of St. Petersburg in English, the current issue of the newspaper, archives of past articles, and detailed photos with a cross-cultural perspective.
 http://www.spb.su/sppress

African National Congress News Briefings

At this site you can read the daily summaries of the world's news, as prepared by South Africa's majority party. This can be a useful site

for geography and social studies.
http://minerva.cis.yale.edu:80/~jadwat/anc

Math

The Geometry Forum

To help with those geometry assignments, check out this site. Tackle the problem of the week, question Dr. Math, and download geometry examples and teaching ideas.
http://forum.swarthmore.edu

Elementary Schools

St. Philomena School

The students and teachers at this school share information over the World Wide Web. You can take part in a rain forest project, view student home pages and art work, and see what's going on in the K–8 classrooms of this school from Des Moines, Washington.
http://www.halcyon.com/dale/Dales.html

The Marion Cross School

Students at this school are creative users of technology. By looking in on their computer, you can learn about Vermont, see kids' Hyper-Studio projects, and meet the students and staff.
http://picard.dartmouth.edu/~cam/MCS.html

The Ralph Bunche School

Students at this school are prolific publishers. Located in Harlem, New York, they and their teachers publish an electronic student newspaper;

they also invite you to participate in on-line experiments and surveys. Last I looked, they were publishing an illustrated Spanish alphabet. http://mac94.ralphbunche.rbs.edu

Middle Schools

Monroe Middle School

Find out what a jackalope is by connecting to this school on the World Wide Web. From Green River, Wyoming, Monroe students publish literature, projects, pictures, opinions, ideas, and surveys. http://monhome.sw2.k12.wy.us

Taylor Road Middle School

Near Atlanta, students at Taylor Road School in Alpharetta, Georgia, publish information on the Atlanta Olympics, engage in joint projects with students, promote pen pals, and provide news about the school. http://www.trms.ga.net

High Schools

Akatsukayama High School

Students and staff at Akatsukayama tell their story—in English. You can tour the school, learn about Kobe, Japan, and read messages from its students. http://www.kobe-cufs.ac.jp/kobe-city/school/akatsuka/akatsuka.html

Branson School

These folks serve as good models for student multimedia projects, such as those described in chapter 8. From Ross, California, Branson

publishes information on the Stone Soup multimedia cooperative, along with student-produced QuickTime movies and a special project called SAREX.
http://www.nbn.com/~branson

Model High School

Located in Bloomfield Hills, Michigan, this school has an on-line newspaper, a student art gallery, a digital imaging lab, and an Internet safari that you can can use for designing your own projects.
http://www.bloomfield.k12.mi.us

Prairie High School

Get ideas for your own projects by reading the school paper, viewing student artworks and sports feats, and visiting clubs from this school in Brush Prairie, Washington.
http://152.157.16.3/phs/doc/PHS.html

Riley High School

From South Bend, Indiana, the science department at Riley shares its multimedia learning applications in chemistry, physics, and earth science, as well as pictures and sounds of the local community.
http://sjcpl.lib.in.us/rhshomepage/riley2.html

Thomas Jefferson High School for Science and Technology

Here you can peruse an on-line student art gallery, gather ideas for computer science projects, and browse student home pages (with many pictures) from this magnet school in northern Virginia.
http://boom.tjhsst.edu:80

University Laboratory High School

This school in Champaign-Urbana, Illinois, publishes great student photos, department home pages, and lists of teacher resources, as

well as information about the school.
http://superdec.uni.uiuc.edu

Colleges

Carnegie Mellon University

At CMU in Pittsburgh, each student is required to own a computer, and the Internet is at the forefront of education. Learn about the university's history, its vision, research, and electronic resources.
http://www.cmu.edu

Escuela Superior Politécnica del Litoral

This site—published entirely in Spanish—provides articles on current events, tutorials on the Internet, and information about Ecuador and the school. It's located in Guayaquil, Ecuador. It's good practice for your next Spanish test.
http://espol.edu.ec

Harvard University

This oldest of American universities provides a directory of its many electronic resources from physics to the arts, from education to business, as well as a student-authored digital magazine.
http://www.harvard.edu

Howard University

You can access Howard's history, browse a Yellow Pages of electronic sources, take a tour with the clickable campus map, and establish links to many other historically black colleges and universities in the United States.
http://www.howard.edu

Institut National de Télécommunications

Published in both French and English, this French site can help you learn about the program of study at the institute, see pictures of the campus, and practice your French.
http://www.int-evry.fr

Istanbul Technical Institute

Some call it Constantinople, and from this site you can learn about education in Turkey, take a tour of Istanbul, or read about the life of a student at ITU. In English.
http://www.itu.edu.tr

Kyoto University

At this site in Japan you can learn about KU's research in physics, African culture, mathematics, and other areas. It's published in English or Japanese.
http://www.kyoto-u.ac.jp

NetCOM Talk

See and hear what's happening at the Boston University College of Communication, from student photojournalism to the multimedia studio.
http://web.bu.edu/COM/communication.html

Oberlin College

Oberlin is a small college in Ohio, one of the first to admit women and black students. At their Internet site you can find out about student life, history, music, and the arts.
http://www.oberlin.edu

Peking University

You can tour the campus, learn the history of the university, and

make Chinese connections at this site. It's a great place to download great photos from China for your next school report.
http://www.pku.edu.cn

Trinity College, Dublin

From Ireland's capital city, you can learn about the Book of Kells, read about the courses at the college, tour Dublin, and browse the newspaper. In English.
http://www.tcd.ie

Yale University

If we put Harvard here, we must also list this site. You can learn about all the courses, departments, research, libraries, art museums, admissions, and even the marching band. Boola boola.
http://www.cis.yale.edu/FrontDoor

Sports

ESPNet

This site provides up-to-date news about all kinds of sports events, from baseball to auto racing. Feature stories, pictures, and statistics that can contribute to a great math project.
http://espnet.sportszone.com

Home Plate

The Seattle Mariners' home page publishes everything about the baseball team and its players, from schedule information to photos, sounds, and 3D movies of the stadium.
http://www.mariners.org/mariner.home.html

San Jose Sharks

Here you will find pictures and history of the Sharks hockey team, with player statistics and biographies, as well as a description of the team's role in the San Jose community.
http://www.sj-sharks.com

U.S. Soccer Page

Maintained by soccer fans, this Internet site contains information on everything from professional teams to youth leagues, with articles, pictures, and statistics.
http://www.cs.cmu.edu/afs/cs/usr/mdwheel/www/soccer/us-soccer.html

Other

Library of Congress

At this site you can find rare works in the historical collections, look up new laws, participate in electronic town meetings, and, of course, search the mother of all catalogs. You'll find facts and ideas for almost every subject here.
http://lcweb.loc.gov/homepage/lchp.html

Scholastic Central

Here you can read *Scholastic* magazines, including one written by and for middle and high school students. Join curriculum projects and sample the Learning Libraries.
http://scholastic.com:2005

Print Resources

■ ■ ■ ■ ■ ■ ■ ■ ■ ■ ■ ■ ■

Books

Bennett, Steve & Ruth. *The Official Kid Pix Activity Book.* New York, Random House Electronic Publishing, 1993.

Brown, Eric. *That's Edutainment! A Parent's Guide to Educational Software.* Berkeley, CA: Osborne McGraw-Hill, 1995.

Kuntz, Margy & Ann. *Computer Crafts for Kids.* Emeryville, CA: Ziff-Davis Press, 1994.

Raskin, Robin, & Carol Ellison. *Parents, Kids & Computers.* New York: Random House Electronic Publishing, 1992.

Salpeter, Judy. *Kids & Computers: A Parent's Handbook.* Carmel, IN: SAMS, 1992.

von Buelow, Heinz, & Dirk Paulissen. *The Photo CD Book.* Grand Rapids, MI: Abacus, 1994.

Wright, June, & Daniel Shade eds. *Young Children: Active Learners in a Technological Age.* Washington, D.C.: National Association for the Education of the Young Child, 1994.

Magazines and Newsletters

Children's Software: A Quarterly Newsletter   713-467-8686
for Parents: Published jointly by Children's
Software Press and Teachers College at Columbia
University (Edited by Diane Kendall)

Children's Software Revue   313-480-0040

Computer Life   800-926-1578

Electronic Learning	212-505-3482
Family Fun	800-289-4849
Family PC	800-289-4849
Home PC	516-562-5309
Mac Home Journal	800-800-6542
Mac User	415-378-5600
Parent's Choice	617-965-5913
PC Novice	800-848-1478
Thinking caps News: A Newsletter for Family Computing	708-241-0322

Mail-Order Software Outlets

One of the best ways to buy software these days is through a mail order catalog. Their prices tend to be 10 to 50 percent off of retail, and they don't have to worry about shelf space in a field that is growing by leaps and bounds. When you get on the phone, they will ask you some questions about your system to make sure the software you are buying is right for your machine, so have the specs for your particular computer handy. Many of them ship overnight for a nominal $3 shipping charge. Unless they have Mac in their name, they all carry both Windows and Macintosh software. Many of them also will take software back within thirty days if it doesn't work. Just call the 800 numbers to get free catalogs.

CD-ROM Warehouse	800-237-6623
Club KidSoft- A subscription catalog and magazine	800-354-6150

Creative Computers Mac Mall	800-222-2808
Educational Resources The most complete catalog. School oriented.	800- 624-2926
Egghead Software	800-EGG-HEAD
Learning Services Largely school oriented, but with a few home products.	800-877-9378
Learning Zone	800-248-0800
Mac's Place	800-260-0009
Mac Connection PC Connection	800-800-2222
MacWarehouse	800-255-6227
MacZone	800-248-0800
PCZone	800-258-2088
Quality Computers	800-777-3642
The Children's Software Company An on-line catalog	800-566-5590
The Edutainment Catalog	800-338-3844
Tiger Software	800-666-2562

Paper

If you don't have a color printer or if your child wants to add a special look to a project, think about using a paper with a preprinted border. Call for free catalogs and samples.

Paper Adventure	800-727-0041
Paper Direct	800-A-PAPERS

appendix B

Software Guide

This is a list of all of the software programs mentioned in this book, plus some additional titles of interest. The list is arranged alphabetically by category or genre. Some titles are mentioned in more than one category. This is not meant to be a comprehensive list of all the software available in any particular genre. We've listed software that we have used and know to work well for various homework projects on most computers. For each entry we have listed the software's title, the platforms it works on, the kind of disk it uses, the publisher's name, and a short annotation. Additionally, a software publishers directory is included at the end of this book. All these titles are available by mail order or at your local computer store. Be sure to have your computer and system information when you go to the store or call to inquire about software—the system requirements for some programs may vary. Each entry is coded as follows:

M=Macintosh   W=Windows   D=Diskettes   CD=CD-ROM

Title	Platform and Format	Publisher	Comment
Animation and Cartooning (Chapter 9)			
Amazing Animation	M/D/CD	Claris	Easy, great backdrops and animated stickers
Kid Pix (Kid Pix Companion, Kid Pix 2, Kid Pix Studio or later)	M/W/D/CD	Brøderbund	Create QuickTime sequences or use the animated stamps on the CD-ROM
Magic Theater	W/D/CD	Knowledge Adv.	Simple! Stickers and backgrounds are limited, hard to edit
Nickelodeon Director's Lab	W/D	Viacom NewMedia	Creates sophisticated presentations
The Cartoon Toolbox Starring Felix the Cat	M/W/CD	Big Top Productions	Felix makes cartooning fun and easy
Atlases (Chapter 4)			
Maps and Facts	W/D/CD	Brøderbund	Quick maps and facts for projects
Pictures Atlas of the World	M/W/CD	National Geographic	Stunning clipable pictures and maps
Small Blue Planet: The Real Picture World Atlas	M/W/CD	Now What Software	A birds-eye-view of the globe
Small Blue Planet: The Cities Below—The Aerial Atlas of America	M/W/CD	Now What Software	Find your neighborhood!
3-D World Atlas	M/W/CD	Electronic Arts	Incredible views of the earth

Title	Platform and Format	Publisher	Comment
U.S. Atlas	M/W/CD	Mindscape	Maps to clip and edit
World Atlas	M/W/CD	Mindscape	Maps ready for projects

Clip Art Images (Chapter 3)

Don't forget that you can also copy clipart off of desktop publishing forums on online services.

Art á la Carte	M/W/D/CD	3G Graphics	Inexpensive and fun images
Best of K–12 Graphics	M/W/CD	Software Sense	Good pictures for school projects
Beyond the Border	M/D	Metro ImageBase	Borders for all kinds of projects
Corel Gallery	M/W/CD	Corel	10,000 clipart images
The Write Companion	M/W/D	The Learning Co.	Add to Student Writing Center

Computer-Assisted Design (Chapter 10)

Kid Cad	W/D/CD	Davidson	Super for creating models for projects

Desktop Publishing (see Word Processing)

Dictionaries (Chapter 4)

The American Heritage Talking Dictionary	M/D/CD	Softkey	Useful for school and home
Random House Webster's School and Office Dictionary	M/W/CD	WordPerfect	Good home resource
Random House Webster's Electronic Dictionary and Thesaurus College Edition	M/W/CD	WordPerfect	Most complete dictionary on this list

Title	Platform and Format	Publisher	Comment
Drawing Programs (Chapters 1, 2, 3, 7, 8, and 9)			
Art Explorer	M/W/D	Adobe	Great tools and textures
Dabbler	M/W/D	Fractal Design	Learn to draw as Fine
Fine Artist	M/W/D	Microsoft	Lots of special effects
Flying Colors	M/W/D	Davidson	Super 3-D effects
Kid Pix (Kid Pix Companion, Kid Pix 2, Kid Pix Studio or later)	M/W/D/CD	Brøderbund	Best all round programs
Kid Works (2 or later)	M/W/D	Davidson	Great for younger kids
Encyclopedias (Chapter 4)			
Compton's Interactive	M/W/CD	Comptons	Best for elementary kids
Encarta	M/W/CD	Microsoft	Great multimedia features
The Grolier Multimedia	MW/CD	Grolier	Our first choice—most depth
Flipbook Creation Programs			
Flipbook	M/D	S.H. Pierce	Tool for making flip books
Clickbook	M/D	BookMaker	Makes any document into a book or even a flipbook
Geography (Chapter 12)			
Cross Country USA	M/W/D	Didatech	Drive a truck across the USA
Where in the USA is Carmen Sandiego?	M/W/CD	Brøderbund	Classic chase across America to learn about geography

Title	Platform and Format	Publisher	Comment
Where in the World is Carmen Sandiego?	M/W/CD	Brøderbund	Chase Carmen around the world and see the sights
ZipZapMap! Canada	M/W/D	National Geographic	Learn the provinces
ZipZapMap! USA	M/W/D	National Geographic	Learn the states
ZipZapMap! World	M/W/D	National Geographic	Learn the world

Grammar Programs (Chapters 3 and 12)

Title	Platform and Format	Publisher	Comment
Correct Grammar	M/D	SoftKey	Check your grammar
Gram*MA*Tik	M/W/D	WordPerfect	Check your grammar
Grammar Games	W/D	Davidson	Learn grammar through games

Images (Chapters 3 and 4)

If you have access to online resources, you can download publicity shots, news pictures, maps, and more.

Title	Platform and Format	Publisher	Comment
Art Gallery	M/W/CD	Microsoft	Copy and clip masterpieces
Corel Photo CD Volumes	M/W/CD	Corel	Separate packages on various topics
Earth's Endangered Environments	M/W/CD	National Geographic	Great rainforest pictures
Mammals: A Multimedia	M/W/CD	National Geographic	Super pictures
Picture Atlas of the World	M/W/CD	National Geographic	Great resource pictures of world nations
Classic Graphics Galleries of Masters	M/W/CD	Planet Art	Classic art and historical masterpieces

333

Title	Platform and Format	Publisher	Comment
The Presidents: A Picture of Our Nation	M/W/CD	National Geographic	Makes history come alive!
The Revolutionary War Gallery of Images	M/W/CD	Fife & Drum Software	Compelling images of the revolution
Worldview/MediaClips	M/W/CD	Aris	Super views of the earth

Journal Keeping (Chapter 12)

Title	Platform and Format	Publisher	Comment
Amazing Writing Machine	M/D	Brøderbund	Lots of idea starters
Keroppi Day Hopper	M/W/D	Big Top Productions	Cute diary/address program
Student Writing Center	M/W/D/CD	The Learning Co.	Complete with password

Math (Chapter 12)

Title	Platform and Format	Publisher	Comment
Alge-Blaster 3	W/D	Davidson	Drill and games for algebra
Alge-Blaster Plus	M/D	Davidson	Mac version of above
Counting on Frank	M/W/CD	Electronic Arts	Innovative math games
Decimal and Fraction Maze	M/W/D	Great Wave	Patient math game
Math Ace	M/W/D/CD	Sanctuary Woods	Fast paced game/tutorial
Math Blaster: Episode 1– In Search of Spot	M/W/D/CD	Davidson	First in the drill series
Math Blaster: Episode 2– Secret of the Lost City	W/D/CD	Davidson	Intermediate math
Math Blaster Mystery: The Great Train Robbery	W/D/CD	Davidson	Good word problems practice

Title	Platform and Format	Publisher	Comment
Math Workshop	M/W/CD	Brøderbund	Runs from drill to logic to patterning games
Measurement in Math	M/D	Learning in Motion	Great graphing tool
Memphis Math: Treasure of the Tombs	W/CD	WordPerfect	Explores mysteries of the tombs and math
Mental Math	W/D	WordPerfect	Math facts at a fast pace
Number Maze	M/W/D	Great Wave	Patient math drill game
Number Munchers	M/W/D	MECC	Practices math concepts
Real World Math: Adventures in Flight	M/W/CD	Sanctuary Woods	Shows math as used in real life
SuperSolvers Outnumbered	M/W/D	The Learning Co.	Word problems in creative context

Multireference CD-ROMs (Chapters 4 and 6)

Title	Platform and Format	Publisher	Comment
Bookshelf	M/W/CD	Microsoft	Our #1 choice in home reference software
Infopedia	W/CD	Future Vision	Contains multiple references

Music (Chapter 11)

Title	Platform and Format	Publisher	Comment
Beethoven's Ninth Symphony	M/CD	Voyager	Interactive music disk
ConcertWare Music Studio	M/WD	Jump Software	Create your own songs
Cubase	M	Steinberg	Sequencer software

Title	Platform and Format	Publisher	Comment
EZ Music Starter Kit w/Music Shop and Band-in-A-Box	M/D	Opcode	Great package to start with
Encore	M/W/D	Passport Designs	Notation software
Finale	M/W/D	Coda	Notation software
Making Music	M/W/CD	Voyager	The Kid Pix of music software
MasterTracks	M/W/D	Passport Designs	Sequencer software
Mozart's String Quartet in C Major	M/CD	Voyager	Interactive music disk
Musical Instruments	M/W/CD	Microsoft	Get acquainted with the orchestra
MusicTime	M/W/D	Passport	Notation software
Rock 'N' Roll your Own	M/W/CD	Compton's New Media	Make your own from sound clips
Rock Rap 'N Roll	M/W/CD	Viacom/Paramount	Play spin doctor
Songworks	M/D	Ars Nova Software	Notation software
Stravinsky's Rite of Spring	M/CD	Voyager	Interactive music disk
The Miracle Piano Teaching System	M/W/D	Mindscape	Learn to play the piano
The Musical World of Professor Piccolo	M/W/CD	Opcode	Musical introduction to the orchestra

Title	Platform and Format	Publisher	Comment
Vision	M/W/D	Opcode	Sequencer software

Photo CD and Photo Editing Software (Chapters 3, 7, and 8)

Easy Photo	W/CD	Storm Software	To use with photo CD or Easy Photo scanner/reader
Kids Studio	M/W/D/CD	Storm Software	Creative tool for cutting and displaying photo CD pictures
Photo CD Access Plus	M/W/CD	Eastman Kodak	Easy way to adapt your computer to read photo CDs

Presentation Programs (Chapters 8, 9, and 10)

ClarisWorks	M/W/D	Claris	Slide show feature
Digital Chisel	M/CD	Pierian Springs	Good for kids, easy to use
Fine Artist	M/W/D/CD	Microsoft	Art program with slide show feature
Impact	M/D	Claris	Adult presentation program
Kid Pix (Kid Pix Companion, Kid Pix 2, Kid Pix Studio or later)	M/W/D/CD	Brøderbund	Art program with slide show feature
Kids Studio	M/W/D/CD	Storm Software	Good for working with photo CD
Multimedia Workshop	M/CD	Davidson	Program with multiple features
Persuasion	M/W/D	Adobe	Adult presentation program
PowerPoint	M/W/D	Microsoft	Adult presentation program

Title	Platform and Format	Publisher	Comment
Print Projects (Chapter 12)			
Print Artist	W/D	Maxis	Lots of projects, easy to use
Print Shop Deluxe	M/W/D/CD	Brøderbund	The classic in the field
Reference Disks (Chapters 4 and 6)			
A Passion for Art Impressionist Art	M/W/CD	Corbis	Impressionist and Post
Ancient Cities	M/W/CD	Sumeria	Look at lost ancient cities
Ancient Lands	W/CD	Microsoft	Egyptian through Roman times
Art Gallery	M/W/CD	Microsoft	Useful general look at art
CNN Global View	W/CD	Compact/SoftKey	Look at facts related to world news
Dangerous Creatures	M/W/CD	Microsoft	Creatures kids love to fear
Dinosaurs	M/W/CD	Microsoft	A look at the Age of Dinosaurs
Exploring the Lost Maya	M/W/CD	Sumeria	Explore an ancient civilization
Eyewitness Encyclopedia of Science	M/W/CD	Dorling Kindersley	Facts galore!
Eyewitness History of the World	W/CD	Dorling Kindersley	Facts, stories, artifacts, and objects bring history to life!
Explorapedia: The World of People	W/CD	Microsoft	Travel the world

Title	Platform and Format	Publisher	Comment
Explorapedia: The World of Nature	W/CD	Microsoft	Excellent nature program for young students
How Animals Move	M/W/CD	Discovery Channel	Encyclopedia of animal motion
In Company of Whales	M/W/CD	Discovery Channel	Lives of the largest mammals
Musical Instruments	M/W/CD	Microsoft	Introduction to instruments
Ocean Life:Volumes 1–5	M/W/CD	Sumeria	Pictures and information about sea creatures
Point of View: U.S. History	M/D	Scholastic	Navigate U.S. history
Sharks	M/W/D/CD	Discovery Channel	The fascinating life of sharks
Space—A Visual History of Manned Spaceflight	M/W/CD	Sumeria	A look at the U.S. space program
Stephen Biesty's Incredible Cross Sections— Stowaway!	M/W/CD	Dorling Kindersley	Stowaway on an 18th century warship
The Animals	M/W/CD	Mindscape	Animals at the SanDiego Zoo
The Perseus Project	M/CD	Yale University Press	Greek art and culture
The Ultimate Human Body	M/W/CD	Dorling Kindersley	Explore the human body
The Way Things Work	M/W/CD	Dorling Kindersley	Probe how machines work
Time Almanac of the Twentieth Century	M/W/CD	Compact/SoftKey	Facts for the century
Time Almanac Reference Edition	MW/CD	Compact/SoftKey	A look at Time magazine issues

Title	Platform and Format	Publisher	Comment
Wild Africa	M/W/CD	Sumeria	A look at the animals of Africa
With Open Eyes: Images from the Art Institute of Chicago	M/W/CD	Voyager	An introduction to art for kids

Scanner Software

Ofoto	M/W/D	Light Source	Scanner connection

Simulations

A.D.A.M.— The Inside Story	M/W/CD	ADAM	Reveal the layers of the human body
AquaZone	M/W/D	Desktop Life	Aquarium simulation
Capital Hill	M/W/CD	Mindscape	Be a member of Congress
DinoPark Tycoon	M/W/D	MECC	Run your own dinosaur park
Discovering America	M/W/D	Lawrence Productions	Explore early Florida
El Fish	M/W/D	Maxis	Aquarium simulation
Fun Physics	M/D	Knowledge Rev.	Experiment with physics
Geography Search	M/W/D	Tom Synder Prod.	Explore the New World
Geometer's Sketchpad	M/W/D	Key Curriculum Press	Plot and graph experiments
Lion	W/CD	Sanctuary Woods	Live like a lion
Odell Down Under	M/W/D	MECC	Live in the sea

Title	Platform and Format	Publisher	Comment
Operation Frog	M/W/D	Scholastic	Bloodless, odorless dissection
Oregon Trail II	M/W/CD	MECC	Life on the early trails across the U.S.
Sim Ant	M/W/D	Maxis	Explore life in an ant colony
Sim City	M/W/D	Maxis	Run a city
Sim City 2000	M/W/D	Maxis	Plan a city-in-computer
Sim Earth	M/W/D	Maxis	Design a planet
Sim Life	M/W/D	Maxis	Design new forms of life
Sim Farm	M/W/D	Maxis	Run your own farm
Sim Town	M/W/CD	Maxis	For kids 8–12, plan a town
The Even More Incredible Machine	M/W/D	Sierra	Build or solve Rube Goldberg style puzzles
The Amazon Trail	M/W/D/CD	MECC	Explore the rainforest
The Tribe	W/D	Lawrence Prod.	Live with a prehistoric tribe
The Yukon Trail	M/W/D/CD	MECC	Relive the Gold Rush
Where in the USA is Carmen Sandiego?	M/W/D/CD	Brøderbund	Chase Carmen around the USA
Where in the World is Carmen Sandiego?	M/W/D/CD	Brøderbund	Chase Carmen around the world
Widget Workshop	M/W/CD/M/D	Maxis	Experiment with devices

Title	Platform and Format	Publisher	Comment
Wolf	W/CD	Sanctuary WoodsLive like a wolf	

Sound Editing Software (Chapters 8 and 9)

Title	Platform and Format	Publisher	Comment
Audio Shop	M/W/D	Opcode	Edit your sound clips
SoundEdit	M/W/D	Macromedia	Edit your sound track

Spelling (Chapter 12)

Title	Platform and Format	Publisher	Comment
SuperSolvers Spellbound	M/W/D	The Learning Co.	Compete in a spelling bee
Spell Dodger	M/W/D	Arcadia/Davidson	Arcade style game

Spreadsheets (Chapter 10)

Title	Platform and Format	Publisher	Comment
The Cruncher	M/W/D	Davidson	Spreadsheet with tutorials

Storybook Creation Programs (Chapters 1 and 3)

Title	Platform and Format	Publisher	Comment
Imagination Express Castle Neighborhood Rain Forest	M/W/CD	Edmark	Modules for creating exciting storybooks
Storybook Weaver Deluxe	M/W/CD	MECC	Create storybooks on any topic

Text Collections (Chapters 4 and 6)

Title	Platform and Format	Publisher	Comment
Barron's Complete Book Notes	W/CD	World Library	101 titles are covered
Great Literature—Personal Library	M/W/CD	Bureau of Electronic Publishing Inc.	943 works plus music and color pictures
Great Mystery Classics	W/CD	Compton's	171 tales of mystery

Title	Platform and Format	Publisher	Comment
Library of the Future	W/CD	World Library	2000 books plus children's classics
Shakespeare Study Guide	W/CD	Compton's	Complete collection

Timeline Programs (Chapter 1)

Timeliner	M/W/D	Tom Synder Prod.	Create personal or historict timelines

Typing (Keyboarding) Programs (Chapter 2)

All the Right Type	M/W/D	Didatech	Traditional approach
Kids Typing	M/W/D/CD	Sierra/Bright Star	Uses a ghost for a tutor
Mavis Beacon Teaches Typing	M/W/D	Mindscape	Best selling program

Video Digitizing Software (Chapters 8 and 9)

VideoBlaster	W/D	Creative Labs	Create video magic
Video Spigot	M/D	Radius	Add video to your Mac
VideoVideo	W/D	Creative Labs	Produce video action

Video Production (Chapter 9)

Premiere video presentations	M/W/D	Adobe Systems	Next step up for creating

Vocabulary (Chapter 12)

Word Attack 3	W/D	Davidson	Game approach
Word City	M/W/D/CD	Sanctuary Woods	Various games

343

Title	Platform and Format	Publisher	Comment
Word Processing and Desktop Publishing Programs (Chapters 2 and 3)			
ClarisWorks	M/W/D	Claris	Integrated software package
Home Publisher	M/W/D	Adobe Systems	Straight forward for the home
Kid Works (2)	M/W/D	Davidson	Talking word processor for younger children
PageMaker	M/W/D	Abode Systems	More expensive and complex
Publisher	M/W/D	Microsoft	Useful for the home
Quark XPress	M/W/D	Quark	More expensive and complex
Student Essentials	M/D	WordPerfect	Great for older kids, comes with templates, help for foreign language papers
Student Writing Center	M/W/D/CD	The Learning Co.	Great for kids—elementary and middle school
Word	M/W/D	Microsoft	Standard word processor
WordPerfect	M/W/D	WordPerfect	Standard word processor

appendix C

Software Publisher's Directory

A.D.A.M.

1600 RiverEdge Pkwy, Suite 800
Atlanta, GA 30328
800-755-2326

Adobe (Aldus) Systems

411 First Ave. South
Seattle, WA 98104-2870
206-622-5500

**Arcadia
Productions/Davidson**

P.O. Box 2961
Torrance, CA 90509
310-793-0620

**Aris Entertainment/
Mediaclips**

310 Washington Blvd. Suite 100
Marina del Rey, CA 92092
800-228-2747

Ars Nova Software

P.O. Box 637
Kirkland, WA 98083-0637
800-445-4866

Big Top Productions, Inc.

548 Fourth Street
San Francisco, CA 94107-6584
800-900-PLAY
Bookmaker Corporation
2470 El Camino Real, Ste. 108
Palo Alto, CA 94306
415-354-8166

Brøderbund

P.O. Box 6125
Novato, CA 94948-6125
800-521-6263

Bureau of Electronic Publishing, Inc.

141 New Road
Parsippany, NJ 07054
800-828-4766

Claris Corporation

5201 Patrick Henry Drive
Santa Clara, CA 95052-8168
800-3CLARIS

Coda Music Software

1401 E. 79th Street, Ste. 2
Bloomington, MN 55425-1126
800-843-2066

Compton's New Media

2320 Camino Vida Roble
Carlsbad, CA 92009
619-929-2500

Corbis

15395 South East 30th Place
Suite 300
Bellevue, WA 98007
206-641-4505

Corel Corporation

P.O. Box 3595
Salinas, CA 93912
800-772-6735

Creative Labs

1901 McCarthy
Milpitas, CA 95035
408-428-6600

Davidson and Associates

19840 Pioneer Avenue
Torrance, CA 90509
310-793-0600

Desktop Life

4400 MacArthur Blvd. 5th Floor
Newport Beach, CA 92660
714-955-4968

Didatech Software Ltd.

4250 Dawson Street
Suite 200
Burnaby, B.C. Canada V5C 481
800-356-6575

The Discovery Channel Multimedia

7700 Wisconsin Avenue
Bethesda, Maryland 20814-3579
310-986-0444

Dorling Kindersley

95 Madison Avenue
New York, NY 10016
800-356-6575

Eastman Kodak

Kodak Information Center
Dept. E, 343 State Street
Rochester, NY 14650-0811
800-242-2424

Edmark Corporation

P.O. Box 97021
Redmond, WA 98073-9721
206-556-8484

Electronic Arts

1450 Fashion Island Blvd.
San Mateo, CA 94404
415-571-7171

Fife and Drum Software

316 Soapstone Lane
Silver Springs, MD 20905

Fractal Design Corp.

Dept. 395 P.O. Box 9050
San Fernando, CA 91341
800-297-COOL

Future Vision

300 Airport Executive Park
Spring Valley, NY 10977
914-426-0400

Great Wave/Interplay

5353 Scotts Valley Drive
Scotts Valley, CA 95066
408-438-1990

Grolier Electronic Publishing

Sherman Turnpike
Danbury, CT 06816
203-797-3530

Jump Software

c/o Home Computer Warehouse
P.O. Box 688
1720 Oak Street
Lakewood, NJ 08701
800-285-7080

Key Curriculum Press

P.O. Box 2304
Berkeley, CA 94702
800-338-7638

Knowledge Adventure

4502 Dyer Street
La Crescenta, CA 91214
800-542-4240

Knowledge Revolutions

15 Brush Place
San Francisco, CA 94103
800-766-6615

Lawrence Productions

1800 South 35th Street
Galesburg, MI 49053-9687
616-665-7075

The Learning Company

6493 Kaiser Drive
Fremont, CA 94555
800-852-2255

Learning in Motion

c/o Apple Computer, Inc.
1 Infinite Loop
Cupertino, CA 95014
800-776-2333

Light Source Computer Images

17 East Sir Francis Drake Blvd.
Lark Spur, CA 94939
800-994-2656

Macromedia

600 Townsend Street, Suite 310
San Francisco, CA 94103
800-288-0572

Maxis

2 Theatre Square
Suite 230
Orinda, CA 94563-3346
510-254-9700

MECC

6160 Summit Drive North
Minneapolis, MN 55430-4003
800-685-MECC

Metro ImageBase, Inc.

18623 Ventura Blvd, Suite 210
Tarzana, CA 91356
800-525-1552

Microsoft Corporation

One Microsoft Way
Redmond, WA 98052-6399
800-426-9400

Mindscape

60 Leveroni Court
Novato, CA 94949
415-883-3000

National Geographic Society

1145 17th St. N.W.
Washington, D.C. 20036-4688
202-775-6585

Now What Software

2303 Sacramento Street
San Francisco, CA 94115
800-322-1954

Opcode

3950 Fabian Way, Suite 100
Palo Alto, CA 94303
415-856-3333

Passport Designs, Inc.

100 Stone Pine Road
Half Moon Bay, CA 94019
415-726-0280

Pierian Spring Software

5200 S.W. Macadam Ave.
Portland, Oregon 97201
800-472-8578

Planet Art

505 South Beverly Drive
Beverley Hills, CA 90212
310-275-5217

Quark

1800 Grant Street
Denver, CO 80203
800-788-7835

Radius

1710 Fortune Drive
San Jose, CA 95131
800-334-3005

Sanctuary Woods

Suite 260
1875 South Grant Street
San Mateo, CA 94402
415-578-6340

Scholastic Inc.

P.O. Box 7502
Jefferson City, MO 65102
800-541-5513

S.H. Pierce and Co.

Suite 323 Building 600
One Kendall Square
Cambridge, MA 02139
617-338-2222

Sierra/Bright Star

3380 146th Place, S. E.
Bellevue, WA 98007
800-757-7707

SoftKey (Compact)

1 Antheneam Street
Cambridge, MA 02142
800-227-5609

Software Sense

180 South Western, Suite 129
Carpentersville, IL 60110
708-888-8417

Steinberg

17700 Raymer Street, Suite
1001
Northridge, CA 91325
818-993-4091

Storm Software

1861 Landings Drive
Mountain View, CA 94043
415-691-6675

Sumeria

329 Bryant Street
Suite 3D
San Francisco, CA 94107
415-904-0800

3G Graphics

114 Second Avenue South,
Suite 104
Edmonds, WA 98020
800-456-0234

Tom Snyder Productions

80 Coolidge Hill Road
Watertown, MA 02172-2817
800-342-0236

Viacom New Media

1515 Broadway
New York, NY 10036
800-469-2539

The Voyager Company

578 Broadway, Suite 406
New York, NY 10012
800-446-2001

WordPerfect/Novell

1555 N. Technology Way
Orem, Utah 84057-2399
800-451-5151

World Library, Inc.

12914 Haster Street
Garden Grove, CA 92640
714-748-7197

Yale University Press

Special Projects
P.O. Box 209040
New Haven, CT 06520
203-432-0912

index